Twilight
of the
Great Lakes
Steamer

Photos and Text
by
Raymond A. Bawal, Jr.

INLAND
EXPRESSIONS

Published by Inland Expressions

Inland Expressions
42211 Garfield Rd. #297
Clinton Township, MI. 48038

www.inlandexpressions.com

First Edition 2009

DISCLAIMER

The photos, and information contained within have been researched thoroughly but while the author and publisher of this book have made every effort to provide accurate information they are by no means responsible for any errors or omissions to the publication.

ISBN-13 978-0-9818157-2-5
ISBN-10 0-9818157-2-3

Printed in the United States of America

Design by Inland Expressions

TABLE OF CONTENTS

Introduction

The use of steam as a motive power for ships has been around since the 1700s, but did not gain wide usage until the last half of the 1800s. Steam power was to remain the most widely used propulsion choice on both the Great Lakes, and the world's oceans until the 1960s. On the inland seas, where at one time there were hundreds of these type of vessels sailing, there are now only twenty active steamers in operation. These ships for the most part represent the pinnacle of steam technology applied to Great Lakes freighters.

Steam power is one of the most basic forms of creating mechanical power. Steam is what helped create the modern world, as it was utilized in a wide array of applications. Besides ships, steam power was heavily used in the railroad industry prior to be supplanted in the 1950s by the diesel electric locomotive. In addition, steam was, and still is, used to produce a good portion of the world's electrical needs.

It could be argued to some degree that nuclear powered ships, and submarines are actually propelled by steam. In general concept, this is correct as a controlled nuclear reaction is used to heat water into steam which in turn is forced through a turbine to produce power. Nonetheless such vessels are termed as nuclear powered, rather than being designated as steamships.

When the concept for this book was envisioned it was decided to include only active steamers as of the end of the 2008 shipping season. In addition to the vessels on the following pages are a handful of retired steam powered freighters tied up in various locations around the Great Lakes, with little chance of returning to service. At least four of these steamers have been utilized as cement storage units. This includes the S. T. CRAPO, J. A.W. IGLEHART, J. B. FORD and C. T. C. No. 1, with the last two reportedly bound for scrapping in the near future.

The histories of some of the ships described in this book have similar histories, in particular the three "AAA" class ships built for the Pittsburgh Steamship fleet. However, effort was made to approach the histories of each vessel from a unique perspective, but with such similarities to deal with, some repetition is necessary.

The newest steamer currently on inland seas is the CANADIAN LEADER which was built in 1967, which makes her 42 years old as of the 2009 season. Every creation by man has a limited life span, and Great Lakes ships are no exception to this fact. In recent years their has been a trend in the American flagged fleet to convert steamers into either diesel powered, or barges after they have reached the end of their economical life. On the Canadian side of the lakes, steam powered ships have received diesel engines in a few cases, but generally have been sold for scrapping.

One day in the not so distant future, it is very likely that one of the ships in this volume will lay up for the last time as a steamer, thus closing an fascinating period in transportation history.

This book is not intended to be a history of the steamship, but rather individual histories of the remaining steam powered ships which in themselves relate the story of the last era for the Great Lakes steam powered freighter.

A Brief History...

The principle of steam power is simplicity itself. The harnessing of steam is based on the physical law that when water boils it expands to around 1,600 times its original volume. If this steam is placed into a confined space it creates massive amounts of pressure which can be utilized to provide power. In a steam engine, the steam is used to push a piston in a cylinder forward to produce mechanical power. Later, when the steam turbine was perfected, the steam was directed into a series of blades attached to a rotor to provide power. The steam turbine is much more efficient than a steam engine, providing more power in less space.

Though simple in concept, the actual application is somewhat complicated. The first practical steam engines appeared around 1700, with the steamboat appearing in France on the Saone River during 1783. The first practical steamship appeared in 1787 when John Fitch demonstrated a paddlewheel steamer on the Delaware River, near Philadelphia, Pennsylvania. Over the next twenty years a series of improvements to the steamboat occurred rapidly culminating with the Robert Fulton's **NORTH RIVER** (later renamed **CLERMONT**) in 1807 which proved itself a commercial success.

The story of steamboats on the upper Great Lakes begin in 1818 when the **WALK-IN-THE-WATER** was built at Black Rock, New York. This 135 foot long steamer was engaged in transportation of passengers between Buffalo and Detroit. As with many other early steamers, this ship was given the rigging of a sailing vessel in this case a two masted schooner. On October 31, 1821 the **WALK-IN-THE-WATER** would come to grief on Lake Erie when it was pushed ashore during a gale. Though the vessel itself was damaged beyond the point of saving, the ship's steam engine was salvaged, and placed into the steamer **SUPERIOR**. This ship began an era which continues to this day, though the **WALK-IN-THE-WATER** bears little resemblance to the steamers now plying the Great Lakes.

Most of the initial steamboats on the lake were of the paddlewheel design. These were replaced slowly by propeller equipped steamers during the later part of the nineteenth century. Although the first screw style steam boats appeared in the early 1800s, they were unable to compete with the paddlewheel steamers until more efficient propeller designs were perfected.

Steam was to replace the age of the sail on the inland seas during the late 1800s, although a small number of schooners continued on until the 1940s. During the early 1900s many schooners were converted into barges to be towed behind steamships, thus enhancing the amount of cargo carried on each trip. This era also marked the switch from building ships with wood, to iron, and then finally steel.

As steam and shipbuilding technology advanced, ships began to be built to larger, and larger specifications. The progression of vessel length of Great Lakes steamers is impressive. In the 1880s the largest ship on the lakes was 300 feet in length, by 1900 this had grown to 498 feet, before making a substantial increase to 600 just six years later. Following reaching the 600 foot mark, vessel growth slowed to the point that by 1942 it had reached 639 feet in length.

One of the most important factors dictating vessel size on the Great Lakes is the size of the locks installed in connecting channels between the lakes. For ships on the upper lakes, the size of vessels allowed to pass through the Soo Locks at Sault Ste. Marie, Michigan largely dictates the maximum size of ship to be built. This is true today, as it was when the first locks opened at that location in 1855 following years of political wrangling.

Steam remained to be preferred choice for vessel propulsion until the 1960s, when diesel engines began to be placed in a large percentage of ships being built. These ships were to be the forerunners of the propulsion standards of today, but they were by no means the first such ships on the Great Lakes.

*The **S. T. CRAPO** was the last hand fired coal powered steam freighter in operation, when she was converted to burn oil in 1995. This cement carrying steamer was launched in 1927, and went on to have a long active career on the inland seas which lasted until 1996. This vessel was powered by a triple expansion steam engine generating 1,800 indicated horsepower. This ship is still in existence, being used a storage barge at Green Bay, Wisconsin. She is seen here passing Marine City, Michigan towards the end of her operating career.*

In 1924, the Ford Motor Company placed both the **HENRY FORD II**, and **BENSON FORD (1)** into service. These two ships were the first large diesel equipped ships to be built for operation on the Great Lakes. The ships were each equipped with a Sun-Doxford diesel engine rated at 3,000 horsepower. These engines were able to give these ships a speed of 13 miles per hour while loaded, and proved dependable as they would go on to power these ships until they were decommissioned during the 1980s. While the **HENRY FORD II**, and **BENSON FORD (1)** provided steadfast service during their careers in the Ford fleet, it is noteworthy that when this firm ordered its third, and last ship for Great Lakes service it was a steamer. This proved to be the **WILLIAM CLAY FORD (1)** which went into operation in 1953 as the last of the "AAA" class.

During the 1950s, when most of today's remaining steamers were constructed, steam turbines were the preferred propulsion choice. The 1950s would see a massive building program on the American side of the Great Lakes as the demand for ore carriage grew during the Korean War. A relatively small number of new ships had been constructed since the 1930s, thus many ships in the American fleet were approaching obsolescence. This had been offset only by the building of 21 steamers during World War II.

In 1950, Inland Steel placed the **WILFRED SYKES** into service, setting the benchmark for many of the ships built during the next decade. During the 1950s no less then 24 new American flagged bulk freighters would be built for Great Lakes service. This does not include a number of salt-water conversions which were accomplished during the same time period. The 1950s shipbuilding boom for the American fleet ended in 1960 with the building of the **ARTHUR B. HOMER**, and **EDWARD L. RYERSON**. Both of these ships were built to the maximum size allowed for Great Lakes operation at the time, with a length of 730 feet, beam of 75 feet, and depth of 39 feet. Both of these ships were rated to carry payload in the range of 27,000 gross tons. These two ships also represent the last steamers to be built for the American fleet.

The Canadian Great Lakes fleet also went through an era of vessel construction during the 1950s, with the building of 16 large bulk steam powered freighters. This does not include a large number of smaller canal sized freighters built during the same period, most of which were diesel powered. These were also the last batch built of the "canaller" type vessels which had a typical length of around 250 feet. These ships would become obsolete with the building of the St. Lawrence Seaway during the late 1950s which would allowed the passage of ships of up to 730 feet in length.

This construction project, one of the largest of its kind to ever have been undertaken enabled ships to travel from the head of Lake Superior to the lower St. Lawrence River. It also allowed for the entry of large salt-water vessels to enter the Great Lakes to load their cargoes directly at ports such as Duluth, Port Arthur, and Fort William. The St. Lawrence Seaway opened in 1959 ushering in a period of growth within the Canadian lakes fleet. Soon several new ships were being built for a number of Canadian fleets as their older canal sized vessels were retired. Most of the ships built during the 1960s were of the 730 foot length, although a number were built to smaller dimensions to better suit their intended trade routes.

The last steamer to be built for Great Lakes service would be the Canadian flagged **FEUX-FOLLETS** which entered service in 1967. This was by no way the beginning of the end for steam powered freighters on freshwater as their numbers still made up the majority of the freshwater fleet. By the 1970s, a new era of shipbuilding began in the American fleet following the opening of the new Poe Lock at Sault Ste. Marie, enabling the passage of ships up to 1,000 feet in length, and beams of 105 feet.

Though the new lock allowed for the construction of a new class of superships, the Welland Canal which connects Lake Erie and Lake Ontario prevented these ships from trading any further than the easternmost part of Lake Erie. This was of little consequence for most of the major US flagged fleets on the lakes as the bulk of their operations involved the movement of raw materials from Lake Superior to discharge ports on Lakes Erie, and Michigan.

*The **ALGOSOUND**, and **ALGOGULF (2)** are tied up at Point Edward, Ontario during a mid-season lull in cargoes in the late 1990s. These two ship are good examples of steamers built for the Canadian fleet during the 1960s for the Great Lakes and Seaway trade. Both were built as steamers during a time at which the switch the diesel power was just starting to gain momentum. Both of these ships no longer sail the Great Lakes. The **ALGOGULF (2)** was sold for scrap in 2002, with the **ALGOSOUND** meeting a similar fate the following year.*

*The **STEWART J. CORT** makes the turn at Mission Point, just below the Soo Locks on September 21, 2008. This ship was the first thousand footer on the Great Lakes, as signified by the "#1" painted on the aft cabin just below and between the stacks. With the ability of carrying double of what the current largest ships could carry at the time it entered service in 1972, this ship was not an evolutionary step in Great Lakes ship design but rather revolutionary. Despite having a profile of a gearless bulk freighter, this ship is equipped with a self-unloading system which utilizes a shuttle boom located at the stern of the vessel. This installation has limited this ship's operation between the upper lakes, and Burns Harbor, Indiana. Since 2005 the **STEWART J. CORT** has been operated by Interlake Steamship.*

In 1972, the 1,000 foot **STEWART J. CORT** entered service for the Bethlehem Steel fleet thus becoming the first supership to enter service. This ship had been built with an unusual construction technique. The bow and stern sections were built at the Ingalls Shipbuilding Corporation in Pascagoula, Mississippi and traveled as one unit, nicknamed "stubby", to Erie, Pennsylvania via the St. Lawrence Seaway. Upon arrival at Erie Marine the bow and stern sections were divided and installed to the ship's mid-section which had been built at Erie. This ship was the only thousand footer to have cabins in the traditional fore and aft style, however all of its living quarters were placed at the bow with the stern section dedicated to the vessel's propulsion, and complicated unloading system. It was also the first ship to enter service with a self-unloading system utilizing a shuttle boom. This type of boom limited the ports that such as ship could unload at, becoming a liability later in the **CORT**'s career. With a carrying capacity of 58,000 tons the **STEWART J. CORT** doubled the carrying capacity of the largest ships then plying the Great Lakes.

The building of 1,000 foot vessels continued until 1981 when the last built thus far, the **COLUMBIA STAR** entered service for Oglebay Norton. While the new lock allowed for the building of the thousand footers, it also enabled the rebuilding of existing steamers through lengthening. These rebuildings provided a substantial increase in the carrying capacity of the ship without the need to construct a new vessel. Such reconstructions also limited the operations of these vessels to the upper lakes, but as mentioned before, this was of little consideration within the American fleet. The lengthening of these steamers, was in many cases followed by a self-unloading conversion in later years enabling the ships to remain economically viable.

Meanwhile, the Canadian fleet continued to also build new vessels during this time period, with none exceeding the maximum allowable length for operation on the St. Lawrence Seaway. This was a reflection in the differing demands in the movement of material between the American and Canadian fleets. One of the primary trade patterns for Canadian flagged ships is the movement of grain from the upper lakes to ports on the St. Lawrence with a return cargo of iron back into the Great Lakes, thus there was no demand for the construction of ships unable to pass through the Welland Canal.

During the 1970s, several other new mid-sized vessels entered the American lakes fleet which were optimized for operations into smaller ports. Several of these were also built to serve unloading docks in locations which larger ships could not reach at harbors such as Cleveland, Lorain, and Toledo. These ships ranged in size from 630 to 770 feet in length. All of these ships were powered by diesel engines and they started to rapidly replace steamers which had previously served along these trade routes.

The last serious thought given to constructing a steam powered vessel occurred in the late 1970s when officials of the Cleveland Cliffs fleet considered the building of a steam powered 1,000 foot vessel. At the time this fleet was in negotiations for both a large ore hauling contract with Republic Steel, and a coal contract with Detroit Edison. Cleveland Cliffs would not be awarded either of these contracts, and the planned thousand footer was not built, with this fleet eventually ceasing operations in 1984.

Upon reaching the end of their productive lives most steamers have gone to the scrapyard, while a small number have been converted into barges. When paired to a tug some of these units have achieved some success in such roles since the late 1980s. Among these in service as of the 2009 season are the **McKEE SONS, JAMES L. KUBER, LEWIS J. KUBER, ST. MARYS CONQUEST, SARAH SPENCER, PATHFINDER (3)**, and **JOSEPH H. THOMPSON**.

*The **CANADIAN TRANSPORT** was built in 1979 for the Upper Lakes Shipping fleet as a modern diesel powered 730 foot vessel for operation on the Great Lakes and St. Lawrence Seaway. So important is the Seaway route for the Canadian flagged Great Lakes fleet that none have been built which are too large to pass through the locks on this waterway. The **CANADIAN TRANSPORT** is downbound on Lake Huron on April 3, 2008.*

*The **McKEE SONS** served as a steamer from 1953 prior to being laid up due to economic reasons in the early 1980s. In 1992 this ship was converted into a self-unloading barge enabling it to operate in the transport of primarily coal and stone cargoes. It is shown on May 24, 2008 downbound on the St. Clair River, and represents one of a small number of steamers which were converted into barges following because they were uneconomical to operate as powered vessels.*

During the 1980s, several steamers were removed from service following a severe downturn in the demand for bulk material transportation on the Great Lakes with the onset of a serious economic recession. A large number of these ships had reached the end of their useful life, and their retirement was of little surprise as many were in excess of 60 years old. There was however many ships which had their careers ended during this time period which were only 20 to 30 years old. Such an age is considered extremely young for a freshwater freighter which usually has a lifespan of at least 60 years. This is in direct contrast to a salt-water vessel which is considered to be near the end of its career after 20 years of service due to the corrosive effects of the ocean. There were many reasons for the retirement of ships built during the 1950s and 60s, including a reduction in the amount of available cargoes, lack of self-unloading equipment, and the building of larger and more efficient vessels.

Several of the older ships to survive the 1980s had previously been converted from steamers into motor vessels. These included the **JOSEPH H. FRANTZ, RICHARD REISS, NICOLET, CALCITE II, MYRON C. TAYLOR,** and **GEORGE A. SLOAN.** All of these ships also received self-unloading conversions during their careers, and would have undoubtedly been retired during the 1980s had they not received these modifications. By 1990 there were 54 bulk freighter steamers in the Great Lakes fleet compared to 101 motor vessels of the same type.

By the 2000 season the number of steamers had been reduced further to 39 freighters. Following the 2000 season several more steamers were retired, or repowered. Steamers removed from service since the beginning of the century include **ALGOGULF (2), ALGORIVER, ALGOSOUND, KINSMAN ENTERPRISE (2), MAPLEGLEN (2), OAKGLEN (2), CANADIAN MARINER, CANADIAN VOYAGER,** and **SEAWAY QUEEN.** All of these ships were gearless straight deckers, and all were Canadian flagged with the exception of the **KINSMAN ENTERPRISE (2).**

*The **OJIBWAY** was converted from a steamer into a motor vessel in 2005, as the **VOYAGEUR INDEPENDENT** following its retirement from the US fleet. It had previously sailed under the American flag as the **KINSMAN INDEPENDENT** (3) in the grain trade.*

Since 2005 four bulk freight vessels have been repowered from steam to diesel. In November of 2005 the **VOYAGEUR INDEPENDENT** entered service following being repowered with a 4,100 brake horsepower diesel engine. This ship had been retired from the US fleet in 2004 as the **KINSMAN INDEPENDENT (3)**. As of the 2009 shipping season this ship sails in the grain trade for the Lower Lakes fleet as **OJIBWAY**. In 2006 the **LEE A. TREGURTHA** received a pair of Rolls Royce Bergen diesel engines with a total of 8,160 shaft horsepower at the Bay Shipbuilding yard in Sturgeon Bay, Wisconsin. Two years later, the **SAGINAW (3)** had her original De Laval steam turbine replaced when Lower Lakes had her repowered at Point Edward, Ontario.

At press time, the **CHARLES M. BEEGHLY** was in the process of being repowered at Bay Shipbuilding with a pair of Bergen engines. This ship had been powered with a General Electric steam turbine capable of generating 9,350 shaft horsepower. The **CHARLES M. BEEGHLY** is expected to return to service by the middle of the 2009 shipping season. This ship is a sister ship to the **JOHN SHERWIN (2)** which is also currently at the Bay Shipbuilding yard for conversion into a self-unloading motor vessel. This ship which has been laid up since 1981 was launched as a steamer, and was in the process of being rebuilt during the last half of the 2008 season when work was suspended due to a severe downturn in global economic conditions. It is probable that once the business climate improves the conversion of this ship will be completed.

The number of steamers has steadily declined to the point a which by the 2009 season there are only 20 operational bulk freight steamers on the Great Lakes. Of these, at least one is slated to be converted to diesel power in the near future. While the operation of many of these steamships will continue for the foreseeable future, there will eventually be a day when the last of this type of ship is retired or repowered.

*The **CUYAHOGA** was repowered from steam to diesel in 2001. She is shown here in the late 1990s while unloading at Zilwaukee, Michigan. This ship is one of 16 ships built in the "Maritime" class during the Second World War. As of 2009 the **CUYAHOGA** remains active in the Lower Lakes Towing fleet.*

*Though not a bulk freight vessel, the carferry **BADGER** is notable is that it still operates as a coal fired steamship. This ship is shown departing Ludington, Michigan on June 8, 2008 on one of its daily trips across Lake Michigan during the summer months. Viewing this ship in operation is much like viewing a time capsule of an era when hundreds of coal fired steamers plied the Great Lakes.*

The ST. MARYS CHALLENGER

In 1904, the Shenango Furnace Company was created to produce steel products out of its primary manufacturing facility located in Pittsburgh, Pennsylvania. Initially, this firm relied upon chartering lake freighters to haul iron ore from its mining interests on the upper lakes to the lower lakes for eventual delivery to its manufacturing operations. Even though this arrangement was initially satisfactory, it was decided within a short period of time that the company would be better served by owning its own vessels, rather then relying on a outside source for carriage capacity.

In 1906, the Shenango created a subsidiary to operate vessels built to its account to serve on the Great Lakes. This firm was named the Shenango Steamship & Transportation Company and took delivery of its first ship, the **WILLIAM P. SNYDER**, that same year. This 552 foot vessel had been built by the Great Lakes Engineering Works at River Rouge, Michigan. At the time, it could hardly be imagined that this ship would still be in active service 102 years later.

This ship had been built to move raw materials from the upper lakes to the lower lakes for delivery to Shenango's steel producing facilities. In her early years this ship was involved in at least three minor mishaps. The first occurred on July 16, 1916 when it struck a dock at Superior, Wisconsin. This ship was later noted as having suffered weather related damages while downbound on Lake Huron on November 22, 1917. While departing Sandusky, Ohio on September 5, 1925 with a cargo of coal this ship struck an underwater obstruction, requiring drydocking at Superior, Wisconsin after unloading of the cargo.

The **WILLIAM P. SNYDER**, was joined in 1907 by the steamer **WILPEN**, which was also built by the Great Lakes Engineering Works. This ship was similar in appearance to the **SNYDER**, but at 579 feet in length it was slightly longer. The **WILLIAM P. SNYDER**, and the **WILPEN** were both equipped with an extra deck on their forward cabins. This deck was used as an observation deck for company guests when they were aboard for a trip on the steamer. This was a feature applied initially to all of the ships built for Shenango. In 1924, **WILLIAM P. SNYDER** received new water tube boilers.

On June 26, 1926, the **WILLIAM P. SNYDER** was sold to the Stewart Furnace Company, with the **WILPEN** being sold to the Pioneer Steamship Fleet on the same date. These transactions liquidated the Shenango Steamship & Transportation Company. In the period of time since the building of these two ships, Shenango had built three other lake carriers. These being the **SHENANGO, COL. JAMES SCHOONMAKER**, and **WILLIAM P. SNYDER, JR.**. The Shenango Furnace Company was the registered owners of these vessels, thus these ships were not effected by the dissolution of the Shenango Steamship & Transportation Company.

Following the sale this ship to Stewart Furnace it was renamed **ELTON HOYT II (1)**, with management being taken over by Picklands, Mather & Company of Cleveland, Ohio. This firm would continue to manage the steamer until 1966 even though it went through two ownership changes. The first of these occurred in 1929 when the **ELTON HOYT II (1)** was sold to the Youngstown Steamship Company. This arrangement did not last long, as ownership was taken over at the end of the 1929 season by the Interlake Steamship Company.

While in service for these firms this ship remained actively engaged in the movement of ore and coal to various ports around the Great Lakes. In 1950 this ship's original 1,665 shaft horsepower triple expansion steam engine was replaced with a Skinner Marine Uniflow steam engine. This power plant is equipped with four cylinders, and generates an indicated horsepower of 3,500. This engine also gave this steamer a operating speed of 12 miles per hour. While being repowered the **ELTON HOYT II (1)** also had two new water tube boilers installed.

Despite this vessel's long career upon the Great Lakes, it has only been involved in one major accident. On November 24, 1950 the **ELTON HOYT II (1)** collided with the **ENDERS M. VOORHEES** in the Straits of Mackinac. The **ELTON HOYT II (1)** had departed South Chicago, Illinois the previous day, without cargo, bound for Two Harbors, Minnesota, while the **VOORHEES** was downbound with ore for South Chicago delivery. The collision occurred during snowstorm conditions, with visibility ranging from 1/4 to 1 mile. Upon approaching the Pittsburgh Steamship vessel the **HOYT** had checked down, while the **VOORHEES** remained running at full speed. The **ELTON HOYT II (1)** struck the **VOORHEES** on the port side between the #14 and #15 hatches. While there were no personnel injuries on either vessel, the **HOYT** suffered extensive damages to its bow, with both vessels anchoring one mile east of Mackinaw City, Michigan. The **ELTON HOYT II (1)** suffered a reported $100,000 worth of damages in this accident, with repairs being completed by Great Lakes Engineering Works at River Rouge, Michigan. Meanwhile, the **VOORHEES** received temporary patching at St. Ignace, Michigan and after unloading at Conneaut, Ohio it went to American Ship Building's Lorain yard for permanent repairs.

In order to free up its name for a new and larger steamer in 1952 this ship was renamed to **ALEX D. CHISHOLM**. This ship remained in active service for Interlake for another decade before being idled at Erie, Pennsylvania in 1962. Despite being a giant when built fifty-six years earlier, this ship was now one of the smaller straight deck bulk carriers in service under the American flag on the Great Lakes. In 1966 this ship was purchased by the Cement Transit Company, a division of Medusa Cement for a conversion into a self-unloading cement carrier. Her small size, which had made her obsolete in the ore trades, was a benefit for the cement trade with numerous docks being located in constricted areas which prevented the employment of larger ships.

This ship was taken to the Manitowoc Shipbuilding yard at Manitowoc, Wisconsin for the before mentioned conversion. This involved the removal of the cargo hatches, with these areas being plated over giving a flush deck appearance with only small circular openings running down the ship's centerline for the loading of cement. A cement unloading boom forty-eight feet long was fitted just aft of the forward deckhouse to enable this ship to off load its cargo without assistance at the company's docks.

Additionally, the ship was converted to burn oil rather than coal. This allowed the removal of the coal bunker, with this space being used for the addition of owner's quarters. A new smokestack was also installed during the reconstruction. This stack was painted in Medusa's colors which consisted of a white stack with an upper black band, and lower gray band, with a figure head of the mythical Greek character Medusa placed upon the middle of the stack. The dark brown hull, so familiar with ships of the Interlake fleet was repainted into a light gray, with "MEDUSA CEMENT" painted in billboard lettering on each side of the hull to represent her new career.

In 1967, this ship entered service in the cement trades as the **MEDUSA CHALLENGER** with Medusa's Charlevoix, Michigan facility being its primary loading point. While many voyages would see this steamer concentrating on Lake Michigan, other ports of call were not uncommon with many voyages involving trips to Lakes Erie, and Huron. At 552 feet in length this ship became the longest cement carrier on the Great Lakes, although her carrying capacity was less the Huron Cement's **J. A. W. IGLEHART** which entered service in 1965 following its conversion from a saltwater tanker.

The **MEDUSA CHALLENGER** would become a common, if not unwelcome sight on the Chicago, and Calumet Rivers. On many occasions this ship would seem to bring bad luck with her while transiting these waterways in regards to the many bridge openings required for her passage. Since part of the trip down the Chicago River to an unloading facility located on Goose Island would bring the **MEDUSA CHALLENGER** through the downtown area of Chicago, traffic delays were inevitable. This was only exaggerated when mechanical failure on the bridge's part caused the structure to become unusable for motorists, necessitating detours, or lengthy delays. In every recorded instance found, the cause for bridge delays in Chicago was blamed on mechanical failure with the bridge, with none being attributed to the ship. This was not always fully appreciated by the citizens working and living in the area whom quickly gained an apprehensive opinion about the **MEDUSA CHALLENGER**.

*The **MEDUSA CHALLENGER** passes downbound at St. Clair, Michigan during May of 1990. As can be seen in the background, she has just passed the upbound **WINNIPEG (4)**, which was operating for Canada Steamship Lines at the time. This latter vessel serves today in the Algoma fleet as the **ALGONTARIO**.*

Cement carriers on the Great Lakes are usually among the earliest ships to fit out each season, and the **MEDUSA CHALLENGER** was no exception to this. Since being converted this ship has not been involved in any major accidents although it did run aground on one occasion, this occurring on December 20, 1976 while transiting Lake St. Clair.

In 1978, Medusa purchased the **STEELTON (3)** from the Bethlehem Steel Corporation. This vessel was never placed into operation as a cement carrier, with Medusa opting to use it as a storage, and transshipment vessel on the Calumet River. This vessel was later renamed **C. T. C. NO. 1** in 1982, following a brief charter to Cleveland Cliffs in 1979 under the name **PIONEER (3)**. This ship has become a common unloading point for the **MEDUSA CHALLENGER**.

This ship has rarely ventured past Lake Erie, but in December 1978 it was recorded as passing through the Welland Canal. While in more familiar waters, on May 31, 1990 the **MEDUSA CHALLENGER** suffered an engine failure on the Calumet River, requiring tugboat assistance to reach the dock. Later that year, on November 20th the **MEDUSA CHALLENGER** arrived at the Miller Paving Dock at Owen Sound, Ontario with that facility's first delivery.

In March of 1998 Southdown Incorporated of Houston, Texas announced that it was acquiring Medusa Cement for 1 billion dollars in stock, thus creating the second largest cement firm in the United States at the time. This transaction did not effect this vessel's operation, although it was renamed to **SOUTHDOWN CHALLENGER** in April of 1999. At this time the Medusa emblems on the stack were also removed.

On September 29, 1999 the Mexican firm Cemex announced that it was to acquire Southdown through a 2.8 billion dollar merger deal. This put the operation of the **SOUTHDOWN CHALLENGER** into question as the Jones Act prohibits foreign owned ships from operating between US ports. This was later solved by the sale of the vessel to the Wilmington Trust Company, with HMC Ship Management, Limited taken over the operation of the **SOUTHDOWN CHALLENGER**.

*The **MEDUSA CHALLENGER** passes upbound at Port Huron, leaving the St. Clair River and entering Lake Huron in the early 1990s..*

*The **SOUTHDOWN CHALLENGER** is downbound on Lake Huron at Port Huron, Michigan during a wintry afternoon bound to a lower lakes port.*

*A bow view of the **MEDUSA CHALLENGER** shows the vessel's classic forward cabins, and placement of its cement unloading boom. When built in 1906 this ship was built to the most modern standards of shipbuilding practices at the time. Currently still in operation as a profitable carrier, 102 years after being constructed it is the oldest operational vessel on the Great Lakes. This has been made possible through two reconstructions during its career. In particular, the conversion to a cement carrier in 1967 when it had become too small in carrying capacity to economically operate in the domestic ore trades. It is also one of the dwindling number of lake steamers in operation on the Inland Seas. Despite many rumors over the years of an impending retirement or conversion to a barge, this ship has proven to be a survivor. This ship is a virtual floating museum celebrating shipbuilding practices of a time gone by.*

In early 2005 Cemex sold its operations in the Great Lakes region, including the **SOUTHDOWN CHALLENGER**, to the Brazilian firm Votorantim Cimentos. This firm placed it into St. Marys Cement of Toronto's United States subsidiary St. Marys Cement Incorporated. Consequently, this ship was renamed to **ST. MARYS CHALLENGER** in May of 2005 before reentering service that season.

In 2006 the **ST. MARYS CHALLENGER** celebrated its 100th anniversary of operation, and was given special markings to commemorate the milestone. This included the painting of "Still Steamin'" on her forward cabins, along with the years 1906 and 2006 painted on her bridge wings, with both of these logos being accompanied by a large red anchor emblem.

In April of 2008 the management of this steamer was given to Central Marine Logistics of Griffith, Indiana. This firm also manages the former Inland Steel vessels **WILFRED SYKES**, **JOSEPH L. BLOCK**, and **EDWARD L. RYERSON**. As of the end of the 2008 shipping season the **ST. MARYS CHALLENGER** is still busy working the Lake Michigan cement trade. Though an elderly ship by any measure, this ship should remain active in the near future.

*The **ST. MARYS CHALLENGER** is shown on May 2, 2009 at Bay Shipbuilding in Sturgeon Bay, Wisconsin undergoing preparations to begin her 2009 shipping season, following a drydocking.*

The ALPENA (2)

The onset of the Great Depression in 1929 would have a serious effect upon the movement of iron ore upon the Great Lakes. As the production of steel plummeted with the global economic collapse, the demand for raw material movement from the upper lakes suffered a significant decline. In 1929, the movement of ore reached 65 million gross tons which in itself set a high level mark for that trade up to that time. The next few seasons would see a noticeable reduction in the movement of ore with the 1930 season ore float being recorded as 46 millions tons, a reduction of 29 percent. So bad was this downhill slide that by the 1932 season the total ore movement on the inland seas was a paltry 3 and 1/2 million tons, before recovering to 21 million tons the following year.

The onset of war fears in the mid to late 1930s caused an increase in the demand for steel production at both home and abroad. This was reflected in the ore movement numbers during this time period, so much so that by 1939 it registered 45 million tons. On September 3, 1939 Britain declared war on Germany following that country's invasion of Poland, thus beginning the Second World War. Though the United States was still neutral at this time, it shortly became involved in supplying Britain with war materials. This, along with a build up in its own military created a huge demand for domestic iron ore movement.

The largest steel producer in the United States at that time was the United States Steel Corporation, with its Pittsburgh Steamship Company being tasked with transporting raw materials from around the Great Lakes to its unloading docks on Lakes Michigan and Erie. It was against these conditions when executives from Pittsburgh Steamship contracted both the American Ship Building Company and Great Lakes Engineering Works to build a new class of five vessels. The American Ship Building Company's Lorain, Ohio yard would build two of these ships, while the Great Lakes Engineering Works would construct three at their River Rouge facility.

In 1938, Pittsburgh Steamship placed the **RALPH H. WATSON**, and **JOHN HULST** into service following their building at the Great Lakes Engineering Works. The new vessels were to be based on an enlarged version of these two ships' design, and were to be built with a length of 639 feet 6 inches, a beam of 67 feet, and 35 feet. They also had other refinements to the cabins, and were equipped with more powerful engines.

On February 28, 1942 the first of these ships was launched at the Great Lakes Engineering works as the **LEON FRASER**. This shipyard went on to launch two additional units of this class that year, these being the **ENDERS M. VOORHEES**, and **A. H. FERBERT (2)**. Meanwhile, American Ship Building launched the **BENJAMIN FAIRLESS**, and **IRVING S. OLDS** in the spring of 1942. All of these ships entered service during the 1942 shipping season.

The entry into service of these five ships could not have happened at a better time for the movement of iron ore. With the attack on Pearl Harbor on December 7, 1941, the United States was now directly involved in the Second World War, and the demand for ore which was growing up to that time skyrocketed to an unheard of 92 million tons in 1942. This record would not be surpassed until 1953 when ore carriage reached in excess of 95 million tons.

While under construction the five ships of this class were often referred to as "Super Freighters" due to their large size. By time they entered service they were more commonly referred to as "Supers". This class was among the largest ships on the lakes at the time, and were 1 foot longer than the infamous **CARL D. BRADLEY (2)** which had been the longest ship on the Great Lakes when it was built in 1927. This group of vessels quickly became primary movers in the Pittsburgh fleet, and were thus responsible for a respectable percentage of that fleet's seasonal tonnage movement.

*These two close-up views of the **ALPENA (2)** illustrate the classic style of shipbuilding used when this vessel was constructed. The photo on the left shows a classic stack design, which was popular until the 1950s. The photo above shows the traditional placement of the pilothouse at the bow, which was a standard design feature for Great Lakes freighters until the 1970s. Built in 1942 as a member of Pittsburgh Steamship's "Super" class with a length of 639 feet, this group of ships strongly influenced the design of the sixteen "Maritime" class built during the Second World War. This latter group of ships were slightly shorter with a length of 620 feet.*

*The **ALPENA (2)** is downbound at St. Clair, Michigan following the conversion into a cement carrier. This conversion done in 1991, has been the last such rebuilding in the American Great Lakes fleet as of 2009.*

On June 21, 1942 the **LEON FRASER** departed Detroit, Michigan upbound for Duluth, Minnesota, where it loaded its initial cargo of iron ore. As originally launched this ship could carry up to 18,500 tons of ore, which was loaded and unloaded through 18 hatches placed on 24 foot centers. Each of these single piece hatch covers measured 43 feet in length, and 11 feet in width. This class also used much more welding for hull construction then had been used in previous classes.

The five ships of the "Super" class would remain among the largest ships in the United States Steel fleet for many years. When they entered service most of the ships in the fleet were able to haul around 12,500 tons of ore, and the "Super" class was only slightly surpassed in carrying capacity by the three ships of the AAA class built in 1952. These were the **ARTHUR M. ANDERSON, CASON J. CALLAWAY,** and **PHILIP R. CLARKE.** In fact, the **LEON FRASER** and her sisters were not surpassed significantly in capacity until 1972 with delivery of the **ROGER BLOUGH** which has the capability to haul 45,000 tons of ore per trip.

On July 11, 1943 the MacArthur Lock was opened at Sault Ste. Marie. The first official commercial passage through this vital facility was the upbound **CARL D. BRADLEY (2)**, which also carried a group of dignitaries for the event. The most reliable sources credit the **ENDERS M. VOORHEES** as the first downbound vessel through the lock, which contradicts some written accounts which indicate the **LEON FRASER** as the first downbound vessel.

The opening of the St. Lawrence Seaway in 1959 created new trade routes for shipping companies on the Great Lakes. By the early 1960s United States Steel envisioned sending many of their vessels up the Seaway to load ore, bringing it back to the unloading centers on the Great Lakes. It was intended that these ships haul grain on the outbound voyage, discharging it at a St. Lawrence River port prior to loading ore for the homebound leg of the trip. This eliminated the penalties of a one way trip without cargo.

To this end, United States Steel chose to start sending many of its more efficient carriers into the long haul Seaway trade, while their smaller ships continued to serve the established Great Lakes trade routes. The first such voyage was pioneered by the **ARTHUR M. ANDERSON** in August of 1962 when it arrived at Port Cartier, Quebec to load ore bound for Gary, Indiana. Shortly, all five units of the "super" class were pressed into service on this trade route. The **LEON FRASER** would carry additional freshwater within her ballast tanks for the engine and crew on these voyages into saltwater. These Seaway voyages would last until the mid-1970s after which they were discontinued. Despite this, the **LEON FRASER** was logged as passing through the Welland Canal on August 3, 1977 to load ore due to a iron mine strike on the upper lakes.

In 1968, the **LEON FRASER** was equipped with a bow thruster, enabling the ship to be less reliant upon tug assistance in tight maneuvers and docking. Another upgrade occurred in 1970 when it was converted from coal to oil fired, and its boilers were also automated at Milwaukee, Wisconsin by the Advanced Boiler & Tank Company.

Traditionally, the Great Lakes season ran from early April to December, with a four month lay-up period in between the shipping seasons. The onset of winter in December creates ice conditions in many areas around the inland seas which makes standard shipping practices impractical. By the late 1960s, United States Steel began exploring ways of breaking the ice barrier by operating many of its top units throughout the winter.

As with its Seaway endeavors, USS choose the ships of the "Super" class to be part of this program. On January 4, 1971 the **LEON FRASER** picked up a delegation of United States Steel officials at Detour, Michigan for a trip up the St. Marys River to observe winter navigation in action. After departing the **FRASER** at Sault Ste. Marie, Michigan, these officials were taken back down the St. Marys the following day on the **BENJAMIN FAIRLESS**. In November of 1972, the **LEON FRASER** arrived at the Fraser Shipyards to have an experimental bubbler system installed upon her hull. Two diesel powered air blowers were installed in the forward part of the ship, and these pushed low pressure air as bubbles through angle plates installed on the hull in an effort to limit ice friction. Testing of this system continued through January of 1973.

The **LEON FRASER** continued to operate in the winter navigation program until the late 1970s. Working in such conditions were hard on these vessels, and this ship suffered ice damage twice on Lake Superior in 1979. In the first instance minor damage was sustained in March of that year, only to suffer similar damages the following month, requiring minor repairs at Sault Ste. Marie, Michigan.

During the 1970s this steamer was involved in at least two other incidents. The first of these occurred on September 13, 1973 when the **LEON FRASER** came into contact with a railroad bridge at Duluth, Minnesota. The second instance, as will be seen, could have had much more serious consequences.

At the base of Lake Huron the lake empties into the St. Clair River on its journey downstream. As this river is very narrow compared to the wider expanses of the lake, it creates significant currents in the area near the Blue Water Bridge, which connects Michigan to Ontario. This location has been the scene of many collisions, and sinkings, not to mention several instances of ships striking the shore. It was at this point on June 6, 1978 that the **LEON FRASER** lost her rudder while upbound. This involved the entire rudder falling off of the ship as it was approaching the bridge. The crew of the **FRASER** were able to maintain directional control through the skillful use of the vessel's bow thruster. This allowed the **LEON FRASER** to continue up into lower Lake Huron and after reaching a point two mile above the Blue Water Bridge, it went to anchor outside of the shipping channel. The following day, tugs arrived on the scene and towed the **LEON FRASER** to Lorain, Ohio for repairs. Meanwhile, Malcom Marine was given the contract to find the missing rudder, which it located on September 20, 1978 just south of the Blue Water Bridge in Canadian waters. The crew of the **LEON FRASER** were commended by the United States Coast Guard in its official bulletin "Marine Spill", for their actions in preventing any damages or disruption in shipping.

By the early 1980s, many of the ships in the United States Steel fleet were becoming obsolete and were taken out of service. Several factors combined at the same time to create this situation. The widespread use of taconite pellets enabled longer shipping seasons, even without year round navigation, allowing for more trips per season. Taconite also allowed for the use of self-unloaders in trades which had been previously been dominated by straight deck bulk carriers. This permitted cargo unloading times to be drastically reduced which also enabled more cargoes per season.

A major jump in tonnage carriage capability within the US Steel Fleet came during the 1970s and early 1980s by four large ships entering service. These were the **ROGER BLOUGH, PRESQUE ISLE (2), EDWIN H. GOTT**, and **EDGAR B. SPEER** which alone have a combined single trip capacity of 249,200 tons of ore. To put this into perspective, to haul the same amount of cargo with a group of ships of the **LEON FRASER** type would require in excess of thirteen ships. This does not include the fact that the newer vessels were all self-unloaders, and could off load their cargoes independently, and at a much faster rate than that with shore side equipment. Additional savings were also realized in crew size, fuel consumption, and maintenance costs to name a few.

All of these factors combined, along with a drastic drop in the demand for domestic steel, created economic conditions not seen on the lakes since the Great Depression. Many lake vessels would be idled in the early 1980s never operate again. The **LEON FRASER** was one of many ships idled by the US Steel fleet in the early 1980s when she was laid up for the last time as an ore carrier on December 20, 1981 at Lorain, Ohio. During this same period, times had become tough enough for United States Steel that it was forced to idle even its thousand-footers at times. In fact the **ROGER BLOUGH** was idle at Sturgeon Bay, Wisconsin from 1981 to 1987.

During the 1980s, United States Steel drastically reduced the size of its Great Lakes fleet. By the end of the 1982 shipping season the fleet had ended straight deck operations, with the laying up of the **FRASER**'s sister **BENJAMIN FAIRLESS** in October of that year. In 1986, the **LEON FRASER** was sold to Spitzer Great Lakes, Incorporated for use as part of its marina development project at the former American Ship Building Company's Lorain Yard. Initial plans called for the **FRASER** to be used as a museum and entertainment center. By 1988 all of the "Super" class had been sold for scrapping, with the exception of the **LEON FRASER** which remained at Lorain.

The curved lines of the ALPENA (2) betray the traditional Great Lakes ore boat design. Shown here in 2000 on a downbound trip on the St. Clair River, this ship is bound for a lower lakes port.

Cement carriers are among the first ships to re-enter service at the beginning of each new shipping season. The ALPENA (2) is no exception to this, and is thus no stranger to encountering ice in its early voyages which usually begin in mid March. In this case this steamer is downbound at St. Clair, Michigan on March 27, 2005.

Spitzer would eventually abandon plans to convert the **LEON FRASER** into part of its redevelopement project, and this steamer was purchased by the Fraser Shipyards in 1989. This was done on behalf of Lafarge Incorporated, which had acquired the Huron Division of National Gypsum in 1987. In late October of 1989 the **LEON FRASER** was towed out of Lorain by the Port Huron, Michigan based tug **MALCOM** on her long journey north to Superior, Wisconsin, where she arrived on October 27th, for conversion into a cement carrier.

On June 5, 1990 the **LEON FRASER** was moved into Fraser's drydock, where she was shortened by 120 feet by removing a midsection of the hull, this shortening would allow for the ship to better serve Lafarge's facilities on the lakes. During the conversion the ship's holds were reconfigured for the carriage of cement, and a topside boom was mounted at the bow, just aft of the forward cabins. The ownership of this vessel was taken over by Lafarge's subsidiary, New Management Enterprises during this timeframe.

The work on this reconstruction proceeded smoothly, and this steamer was renamed **ALPENA (2)** in honor of the location of Lafarge's large cement facility. On May 28, 1991 the **E. M. FORD** arrived at Superior and unloaded a partial cargo into the **ALPENA (2)** to allow the testing of the newly installed cement handling equipment. On June 6, 1991 the **ALPENA (2)** departed Superior, following having experienced boiler problems, bound for Alpena, Michigan. While on her first trip under power since laying up in 1981 nagging boiler issues were encountered, forcing the steamer to cross Lake Superior at a reduced speed.

On June 10, 1991 rechristening ceremonies were held at Alpena, for this vessel. Following the conclusion of these festivities, the **ALPENA (2)** departed with 12,529 tons of cement bound for Superior. When it reentered service this ship was part of the Inland Lakes Transportation, Incorporated fleet, and was operated by Inland Lakes Management, Incorporated.

The 519 foot, 6 inch freighter quickly found herself hard at work servicing Lafarge's facilities around the lakes. Ports such as Detroit, Cleveland, Green Bay, Carrollton, Milwaukee and Muskegon were popular unloading destinations. With a carrying capacity of 13,900 tons at a mid-summer draft of 25 feet 9 inches, this ship just barely edged out its fleet **J. A. W. IGLEHART** by 700 tons as the largest ship in the Inland Lakes Transportation fleet in terms of capacity.

While trips on the upper lakes were the most common for the **ALPENA (2)**, voyages through the Welland Canal were not unheard of, with the first of these occurring on July 17, 1993. In September 1996, Andrie Incorporated obtained principal ownership of Inland Lakes Management.

On December 29, 1996 the **ALPENA (2)** was called upon to assist the **J. A. W. IGLEHART** which had ran aground in Saginaw Bay while carrying a load of cement for Carrollton, Michigan. After unloading a portion of her cargo into the **ALPENA (2)**, the **J. A. W. IGLEHART** was released with tugboat assistance.

On April 18, 2000, the **ALPENA (2)** briefly grounded at Grand Haven, Michigan while inbound with cement. After shifting ballast, the cement carrier freed herself and continued to the Lafarge dock to unload. A little over a year later on July 7, 2001 the **ALPENA (2)** rescued two divers in upper Lake Huron off of Alpena near the wreck of the salt water vessel **NORDMEER**. The divers had been underwater when their boat drifted away, thus stranding them.

In October of 2005, the **ALPENA (2)** lost her rudder in Lake Michigan, requiring a tow into the Bay Shipbuilding yard at Sturgeon Bay, Wisconsin. Demand for cement was significant enough at this time that it prompted the towing of the inactive cement carrier **S. T. CRAPO** from Green Bay, Wisconsin to Alpena to carry cement, while the **ALPENA (2)** was out of service. This ship had been inactive since 1996, and was used to haul at least one cargo, while repairs to the **ALPENA (2)** were completed. Meanwhile the lost rudder was located by the American Diving & Salvage Company and shipped to Bay Shipbuilding arriving there on October 14th. Repairs were completed rapidly, with the **ALPENA (2)** arriving at her namesake port on October 24, 2005 to load a cargo of cement.

One of Lafarge's facilities is located along the Saginaw River at Carrollton, Michigan which is around 120 miles southwest of Alpena. This river has been in recent years, the scene of many vessels having difficulties due to low water levels, combined with a lack of dredging. On April 4, 2006 this location was the scene of the **ALPENA (2)** running aground while attempting to turn just upriver from the Lafarge facility following the unloading of her cargo. This grounding was minor in nature, with the stranded vessel being freed shortly with tug assistance.

In 1996, the American flagged cement trade on the Great Lakes changed with the building of the barge **INTEGRITY** for Lafarge. This self-unloading barge had a capacity of 17,600 net tons, prompted the retirement of the **E. M. FORD**, and **S. T. CRAPO**. It also effected the operation of the **PAUL H. TOWNSEND**, and **J. A. W. IGLEHART** which would find themselves being utilized less then they had in previous seasons. In 2006, Lafarge placed another cement carrying barge, **INNOVATION**, into service. This second barge would in part prevent the reactivation of the **PAUL H. TOWNSEND** at Muskegon, Michigan which had been idle since the end of 2005 season, and the idling of the **J. A. W. IGLEHART** at Superior, Wisconsin in 2006.

This left only the **ALPENA (2)**, and **ST. MARYS CHALLENGER** as the last self-powered vessels committed to the cement trade under the American flag. The **ALPENA (2)** is powered by a 4,400 shaft horsepower De Laval steam turbine, giving an operating service speed of 14.1 miles per hour. This ship's cargo hold is divided into seven compartments, and is rated to carry 13,550 tons of cement through the St. Lawrence Seaway System.

The **ALPENA (2)** remains active as of the end of the 2008 shipping season. It tied up for the winter at the end of that season on December 24, 2008 at her usual lay-up location of Cleveland, Ohio. This ship is usually one of the first US flagged vessels to enter service each season, and time will tell what the future holds for this steamer. Repowering to diesel, or conversion into a barge may be possibilities.

*This view of the **ALPENA (2)** shows the classic lines of the Pittsburgh Steamship's "Super" class. Though converted into a self-unloading cement carrier in 1991, this ship appears much unchanged from the time it was built. The shortening of this ship by 120 feet during the before mentioned conversion, certainly makes this vessel appear much shorter than it was while serving for US Steel as the **LEON FRASER**. This is not as noticeable from this perspective due to the closeness of the photographer's boat, to the **ALPENA (2)**.*

The WILFRED SYKES

Following the end of the Second World War, demand for iron ore continued to be strong as the world rebuilt itself from the ashes of conflict. Despite the construction of the five ships of the **LEON FRASER** class, along with sixteen "Maritime" class freighters during the war, the majority of the American flagged fleet was becoming increasingly aged. Most ships in operation at the end of 1945 had been built prior to the 1930s, due to a shipbuilding slump that began during the Great Depression.

In 1948, the Inland Steel Company contracted the American Ship Building Company at Lorain, Ohio to construct a new 678 foot freighter. This ship was to be revolutionary in design, with no equals then in service or being built on the lakes. Inland Steel vessels were primarily engaged in the hauling of raw materials from the upper lakes into Inland's steel making facilities at Indiana Harbor, Indiana. This new ship was built for just that purpose.

Inland Steel had entered into the vessel owning business in 1911 when it created the Inland Steamship Company with the purchase of the Hawgood vessels **ARTHUR H. HAWGOOD**, and **W. R. WOODFORD**. These two steamers were renamed **JOSEPH BLOCK**, and **N. F. LEOPOLD**, and were placed into operation under the management of Hutchinson & Company. In 1936, the Inland Steamship Company was dissolved and the ships of this fleet became owned by Inland Steel outright. By the late 1940s the need for new capacity to satisfy its needs was recognized by company officials and thus prompting the building of a new ship. This would be the first ship to be ordered for Great Lakes use by an American fleet since the end of the Second World War.

This ship was also the first ship built for the US flagged Great Lakes fleet with a beam of 70 feet. While this beat US Steel's "Super" class by only 3 feet, it must be considered that most of the largest ships in service on the lakes at the time had an average beam of around 60 feet. This ship's after cabins stretched completely across the beam of the ship, providing an enclosed stern. This allowed for inside passageways for access to the compartments in the after cabins, rather then the need to go outside to gain access to individual rooms as was common at the time with traditional designs. The forward cabins were mounted at bow, as was tradition, but the pilot house was much more spacious then what was common. Overall, the ship was given a streamlined appearance, which still today provides a modernistic flare.

Widely touted at the time as the "Prototype of Today's Lakes' Vessel", this vessel ushered in a new philosophy in shipbuilding practices on the Great Lakes in both the American and Canadian designs for the next two decades. The construction of this steamer progressed with a steady pace at Lorain, with the ship's name, **WILFRED SYKES**, being painted on the ship while still on the ways. The building of this ship was a hugely important event at the time, and attracted much publicity. It was against this backdrop that it was launched on June 28, 1949, following the traditional breaking of a champaign bottle against the bow of the ship.

Following the launching into the Black River, the **WILFRED SYKES** was berthed so that the remaining fitting out tasks could be completed. This vessel introduced a new color scheme for the Inland Steel fleet, becoming one of the most popular to be used on the inland seas. The **SYKES** was painted with a dark brown hull, with white, gray, and dark blue bands on the forecastle, and stern. The hull colors incorporated a white sheer band which ran completely around the vessel, a few feet below the spar deck. The words "INLAND STEEL" were painted in large block letters on the sides of the ship, with Inland Steel's diamond logo placed between "INLAND" and "STEEL". The ships white cabins were also given a gray band. The streamlined stack was white with a stainless steel band about 1/3 the height of the stack. Above and below this band was a red band, and blue band respectively. Place upon the steel band was Inland's diamond logo. Within a short period of time the other members of the Inland fleet were also given these colors.

On November 28, 1949 the **WILFRED SYKES** departed Lorain and ventured into Lake Erie to begin her sea trials. These were successful and following finishing touches this steamer was formally transferred to its owners on January 20, 1950. In command of the **SYKES** during her sea trials was Captain Henry Kaizer. He had been involved very intimately with the construction of the vessel, and was assigned to command the **SYKES** when it entered operational service in 1950. Unfortunately, Captain Kaizer passed away in early 1950, and Inland assigned Captain George Fisher to command the **WILFRED SYKES**.

This steamer began its operational life when it departed Lorain on April 19, 1950 bound to load a cargo of coal at Toledo, Ohio. As the **WILFRED SYKES** proceeded on her maiden trip up the Detroit, and St. Clair Rivers she attracted much attention with crowds lining the shores to witness the historic first voyage. This amount of publicity would not be equaled, until the upbound voyage of the **STEWART J. CORT** in 1972.

Inland Steel had invested a reported 5 million dollars to build the **WILFRED SYKES**, and they quickly put the ship into operation in the ore trade to generate a return on this investment. With a carrying capacity of 22,000 gross tons of iron ore, she had the largest carrying capacity of any ship then on the Great Lakes. As the **SYKES** represented a substantial increase in vessel capacity, it is not surprising that she would set many cargo records early in her career. On September 7, 1950 the **SYKES** loaded a record 19,120 gross tons of ore at Superior, Wisconsin for Indiana Harbor. Over the next two seasons, she would beat her own record on numerous occasions, culminating with a record of 21,223 gross tons of ore loaded at Superior on August 27, 1952.

As mentioned earlier, the ships of the Inland Steel fleet were owned by Inland Steel, but were managed by Hutchinson & Company. But by the early 1950s, Inland Steel was starting to move in the direction of managing their own ships. On December 31, 1956 the management of this fleet was taken over formally by Inland Steel, thus ending the long term relationship with Hutchinson.

The **WILFRED SYKES** remained the largest ship in the Inland Steel fleet until 1960 when the **EDWARD L. RYERSON** entered service following her construction at Manitowoc, Wisconsin. The **RYERSON** has the distinction of being one of the few 730 foot vessels built for an American shipping company on the lakes, it was also the last ship built at Manitowoc.

Despite having a relatively quiet career, this steamer has been involved in a number of incidents since entering service. The 1973 season would see the **WILFRED SYKES** being involved in two incidents at Thunder Bay, Ontario. During the summer of that season this ship struck an ore dock at that port, requiring a trip to the local shipyard. Later, on August 5, 1973 the **SYKES** suffered hull damages to roughly 150 feet of its bottom, when it grounded at Thunder Bay.

*The forward cabins of the **WILFRED SYKES** heavily influenced later ships built during the 1950s, and 60s. Easily apparent in this view is the spacious pilot house, and attractive color scheme applied to the vessel. The colors of the Inland Steel fleet were considered one of the most attractive to have been used on the lakes. This made the ships of this fleet easily identifiable from a distance. While not easily seen in this photo, the windows in the ship's pilothouse are angled in such a way to reduce interior reflections.*

During this time, the **WILFRED SYKES** had remained in active service carrying ore from the upper lakes into Indiana Harbor. But by the early 1970s this steamer was being surpassed by newer vessels with significantly larger carrying capacities. This along with the emergence of taconite pellets which were easily unloaded by self-unloading vessels, caused Inland Steel officials to consider the future of the **WILFRED SYKES**. Having the insight that the future of the Great Lakes commerce would see heavy use of self-unloading vessels, it was decided to have the **WILFRED SYKES** receive such a conversion.

In 1975, the **WILFRED SYKES** was converted into a self-unloader by the Fraser Shipyards, at Superior, Wisconsin. While the conversion of straight deck bulk carriers into self-unloaders was nothing new, the conversion of this ship incorporated a stern mounted boom, rather then a bow mounted boom directly behind the forward cabins as was standard up to that time. Also given a similar conversion that year was Interlake's **HERBERT C. JACKSON**, which received her rebuilding at the Defoe Shipyard in Bay City, Michigan. Stern mounted unloading booms became a popular design for such reconstructions of American Ships as all converted since 1975 have had the stern mounted design, although the planned conversion of the **JOHN SHERWIN (2)** is to incorporate a bow mounted boom. However, this conversion was placed on hold near the end of the 2008 season due to severe economic conditions.

By July 1, 1975 the **WILFRED SYKES** was undergoing sea trials with her new unloading gear, and on July 9th she unloaded her first cargo as a self-unloader when she offloaded 23, 905 tons of taconite at Indiana Harbor. Later that season, this steamer participated search operations following the sinking of the **EDMUND FITZGERALD** on November 10, 1975. The **SYKES** had been downbound from Superior with a cargo of ore, which had been loaded at the same facility at which the **FITZGERALD** had loaded her last cargo.

This would not be the first time that the **WILFRED SYKES** was involved in a ship sinking in Lake Superior, as it had participated in the rescue of crewmembers from the **HENRY STEINBRENNER** which sank on May 11, 1953 during a spring storm. The **WILFRED SYKES** rescued two crewmembers from the sunken steamer, one after some dramatic ship handling. During this rescue the **WILFRED SYKES** was also maneuvered in such a way to provide a lee in the rough seas to allow the rescue of additional crewmembers from the **STEINBRENNER** by the **JOSEPH H. THOMPSON**. Following the rescue, the crew of the **SYKES** was recognized by the Inland Steel with the issuance of savings bonds.

Not only did the self-unloading conversion enable the **SYKES** to dramatically decrease turnaround time while unloading, it also allowed the vessel to be used in transporting cargoes outside of those required by its owning firm. Soon the **WILFRED SYKES** began making common trips into Lake Michigan ports such as Milwaukee, Muskegon, Holland, and Grand Haven.

The 1980s were a rough period for Great Lakes shipping, with many ships built during the 1950s, and 60s being idled, some never to operate again. During the time period the **SYKES** was not immune to being idled, and she did spend some time at the wall. However, for the most part Inland Steel was able to find work for this steamer, minimizing these inactive periods. By this time the **WILFRED SYKES** had been joined by the **JOSEPH L. BLOCK** which was constructed in 1976. During the 1980s these two vessels were the most active Inland ships, with the **EDWARD L. RYERSON** being idled several times, primarily due to not being a self-unloader.

One unique trip for the **WILFRED SYKES** during the 1980s took place on September 14, 1986 when it arrived at the Great Lakes Steel dock on the Detroit River with a cargo of limestone. Since this ship had concentrated on the Lake Superior to Lake Michigan run for most of her career up to that point, this was apparently the first trip thru the Detroit area since the late 1960s when she made passage with a load of ore for Cleveland, Ohio.

On April 26, 1994 the **WILFRED SYKES** began to take on water through its stern tube, following her departure from Port Inland, Michigan. After unloading her stone cargo at Green Bay, Wisconsin it went to Sturgeon Bay where it was found that she had tangled a cable around her propeller, causing the leakage.

*The **WILFRED SYKES** is shown just after departing Marine City, Michigan following the delivery of a stone cargo on May 28, 2005. This ship carries a large amount of aggregate payloads throughout a normal shipping season. Following its conversion into a self-unloader in 1975 this ship was able to serve many ports which it had been previously been unable to unload at. The before mentioned delivery into Marine City is a good example of this ship's added versatility following its reconstruction thirty years previously.*

*The **WILFRED SYKES** is downbound at Port Huron on December 30, 2006 on its way to Lorain, Ohio with a cargo of taconite. Despite being 60 years old, this vessel continues to be one of the busiest on the Great Lakes.*

The **WILFRED SYKES** is usually one of the earliest vessels to reenter service following the winter lay-up, while also being one of the last to tie up for the winter. While opening the navigation season at Grand Haven, Michigan on April 2, 1997 this ship struck a seawall at that port, causing damage to 60 feet of that structure. Strong winds, combined with tricky currents were determined to be the cause of this incident. This ship's adventures at Grand Haven would continue the following year when it ran aground there on August 11, 1998. No damages were reported to have been suffered by the **WILFRED SYKES** in this incident.

On April 10, 1998 the **WILFRED SYKES** passed downbound at Port Huron, Michigan on her first trip through this area since 1986. On this trip the **SYKES** was downbound with a cargo of ore for Ashtabula, Ohio. While this was an unusual trip for this vessel, as later events would show, the **WILFRED SYKES** would become somewhat of a common visitor to the lower lakes in seasons to come.

In 1998, Ispat International completed the purchase of Inland Steel. Since this was a Dutch owned corporation, the issue of the Jones Act came into play concerning Inland's remaining vessels **JOSEPH L. BLOCK**, **EDWARD L. RYERSON**, and **WILFRED SYKES**. Since the Act prohibits foreign owned ships from carrying cargoes between two US ports, this had a direct impact upon the operation of these vessels. To satisfy these regulations the ownership of the ships was transferred to the Indiana Harbor Steamship Company of Griffith, Indiana. Management of the vessels was taken over by Central Marine Logistics.

While the ownership of the **WILFRED SYKES** had changed, her duties continued much as before with her primary duty of supplying Ispat's manufacturing facility at Indiana Harbor. The most noticeable changes involved the **SYKES** color scheme. While the **SYKES** retained the old Inland Steel hull colors, the Inland diamond stack logos were removed, and the "INLAND STEEL" billboard lettering was painted over.

At the beginning of the 1999 season the **WILFRED SYKES** was approaching the 50th anniversary of its launching. To symbolize this, scripted text in the form of "50 Years of Smooth Sailing!" was painted upon each side of her pilot house.

In April of 2002, the **WILFRED SYKES** entered the Saginaw River with a load of stone to be split between Bay City and Saginaw, Michigan. This was the first time this ship had entered the Saginaw River area, but over the next three seasons the **WILFRED SYKES** would deliver numerous cargoes of the stone to docks on this river.

Also, during the period of the 2002 to 2005 seasons the **WILFRED SYKES** was utilized to carry taconite from Marquette, Michigan to River Rouge, Michigan. On occasion, the **SYKES** would go to Toledo, Ohio for a cargo of coal following the unloading of her cargo. Many of these coal cargoes were carried into Holland, Michigan.

Since the end of the 2005 season the **WILFRED SYKES** has concentrated her activities on Lake Michigan. Despite this, she has passed through the St. Clair River area on a few occasions. The latest such trip occurred on December 30, 2006 when she passed downbound with taconite for Lorain, Ohio. The **WILFRED SYKES** can carry 21,500 gross tons of ore at a mid-summer draft of 27 feet, 7 inches. Cargo is placed into the vessel's hold through 18 hatches, placed on 24 foot centers. Each of these hatches measure 44 feet in length, and 11 feet in width. This steamer is powered by its original Westinghouse steam turbine with a rated 7,700 shaft horsepower. The **WILFRED SYKES** can obtain a speed of 16.1 miles per hour. This vessel is also equipped with 17 ballast tanks.

As of the conclusion of the 2008 shipping season, the **WILFRED SYKES** remains very active in transporting raw materials on Lake Michigan. She is now sailing with Arcelor-Mittal stack markings, and is a frequent visitor to Escanaba, Michigan. During a regular season this ship will very rarely travel into Lake Superior, although such trips are not unknown. It is probable that the **SYKES** may one day receive a repowering to diesel to maintain its efficient operation. Regardless of what the future holds for the **WILFRED SYKES**, she will always be considered a turning point in the construction practices of the Great Lakes freighter.

The PHILIP R. CLARKE

In 1947, the Pittsburgh Steamship Company contacted the American Ship Building Company at Lorain, Ohio to design a new class of lake vessel. This class was to be based on that fleet's previous experience with the Miller, and Maritime Class vessels that had been placed into service from the late 1930s to the mid-1940s. The dimensions of the projected ships would be 647 feet in length, 70 foot beam, and a depth of 36 feet. This would provide a carrying capacity of 20,150 gross tons of iron ore. The length of 647 feet was determined as being the maximum length which could accommodated at the Conneaut, Ohio turning basin.

Pittsburgh Steamship would later decide not to proceed with this class of vessel, though the design had reached an advanced stage. This would change in 1950 when Pittsburgh revived this design, and contracted American Ship Building to build two ships, and the Great Lakes Engineering Works to build one vessel. The **PHILIP R. CLARKE** was to be the lead unit of this class, and it was launched on November 26, 1951 at Lorain. This was the next vessel to be built by that yard following the construction of the **WILFRED SYKES**. Although, the **CLARKE** had many things in common with the **SYKES**, it was built with much less flair than the Inland Steel vessel.

The **PHILIP R. CLARKE**, would be followed by seven other ships built to the same general design, split between the American Ship Building Company, and the Great Lakes Engineering Works. The other ships built by American Shipbuilding Company were the **ARTHUR M. ANDERSON, ARMCO**, and **EDWARD B. GREENE**. Those built at River Rouge, Michigan include the **CASON J. CALLAWAY, J. L. MAUTHE, RESERVE**, and **WILLIAM CLAY FORD (1)**. While all shared identical dimensions when built, there were some noticeable differences between the ships.

On May 10, 1952, the **PHILIP R. CLARKE** underwent sea trials off of Lorain, and departed on May 15th to begin her first trip. The first trip would be for a load of iron ore from Duluth, Minnesota destined for delivery to Conneaut, Ohio. The Pittsburgh Steamship Company designated this class of ships "AAA" for internal tracking purposes, and this class is commonly referred to as the "AAA" class, or in some quarters, the Pittsburgh class.

The **CLARKE** and her sisters were among the largest on the lakes when built, and as time would show these ships would be highly successful, and versatile in a number of roles. As with the other carriers in the Pittsburgh Steamship fleet the **CLARKE** would be primarily tasked with the movement of raw materials from the upper lakes into the US Steel's unloading facilities on the lower lakes.

The construction of the St. Lawrence Seaway during the 1950s, brought upon a period of optimism on the Great Lakes. United States Steel saw this as a avenue for the hauling of iron ore from the Lower St. Lawrence into their dock facilities on the Great Lakes. Another benefit of the Seaway system was the fact that grain cargo could be carried on the outbound trip to be unloaded at St. Lawrence River port, prior to be loaded with ore for the return voyage. This eliminated a costly, and inefficient trip in ballast without a paying cargo.

Being one of Pittsburgh's premier units, the **PHILIP R. CLARKE** was chosen to participate in the movement of ore through this trade route starting in the early 1960s. Also included in this program were the **CASON J. CALLAWAY, ARTHUR M. ANDERSON, LEON FRASER, BENJAMIN FAIRLESS, A. H. FERBERT (2), IRVING S. OLDS, ENDERS M. VOORHEES, EUGENE W. PARGNY, HOMER D. WILLIAMS, THOMAS W. LAMONT**, and **EUGENE P. THOMAS**. The use of these ships, allowed for less efficient vessels to concentrate on the movement of ore between Lakes Superior, and Lakes Michigan, and Erie.

The **PHILIP R. CLARKE** is downbound at Marine City, Michigan in the mid-1990s. By this time she had been lengthened to 767 feet, and converted into a self-unloader. All eight ships of this class, with one exception were lengthened by 120 feet during the 1970s.

The **PHILIP R. CLARKE** is upbound at Port Huron, Michigan during the early 1990s. It is about to pass under the span of the original Blue Water Bridge which was built in 1938 to connect the United States and Canada.

These seaway trips were significantly longer in distance then the traditional trade routes between ports these ships had normally traded between. A normal run between Duluth and Conneaut has a distance of 890 miles, while from the same departing point the distance to Port Cartier, Quebec is roughly 1,749 miles. On the Seaway run, the **CLARKE** would also pass through the eight locks of the Welland Canal system, and the seven locks of the St. Lawrence Seaway.

It was on one of these trips when the **PHILIP R. CLARKE** would suffer damages in a serious grounding. This occurred on October 1, 1972 when the **CLARKE** struck an obstruction near the Snell Lock. Following this accident, this steamer went to the Canadian Vickers yard at Montreal for extensive hull repairs. The **PHILIP R. CLARKE** departed the shipyard and resumed service on November 8, 1972.

In July 1964, the contract for the construction for the new Poe Lock at Sault Ste. Marie, Michigan was awarded. This had followed the excavation of the old Poe Lock at that site which took place between 1961, and 1964. This new lock would have a length of 1,200 feet, and a width of 110 feet. Ships of the Great Lakes had been traditionally limited in size by the dimensions of the locks at Sault Ste. Marie, and the new lock enabled ships to be built of up to 1,000 feet in length, and 105 feet in beam.

The **PHILIP R. CLARKE** became the first commercial ship to use the enlarged Poe Lock when she entered it on October 30, 1968. This passage was to validate the functionality of the new lock, with the **PHILIP R. CLARKE** returning on June 26, 1969 to participate in the official dedication ceremony. The **CLARKE** was opened for tours during the ceremonies, which also included the United States Coast Guard icebreaker **MACKINAW**, which was moored in the adjacent MacArthur Lock.

In the late 1960s United States Steel began advocating year round navigation on the Great Lakes. Up to that time the Great Lakes shipping season ran from about mid-April to mid-December, when the lakes and rivers began to freeze over. United States Steel thought it was possible, and profitable to run ships year round hauling materials into their steel processing centers. This would eliminate the need to stockpile during the season in anticipation of the four month gap of no waterborne transportation. As only the newest and strongest of their vessels would be involved in winter operations, it is no surprise that the **PHILIP R. CLARKE** would be one the ships chosen to participate.

Starting in 1968, the Soo Locks were kept open later into winter, until 1974 when a full year of navigation was possible through that facility, which is a key link in the movement of taconite from Lake Superior to the lower lakes. Year round operations on the Great Lakes would continue until 1979 when the mid-January closing date at the Soo Locks was established.

The **PHILIP R. CLARKE**'s winter operations would not be without incident, she was involved in at least two notable incidents during this time. On January 11, 1973 the **PHILIP R. CLARKE** was struck by its fleet mate **ROGER BLOUGH** in the Straits of Mackinac. This occurred when the **CLARKE**'s forward progress had been stopped by heavy ice, and the **BLOUGH** was unable to stop in time to avoid colliding with the 647 foot steamer.

A second accident occurred on March 21, 1976 the **CLARKE** was transiting on Whitefish Bay under the escort of the icebreaker **MACKINAW**. The **MACKINAW** encountered an ice ridge and came to sudden stop, and the **PHILIP R. CLARKE** was unable to avoid striking the icebreaker. The weather conditions at the time were less than perfect, with heavy snow and high winds. Both vessels later made it to Sault Ste. Marie, Michigan where it was discovered that the **CLARKE** had sustained a crack in her bow plating just above the waterline. This damage was patched prior to proceeding, with permanent repairs being done at Lorain, Ohio. The **MACKINAW** sustained more extensive damages to her starboard side, but was able to continue in operation.

In the early 1970s, several fleets began to build new carriers and lengthen others to take advantage of the Poe Lock. United States Steel placed the 858 foot **ROGER BLOUGH** into service in 1972, and had decided to lengthen the **CLARKE, ANDERSON, CALLAWAY,** and **MUNSON** during the 1974 to 1976 timeframe. All of these conversions were to be done at Superior, Wisconsin by Fraser Shipyards, Inc..

In October of 1974, the **PHILIP R. CLARKE** arrived at Superior and entered the shipyard to be lengthened by 120 feet with the insertion of a new mid-section. She had been preceded by the **CASON J. CALLAWAY** which had undergone the same process earlier that year. This reconstruction was accomplished rather quickly with the **PHILIP R. CLARKE** departing Superior on December 4, 1974. This lengthening allowed this ship to carry 26,525 gross tons of ore, an increase of 31% over its original carrying capacity. With a new length of 767 feet, the **CLARKE** was now unable to operate past the Welland Canal, thus limiting her area of operation no further east then Lake Erie. This was not to be a major factor in her career as US Steel's Seaway operations were winding down during this period.

Shortly after returning to service, on December 8, 1974, the **PHILIP R. CLARKE** collided with the **MERLE M. McCURDY** on Lake St. Clair. Both ships were downbound on the lake when the incident took place, with the **CLARKE** attempting to pass the **McCURDY**. No significant damages were reported following this collision and both vessels were able to proceed following an inspection.

By the early 1980s the economic benefits of operating self-unloaders in the taconite trade forced many ship operators to convert several of their vessels into self-unloaders. After just investing in their lengthening just a few years prior to this time, officials at United States Steel decided in 1981 to have all three of their AAA class converted. Again, the Fraser Shipyards was contracted to modify all three vessels of this class owned by US Steel.

At the end of the 1981 season, the **PHILIP R. CLARKE** laid up at Superior, Wisconsin following her last trip as a gearless vessel. Over the winter this ship's holds were modified to accommodate cargo gates which fed cargo onto conveyor belts running under the cargo hold. This in turn fed a topside boom mounted at the stern which is 250 feet in length, enabling cargo to be discharged onshore without assistance. Not only did this conversion enable the **CLARKE** to reduce its time dockside while unloading from 18 hours, to less then 6, it also allowed for operations outside of US Steel's ore trades.

During the 1980s, a ship's versatility was a significant factor in keeping that vessel in active service. Now that the **PHILP R. CLARKE** and her sisters were self-unloaders they could be employed in a wide array of trades. These ships were soon common sights at locations around the lakes, which they would not have been able to serve previously. Ports such as Green Bay, Manitowoc, St. Clair, and Ontonagon are some examples to name a few. In fact the **PHILIP R. CLARKE** became the first large freighter to enter the port of Ontonagon in over eight years when she arrived with a limestone cargo on May 11, 1983.

As the **PHILIP R. CLARKE** was arriving at the Reiss Coal dock at Superior, Wisconsin on August 30, 1983, a sudden gust of wind came up forcing the dropping of one the ship's bow anchors. After the **CLARKE** had secured herself to the dock, the anchor was pulled up which had entangled an automobile containing two bodies. Amazingly, these two individuals had been reported missing exactly five years previously on August 30, 1978.

While arriving at Corunna, Ontario to refuel on December 20, 1983 the **PHILIP R. CLARKE** collided with the Shell Fuel dock. The dock was heavily damaged, with approximately 75 feet of the structure destroyed. Damage to the **CLARKE** was reported to be of a minor nature.

The **PHILP R. CLARKE** was transiting the Black River at Lorain, Ohio on September 3, 1985 when it struck several small craft at a marina. Damages were reported in range of $40,000 to $60,000. In 1988, the **PHILIP R. CLARKE** received a stern thruster at Superior, Wisconsin by the Fraser Shipyards while in winter lay-up.

During the beginning of the 1989 shipping season the **PHILIP R. CLARKE** touched the bottom of the St. Marys River while upbound. Following a brief delay at Sault Ste. Marie, Michigan the **CLARKE** was allowed to proceed to the twin ports. On May 9, 1995 the **PHILP R. CLARKE** was downbound on Lake St. Clair in foggy conditions when she suffered a collision with the **SEA BARGE ONE**. This barge was the former **ADAM E. CORNELIUS (3)**, and was being pushed by the tug **ATLANTIC HICKORY** at the time of the accident. The **SEA BARGE ONE** suffered only minor damages in this incident, the **CLARKE** however received significant damages to her port side, requiring the replacement of several hull plates by the Fraser Shipyards.

While unloading salt at Sandusky, Ohio on September 2, 2000 the **PHILIP R. CLARKE**'s unloading boom suffered a failure allowing it to fall onto the top of the pile of cargo which had been unloaded. The unloading process was halted with 6,000 tons of salt still aboard, and the **CLARKE** departed for Sturgeon Bay for repairs by Bay Shipbuilding.

The ownership of this ship has undergone a number of changes since its construction in 1952. The Pittsburgh Steamship Division was consolidated directly into the Unites States Steel Corporation in 1964, and renamed the Pittsburgh Fleet. In 1967, a further consolidation was completed when the operations of the Pittsburgh Fleet, and those of the Bradley Transportation fleet were combined forming the United States Steel Great Lakes Fleet. This would last until 1988, when US Steel sold the majority of its stake in its shipping fleet to Blackstone Partners, Inc..

Once sold to Blackstone, the ships of the fleet were given a new color scheme. All of the ships operated by this fleet now sported red hulls, in contrast to the previous practice of having the former Bradley units retaining a light green hull. With the exception of the **PRESQUE ISLE (2)**, all of these ships had two diagonal stripes, one black the other gray, painted upon each side of the bow.

This arrangement with Blackstone Partners continued until October 2003 when it was announced that Canadian National had agreed to purchase the ships in this fleet, along with other transportation oriented properties owned by Blackstone. In May of 2004 this deal was finalized and the management of the **PHILIP R. CLARKE** was passed to the Keystone Shipping Company of Bala Cynwyd, Pennsylvania.

Regardless of these ownership changes the primary duty of the **PHILIP R. CLARKE** has remained the same in the 57 years since her entry into service, this being the transporting of raw materials into facilities owned by United States Steel. This steamer is powered by a Westinghouse Electric Corporation steam turbine with a rating of 7,700 shaft horsepower. The **CLARKE** is able to reach a speed of 16.1 miles per hour.

While the **WILFRED SYKES** brought several innovations in ship design to the Great Lakes when built in 1949, the **PHILIP R. CLARKE** will be remembered as the lead unit of one of the most prolific and versatile classes of steamers to ever have been built for service on the inland seas.

*The **PHILIP R. CLARKE** is downbound on the St. Clair River on December 18, 2005. As can be seen in this picture, the vessel is in need of a paint job. The **CLARKE**, and her sister ships are among the most versatile and hard working vessels on the Great Lakes.*

The KAYE E. BARKER

The Cleveland Cliffs Steamship Company had a long history of operating vessels upon the Great Lakes. This fleet can trace its roots back to 1867 when the Cleveland Iron Company purchased a 50% interest in the schooner **GEORGE SHERMAN**. This would start a series of transactions which by the start of the 1950s would see Cleveland Cliffs operating a large number of steamers engaged primarily in the movement of iron ore from the upper lakes to the lower lakes. A large amount of these cargoes would originate through Cleveland Cliffs' extensive holdings in Michigan, and Minnesota.

A steady demand of ore during the late 1940s, and into the 1950s coupled with an aging fleet compelled Cleveland Cliffs to acquire additional tonnage through construction. The newest vessels in the fleet at the time were the **CHAMPLAIN (3)**, and **CADILLAC (3)** which had both been built in 1943. Both of these ships were of the "Maritime" class, and had been acquired in part by the trade in of older tonnage the fleet owned during the Second World War. Cliffs had traded in five steamers to United States Maritime Commission as part of the acquisition process. These ships were the **CADILLAC (2), COLONEL, MUNISING, NEGAUNEE, YOSEMITE**. In order to free its name up for one of the new ships, the **CADILLAC (2)** was subsequently renamed **CHACORNAC**. After being traded in, these five steamers were chartered back to Cleveland Cliffs which operated them until 1953 when they were sold for scrapping.

To address the issue of obtaining new tonnage Cleveland Cliffs contracted with the American Ship Building Company to build a ship from a modified design of the "AAA" class, then being built for the Pittsburgh Steamship Company. Although, this vessel would share the same dimensions as the Pittsburgh steamers, it would have a more distinctive cabin arrangement. This ship would also be the first ship to be built at American Ship Building's yard in Toledo, Ohio following this shipbuilder acquiring the facility in 1945.

This vessel was christened on January 10, 1952 as the **EDWARD B. GREENE**. It departed the shipyard for sea trials on June 18, 1952, but due to a steelworkers strike this ship did not depart on her maiden trip until July 29, 1952. The first payload for this ship was a load of ore from Marquette, Michigan for Cleveland, Ohio.

Compared to the other vessels in her class the **EDWARD B. GREENE** had very distinctive forward cabins. This vessel had a much larger pilot house, when compared to the **PHILIP R. CLARKE**, additionally the forward cabins also had an extra deck with guest quarters. The **GREENE**'s smokestack was also more stylish when compared to the other seven ships built along the same lines.

Cleveland Cliffs also had a very pleasing color scheme for their freighters. This encompassed a black hull with white lettering for the ship's name, with large billboard "CLEVELAND CLIFFS" lettering placed on the each side of the hull. When entering service in 1952 Cleveland Cliffs also had a large diamond emblem with a large letter "C" centered within it at the amidships position. The cabins were painted olive drab, with white trim. The smokestack was entirely black with a large red "C" placed upon it.

With such colors the **EDWARD B. GREENE** made an unforgettable sight as she ventured out of Toledo for that first time, fully decorated with signal flags. The management of the Cleveland Cliffs Steamship Company had a history of being critical concerning the appearance of their vessels, and to see one with its paint in poor shape was truly a rare occurrence. The **EDWARD B. GREENE** quickly became a familiar sight passing through the Soo Locks, as she made her way to and from Lake Superior. Many of these trips would be into Marquette to load ore, although trips to Duluth, and Superior were common as well.

The **EDWARD B. GREENE**'s entry into service for the Cliffs fleet was preceded by that of the **CLIFFS VICTORY** which had entered operation on June 4, 1951. This ship had been rebuilt from a saltwater "Victory" class vessel built during World War II. Originally constructed in 1945 at Portland, Oregon by the Oregon Shipbuilding Company as the **NORTE DAME VICTORY** it had been laid up shortly following the cessation of hostilities as excess tonnage. Christened at Baltimore, Maryland on March 21, 1951 as the **CLIFFS VICTORY**, this ship was brought into the Great Lakes via the Mississippi River, and Chicago Sanitary Canals. This ship was acquired in part due to the fact that at the time all of the available American shipyards on the Great Lakes were backlogged with orders, thus creating a serious time lapse between the ordering of a ship and its entry into service. This situation was exaggerated by the material demands of the ongoing Korean War.

The **EDWARD B. GREENE** was the last ship constructed from the keel up for Cleveland Cliffs, and the second to last to be acquired through construction. The last ship to built for Cleveland Cliffs was the **WALTER A. STERLING** which entered service in 1961, following being reconstructed from a salt water tanker. As will be related later, these two ships would have similar histories in the upcoming decades.

During the early 1970s there was an energy crisis in the United States due to OPEC embargoes, causing the reassessment of alternative fuel sources. One of these was to create oil processed from shale rock, and in 1975 the **EDWARD B. GREENE** was chosen to use such a fuel on a trip starting in Cleveland to Marquette, and ending in Ashtabula. While on this voyage the **GREENE** flew a flag off of her forward mast with the words "SHALE OIL" affixed upon it. Though this trip proved that the use of shale oil was technically possible, the extreme cost difference when compared with conventional fuels made it very uneconomical.

Following the opening of the new Poe Lock in 1968, Cleveland Cliffs like many other American shipping companies looked into lengthening some of its more economical units to increase their capacities thus taking advantage of the dimensions allowed by the new lock. Both the **EDWARD B. GREENE**, and **WALTER A. STERLING** would a receive lengthening. The **EDWARD B. GREENE** was lengthened by 120 feet in 1976 at Superior, Wisconsin by the Fraser Shipyards. This reconstruction was similar to those given to all but one of the ships built of the "AAA" class.

By mid-June of 1976 the **EDWARD B. GREENE** was undergoing her sea trials with the new length of 767 feet. This had increased her carrying capacity from 20,150 gross tons to 26,750 gross tons of taconite. The first voyage following the lengthening would not be uneventful however. While downbound on Lake Superior on June 20, 1976 it was discovered that the **EDWARD B. GREENE** was taking on water through a crack in the hull. The Cliffs steamer made it safely to Sault Ste. Marie, where part of the cargo was off loaded, prior to proceeding downbound for Conneaut, Ohio. Following the unloading of the remaining cargo, the **EDWARD B. GREENE** went to Lorain for permanent repairs at the American Ship Building Company.

By the early 1980s, the trend towards the use of self-unloaders in the ore trade was causing ship owners once again to look at modernizing their premier units. Cleveland Cliffs had only one self-unloader in operation at the beginning of the 1980s, this being the **WALTER A. STERLING,** which had been converted in 1978. The remainder of its vessels were straight deck bulk carriers, and thus tied to onshore unloading facilities. As many of these facilities began to eliminate their unloading equipment, in favor of receiving self-unloading vessels, many of the ships in the Cleveland Cliffs fleet began to be at a disadvantage during a time at which the demand for iron ore transportation was itself declining. This was accompanied by a number of other factors, one of which was Cleveland Cliffs' loss of the Republic Steel ore hauling contract in 1980. The loss of this very important contract essentially ended the careers of all the smaller steamers in the fleet. As the **WALTER A. STERLING** was showing it was able to operate in a number of trade routes with its unloading capability, Cleveland Cliffs officials decided to perform a similar reconstruction to the **EDWARD B. GREENE**. The **STERLING** had been converted by the American Ship Building Company, and this firm was contracted to perform a similar operation to the **GREENE**, which would be undertaken at their Toledo yard.

On August 6, 1980 the **EDWARD B. GREENE** arrived at Toledo following unloading her last cargo as a straight decker at Conneaut the previous day. Interlake Steamship had won the Republic Steel ore contract which Cleveland Cliffs had been unable to successfully secure. So it was ironic that when the **GREENE** entered the shipyard she tied up next the Interlake's **ELTON HOYT 2nd (2)** which was also being converted into a self-unloader, in large part to that firm winning the lucrative Republic contract.

By 1981, the **EDWARD B. GREENE** had returned to service as a self-unloader, and she along with the **WALTER A. STERLING** were the only active carriers in the Cleveland Cliffs fleet. Despite only operating two of their ships, Cleveland Cliffs was still active in trying to pursue new contracts, with many hopes being pinned on winning a coal hauling contract for Detroit Edison. This contract would eventually be won by the Interlake Steamship Company, with deliveries starting in 1984.

On June 8, 1982 the **EDWARD B. GREENE** ran aground in the St. Clair River, following a loss of power. The **GREENE** was upbound at the time and was able to free herself after being stranded for around four hours.

While the decade of the 1970s had been a period of great optimism for the Cleveland Cliffs fleet, the 1980s would prove to be its demise. During the 1970s it had not built any new tonnage, and in particular no 1,000 foot vessels, as many other American shipping companies had. In fact no major US flagged company that had not acquired new tonnage during the 1970s would survive the 1980s intact. Cleveland Cliffs officials had considered building a 1,000 foot ship, but without securing the Republic or Detroit Edison contract this idea was dropped.

In May of 1984 both the **EDWARD B. GREENE**, and **WALTER A. STERLING** made several trips carrying ore into the Ford Plant on the Rouge River. The **GREENE** had made at least one similar trip previously in June of 1982. In a few months, both the **GREENE**, and **STERLING** would be committed to providing the transportation of ore into the Rouge River supplying the demands of the Ford Motor Company.

In October of 1984, the Cleveland Cliffs Steamship Company ceased operations with the sale of the **EDWARD B. GREENE**, and **WALTER A. STERLING** to the Rouge Steel Company. During its long history of over 110 years, this fleet had operated only one diesel powered freighter, this being the **RAYMOND H. REISS** which served in the fleet from 1972 to 1980. Following their purchase both steamers went to the Fraser Shipyards, where they were repainted and renamed.

The **EDWARD B. GREENE** was renamed **BENSON FORD (3)**, while the **STERLING** became **WILLIAM CLAY FORD (2)**. By the start of the 1985 shipping season both ships had received the colors of the Rouge Steel fleet, and had their new names painted on. As part of its new fleet the **BENSON FORD (3)** was engaged primarily in the transport of ore and coal into the Rouge Steel Plant at Dearborn, Michigan.

Despite being committed to the Rouge Steel run, the **BENSON FORD (3)** did operate outside of this route as demands warranted it. On one such trip this steamer became the largest ship to enter Manistee, Michigan when she arrived on August 2, 1985 with coal. Later, on May 4, 1988 the **BENSON FORD (3)** was noted as being the first ship of the season into Ashland, Wisconsin.

Service in the Rouge Steel fleet did not last long however as the **BENSON FORD (3)**, and **WILLIAM CLAY FORD (2)** were sold on March 13, 1989 to the Interlake Steamship Company, who placed them into its newly formed subsidiary, the Lakes Shipping Company. This transaction also included the **HENRY FORD II** which would never operate again. At the time of the sale a long term contract was secured with Rouge Steel to provide its raw material transportation needs, thus bringing to a close of Ford Motor Company's marine transportation activities which dated back to 1923.

Immediately following the sale, the **BENSON FORD (3)** was renamed **KAYE E. BARKER**. Meanwhile, the two other ships involved in the sale were also renamed with the **WILLIAM CLAY FORD (2)** becoming **LEE A. TREGURTHA**, and **HENRY FORD II** being renamed **SAMUEL MATHER (7)**. As mentioned earlier the latter ship would remain idle, after being towed to Toledo in June of 1989, and finally sold for scrapping in 1994.

*The **KAYE E. BARKER** is downbound on the St. Marys River in the mid-1990s in Lakes Shipping Company colors.*

*The **KAYE E. BARKER** awaits its turn to lock downbound in the Poe Lock during the 1990s. With a length of 767 feet, this steamer is limited to utilizing only that lock at Sault Ste. Marie, Michigan.*

The **KAYE E. BARKER** was repainted into her new fleet colors prior to reentering service in 1989. The fleet colors of the Lakes Shipping Company were identical to those of the Interlake Steamship Company, with a dark brown hull, white cabins, and a black stack with an orange ring. As planned, this ship would concentrate on the carriage of ore from the upper lakes to the Rouge Steel Plant.

On March 15, 1994 the **KAYE E. BARKER** departed Erie, Pennsylvania on its first trip of the season. At the time the **BARKER** was bound for Sandusky, Ohio to load coal, but soon ran into heavy ice on Lake Erie. The steamer encountered ice of up to five feet thick, requiring the assistance of the United States Coast Guard cutter **NEAH BAY**, and the Canadian Coast Guard icebreaker **GRIFFON**. Despite the efforts of the icebreakers, the **KAYE E. BARKER** was not freed until March 20th. This steamer would remain active that season until January 25, 1995, which was reportedly the longest season for any Interlake Steamship owned vessel up to that time.

*Easily seen in this view is the extra deck built into the **KAYE E. BARKER**'s forward cabin, as compared to other vessels of the "AAA" class pioneered by the **PHILIP R. CLARKE**. This ship is shown on April 29, 2007 while downbound on the St. Clair River. Beginning in 1984 this ship has been engaged heavily in the movement of taconite from the upper lakes and into Ford Motor Company's Rouge Steel plant in Dearborn, Michigan. This steel plant which was sold to Severstal International in 2004 is still served by this vessel. This ship was one of the eight vessels of the "AAA" class, all of which were modified at some point during their careers. This ship has had two major rebuildings since her construction in 1952.*

The steamer **KAYE E. BARKER** has the distinction as delivering the last load of limestone into the Dow Chemical Plant at Ludington, Michigan when she arrived there on August 8, 1998. Following this delivery future needs were to be transported by rail.

On December 19, 2000 the **KAYE E. BARKER** damaged the Shell Fuel Dock at Corunna, Ontario while arriving to refuel. The dock received extensive damages, with repairs costing an estimated $300,000. The fuel dock which is a popular refueling stop along the upper St. Clair River for upbound vessels was put out of service until repairs could be completed. This dock has been hit by numerous docking vessels over the years.

As with many other ships of her class, the **KAYE E. BARKER** is very active in many different ports on the Great Lakes. Confined to operating no further east than Lake Erie by her 767 foot length, which prevents passage through the Welland Canal this ship can be found in places such as Grand Haven, South Chicago, Stoneport, Toledo, Sandusky, Green Bay, Marquette, and Escanaba. This is in addition to her runs into the Rouge River with ore for the Severstal steel plant (formerly Rouge Steel), which has been a mainstay of her activities since 1984.

While downbound on Lake Superior, and just approaching Whitefish Point on November 5, 2006 the **KAYE E. BARKER** suffered a boiler explosion causing serious injuries to two crewmembers. Injuries sustained by the two persons were significant enough to require an airlift for medical treatment from a United States Coast Guard HH-65 Dolphin helicopter. Following the explosion which occurred at eight o'clock in the morning, the **KAYE E. BARKER** went to anchor in Whitefish Bay. Engineers aboard the disabled steamer were successful in restoring motive power to the ship, and the **BARKER** was allowed to continue downbound through the Soo Locks, arriving at the Carbide Dock at Sault Ste. Marie where she was docked for inspection. The following day the **KAYE E. BARKER** was permitted to leave, and continued her trip downbound on the St. Marys River in the early afternoon. While a boiler explosion is an extremely rare occurrence in current Great Lakes shipping, it was a relatively common event in the early days of steamship operations.

The **KAYE E. BARKER** is capable of carrying 25,900 gross tons of taconite at its maximum draft of 27 feet. Cargo is loaded into a five sectioned cargo hold through 23 separate hatches, each measuring 46 feet by 11 feet. This steamer is capable of off loading its cargo via a 250 unloading boom mounted on a pivot point 150 feet from the stern of the vessel. To increase her maneuverability and ease its docking operations, the **KAYE E. BARKER** has been fitted with both bow and stern thrusters.

For motive power, this 57 year old steamship utilizes its original De Laval steam turbine with a rating of 7,700 shaft horsepower. With this power plant the **BARKER** is able of achieving speeds of up to 17 miles per hour. Continued operation on steam power may be coming to an end in upcoming years as Interlake continues a modernization program of repowering its vessels. In 2006 it repowered the **LEE A. TREGURTHA** from steam to diesel, with similar repowering of the **CHARLES M. BEEGHLY** being done in 2009. Along with these two modernizations, Interlake had begun the rebuilding and repowering of the long idle **JOHN SHERWIN (2)**. This project was put on hold in late 2008 due to economic conditions, but should resume once conditions become more favorable. These before mentioned repowerings leave only the **KAYE E. BARKER**, and **HERBERT C. JACKSON** as the last steamers owned by Interlake. Both of these ships are excellent candidates to also receive diesel engines allowing for continued economical operation.

*The **KAYE E. BARKER** is downbound on the St. Clair River during the 2007 shipping season with a cargo of taconite for the lower lakes.*

The ARTHUR M. ANDERSON

The **ARTHUR M. ANDERSON** became the second of three "AAA" class steamers to enter service for US Steel's marine division, the Pittsburgh Steamship Company when it departed Lorain, Ohio on August 10, 1952 bound for Two Harbors, Minnesota to load a cargo of iron ore. It had been third of this class to be built by the American Ship Building Company, and its construction was completed at Lorain as hull #868 immediately following that of the **PHILIP R. CLARKE**.

As with other members of her class, the **ARTHUR M. ANDERSON** concentrated on the hauling of raw materials from the upper lakes to the lower lakes. Though not the largest on the lakes in any sense of the distinction, the **ANDERSON** at 647 feet in length was tied with the **CLARKE** as being the longest ship in the Pittsburgh Steamship fleet at the time of her maiden voyage. The title for the longest ship owned by US Steel would change later in August of 1952 with the entry into service of the **JOHN G. MUNSON (2)** which was built for that firm's Bradley Transportation Line subsidiary. This ship was slightly longer then the "AAA" class, at 666 feet, 3 inches. It was also the largest self-unloading vessel on the Great Lakes at the time.

The **CALLAWAY, ANDERSON,** and **CLARKE** would all have similar careers, with the **ANDERSON** becoming the most famous of the trio primarily due to her involvement with the sinking of the **EDMUND FITZGERALD** in 1975 which will be related later. In 1953, the Pittsburgh Steamship Company was integrated directly into United States Steel's corporate structure as the Pittsburgh Steamship Division. This transition did not effect the operation of the **ANDERSON**, and her seasonal duties remained unchanged.

The opening of the St. Lawrence Seaway in 1959, created the opportunity for United States Steel to haul iron ore through that system into their unloading facilities on the lower lakes. To do so, the most efficient vessels in the Pittsburgh Steamship fleet were utilized. The **ARTHUR M. ANDERSON** would inaugurate these voyages when she arrived at Port Cartier, Quebec on August 17, 1962 to load ore for delivery to Gary, Indiana.

Shortly, ships of the Pittsburgh Steamship Division became a common sight in the Welland Canal, and St. Lawrence Rivers. A side benefit of the Seaway was the fact that cargo could be carried both ways through the system, thus eliminating the necessity of a trip in ballast, without a paying cargo. Thus, several of the ships in this fleet would carry grain to St. Lawrence ports, and then carry ore back through on its return trip. As stated before, only the most efficient ships were routinely engaged in these Seaway trips. Included were all three of the "AAA" class, along with all of members of the **FRASER** class, and four ships repowered during the 1950s and 60s, these being the **EUGENE W. PARGNY, HOMER D. WILLIAMS, THOMAS W. LAMONT,** and **EUGENE P. THOMAS**. Seaway operations for the US Steel fleet would continue until the late 1970s when they concluded following a steady decline during that decade.

In 1964, the Pittsburgh Steamship Division was dissolved with ships being absorbed directly into the United States Steel Corporation. This arrangement would continue until 1967 when the operations of the Pittsburgh Fleet were combined with those of the Bradley Transportation fleet, thus becoming the United States Steel Corporation Great Lakes Fleet. During the 1960s the demand for iron ore transportation on the Great Lakes had remained relatively strong with the lowest demand occurring in 1961 when 60,897,367 gross tons were moved, and the highest movement occurred in 1969 when 86,307,605 gross tons were carried to ports on the inland seas.

In the late 1960s United States Steel was studying the feasibility for the extension of the navigational season into late winter. Starting with the 1968 shipping season, the Army Corps of Engineers began to keep the locks at Sault Ste. Marie, Michigan open past the traditional December closing date. That year the 1968 shipping season would come to an end on January 9, 1969 with the passage of the **ENDERS M. VOORHEES**. During the next few seasons the closing of the locks was pushed back, until the 1974 season when the Soo Locks were kept open year round. The **ANDERSON** and her sister ships were actively engaged in this year-round navigation program throughout its tenure which ended in 1979 with the establishment of the mid-January closing date of the Soo Locks.

By the end of the 1960s the opening of the Poe Lock at Sault Sainte Marie which allowed the passage of ships up to 1,000 feet in length, heralded a new era of growth within the US flagged fleet on the Great Lakes. As shipping firms examined their fleets to determine how best to stay competitive with the opportunities provided by the new lock, many began modernization programs to update their fleets. In 1967, United States Steel placed an order with the American Ship Building Company for a 858 foot supership, which was to become the **ROGER BLOUGH**. Besides ordering this ship, US Steel decided by the early 1970s to lengthen four of their steamers built during the 1950s. These ships were the **ARTHUR M. ANDERSON, CASON J. CALLAWAY, PHILIP R. CLARKE**, and **JOHN G. MUNSON (2)**.

In 1975 the **ARTHUR M. ANDERSON** was lengthened by 120 feet to 767 feet in length at the Fraser Shipyards in Superior, Wisconsin. This reconstruction allowed this steamer to carry an additional 6,375 tons of cargo per trip, an increase of 31 percent over its previous capacity of 20,150 gross tons. While this rebuilding allowed the **ANDERSON** to haul significantly more cargo per year, it also constricted her movements to no further than Lake Erie as she was now too long to pass through the Welland Canal. This eliminated the **ANDERSON**'s capability to haul ore on US Steel's Seaway trade routes, but as mentioned earlier these trade patterns were on the decline by the time and were not to be a overriding consideration in this ship's future.

On November 9, 1975 the **ARTHUR M. ANDERSON** departed Two Harbors, Minnesota with a load of ore. Though the weather earlier that day was mild, storm warnings were posted for later that day. Shortly after leaving port the **ANDERSON** made radio contact with **EDMUND FITZGERALD** which had departed Superior, Wisconsin and the two decided to take a northern route on their voyage across Lake Superior due to the expected change in the weather. Throughout that day and into the following morning the two ore carriers made steady progress across the lake. Though the **FITZGERALD** had been behind the **ANDERSON** when the two met, the former vessel was somewhat faster and it later overtook the **ANDERSON** opening up a lead of about 15 miles by the afternoon of November 10th.

The forward cabins of the ARTHUR M. ANDERSON are basically unchanged since her construction in 1952. There are some noticeable differences however. Most prominent is the addition of bridge wings added following the ship's conversion to a self-unloader in 1982. Though built shortly after the WILFRED SYKES, the eight ships of the "AAA" class do not have the dramatic flare incorporated into the Inland Steel vessel. This does not detract from their usefulness, as lake freighters are built to haul cargo efficiently and this class has proven to be quite able to do just that for over 50 years.

This particular storm was relatively small in size, but what it lacked in mass was more then made up by the severity of the winds it was composed of. Some of the gusts recorded during this storm were in the range of 90 miles per hour, with sustained winds of 60 miles per hour. By late afternoon, both ships were on the final leg of their path across Lake Superior, when the **EDMUND FITZGERALD** contacted the **ANDERSON** indicating that they had sustained some topside damage, and were taking on some water causing a list. The **FITZGERALD** also requested that the **ANDERSON** provide navigational aid, as the stricken freighter had also lost the use of her radars. The **FITZGERALD** had slowed down slightly to allow the **ANDERSON** to close the gap between the two ore carriers.

By late afternoon sustained winds were being recorded in the 80 miles per hour category, and both ships were taking massive waves from astern. By 7:00 PM on November 10th, the **FITZGERALD** was about 20 miles north of Whitefish Point. At approximately 7:10 PM, the last radio communication from the **FITZGERALD** was received by the **ANDERSON** in response to an inquiry as to what the situation was with its difficulties. The reply was simply, "We are holding our own."

Shortly after this the radar operators watched the **FITZGERALD** sail into a blob of radar returns caused by the heavy wave action, and a snow squall. After this cleared a few minutes later, the image of the **FITZGERALD** had disappeared from the radar scopes. Over the next few minutes the **ANDERSON** attempted to contact the **FITZGERALD** without success. It then contacted some vessels in Whitefish Bay to verify that its radio was working. Upon receiving an affirmative response, Captain Jesse Cooper then contacted the Coast Guard Station at Sault Ste. Marie.

The Coast Guard was initially reluctant to believe that the **FITZGERALD** had been lost, and it was not until around 9 PM that evening that search and rescue operations were initiated. Since the nearest rescue forces were literally hours away, the Coast Guard contacted freighters in Whitefish Bay to request that these ships participate in a search for survivors. Initially, the only ships able to respond to this request were the **ARTHUR M. ANDERSON, HILDA MARJANNE** and the **WILLIAM CLAY FORD (1)**. However, the **HILDA MARJANNE** soon returned to the safety of Whitefish Bay, leaving the **ANDERSON**, and **FORD** to continue out into the lake. Over the next several hours these two ships searched the area where it was believed that the **FITZGERALD** had gone down, but no survivors were found. A total of 29 crewmembers were lost in this sinking.

As news got out about the **FITZGERALD** sinking, Captain Cooper found himself in the spotlight as being in command of the ship which had sailed basically in tandem with the sunken ship through the storm. For the rest of his life Captain Cooper would be sought out for his views on the cause of the wreck, and his recollection of that trip. Since the crew of the **FITZGERALD** never elaborated on the cause of its sustained damages or their severity, several theories have come forward to explain the sinking. Had the **ARTHUR M. ANDERSON** not been in close proximity to the **EDMUND FITZGERALD** during that November storm, most likely even less would be known as to the events leading up to the demise of that lake carrier.

The **ARTHUR M. ANDERSON** has had very few incidents during her career. On July 18, 1961 this steamer suffered a minor grounding in the St. Marys River during heavy fog. Following the lightering of some of her cargo, the **ANDERSON** was released from the stranding. A more serious accident occurred on January 31, 1979 while the **ANDERSON** was engaged in the winter navigation program. The **ANDERSON** ran into the stern of the United States Coast Guard icebreaker **WESTWIND** during icebreaking operations near Ashtabula, Ohio. The **ANDERSON**'s damages included a hole in her bow starting at the 29 foot draft mark, extending upwards for about 12 feet, along with buckling to her forecastle deck.

As with many other fleets at the beginning of the 1980s, US Steel began to explore the option to rebuild its most efficient straight deckers into self-unloaders. Despite having a large fleet of gearless bulk carriers at the time, it was decided to only convert the **ARTHUR M. ANDERSON, CASON J. CALLAWAY**, and **PHILIP R. CLARKE** into self-unloaders. The other ships in the fleet at the time were considered to have too small of a carrying capacity, or overly advanced in age to justify the expenditure for such conversions.

*The conversion of the **ARTHUR M. ANDERSON** into a self-unloader in 1982 enabled this vessel to remain an efficient carrier in the movement of bulk materials around the Great Lakes Visible in this view are the extensions added to the stack to address updraft problems associated with the unloading structure added just forward of the after cabins during the self-unloading conversion.*

*The steamer **ARTHUR M. ANDERSON** is shown downbound on the St. Clair River on May 30, 2005. Since her entry into service in 1952 such a passage has occurred hundreds of times. This steamer is one of the most well known ships on the Great Lakes, in large part due to her role in the **EDMUND FITZGERALD** sinking.*

The **ANDERSON** along with her sisters would undergo these conversions at the Fraser Shipyards, with all of them converted by early 1982. The **ANDERSON** entered service as a self-unloader on May 1, 1982. As with many other ships of her class, the conversion to a self-unloader enabled cargoes to be carried into locations which had previously been impossible to serve due to the lack of unloading equipment. Thus, the **ANDERSON** would commonly begin to operate in trades outside of US Steel's iron ore movement when tonnage.

With the downturn in the steel industry during the early 1980s, the conversion that the **ARTHUR M. ANDERSON** received could not have come at a more opportune time. With the ability to operate in the stone, and coal hauling trades the **ANDERSON** was able to stay active when the demand for ore decreased. This aspect of US Steel's shipping operations on the Great Lakes had been traditionally been served by the ships in the Bradley Division. If this ship had not received the conversion when it did, it is very probable that it would have spent much of the decade idle, and may not have survived this turbulent era.

In 1988, US Steel sold a majority of its stake in their shipping fleet to the Blackstone Partners Group. With this change the ships of the fleet were given new colors of the familiar ore red hull, but with a gray and black diagonal strip on the bow. This color scheme change was also applied to the ships of the former Bradley fleet which up to this time had retained the green colored scheme. By 2000, US Steel had sold the balance of its share in the fleet to Blackstone.

On May 28, 1994 the **ARTHUR M. ANDERSON** docked at the Canada Starch dock at Port Colborne, Ontario, thus becoming the longest ship to have docked there up to that time. A second trip to that location occurred in June of the same season. In June of 1997 the **ANDERSON** arrived at Sturgeon Bay, Wisconsin to receive repairs to its portside ballast tanks at Bay Shipbuilding following a reported grounding.

Another trip to Bay Shipbuilding was necessary on April 8, 1999 following a grounding at Rogers City, Michigan two days earlier. The **ANDERSON** had just loaded 26, 259 tons of limestone at that port bound for Buffington Harbor, Indiana when she stranded just outside of the breakwall while departing. The **ANDERSON** was later freed after unloading around 7,000 tons of cargo into the **WOLVERINE (4)**. The **ANDERSON** then went back to the dock at Rogers City where she offloaded the remainder of its cargo, before departing for Sturgeon Bay.

The beginning of the 2001 shipping season would not be without incident for the **ARTHUR M. ANDERSON**, as she ran into engine troubles in the Straits of Mackinac on March 24, 2001. Problems with a steam throttle valve forced the anchoring of the 767 foot freighter. On March 25th the **EDGAR B. SPEER** arrived on the scene and took the **ANDERSON** into tow, arriving at Sturgeon Bay on March 26, 2001. Following repairs the **ANDERSON** departed the following day, only being forced to return for additional repairs after experiencing more engine problems.

In October 2003, it was announced that Canadian National had agreed to purchase the ships of the Great Lakes Fleet, Incorporated fleet along with several other properties owned by the Blackstone Partners Group. This transaction was finalized in May of 2004, with the Keystone Shipping Company of Pennsylvania taking over the management of the **ARTHUR M. ANDERSON**.

This ship can carry 25,300 gross tons of cargo at her mid-Summer draft of 26 feet. This cargo is discharged by the **ANDERSON**'s unloading gear at a rate of 6,000 tons per hour, via a 262 foot boom. This vessel is powered by its original steam turbine engine capable of producing 7,700 shaft horsepower. This engine was built by the Westinghouse Corporation and is able to give the **ANDERSON** an operating speed of 16.1 miles per hour.

The **ARTHUR M. ANDERSON** is one of the most active ships on the Great Lakes. She remains engaged in the ore, stone, and coal trades. The **ANDERSON** can be expected to be in operation for several more seasons.

The CASON J. CALLAWAY

The steamer **CASON J. CALLAWAY** was the third, and final, "AAA" class vessel to enter service for the Pittsburgh Steamship Company. It would also be the final new vessel added to United States Steel Corporation's freshwater shipping operations until 1972 when the **ROGER BLOUGH** was delivered. In contrast with the **ANDERSON** and **CLARKE**, the **CASON J. CALLAWAY** was built by the Great Lakes Engineering Works, at River Rouge, Michigan rather than the American Ship Building yard at Lorain, Ohio.

Launching of the 647 foot steamship occurred on March 22, 1952, with the maiden voyage commencing on September 16, 1952 when it departed River Rouge bound for Duluth, Minnesota to load iron ore. As with the other ships of the Pittsburgh Steamship fleet the **CASON J. CALLAWAY** was placed into operation bringing raw materials from the upper lakes down the US Steel's unloading facilities on the lower lakes. Common unloading ports being Gary, Indiana and Conneaut, Ohio.

Early in her career the **CASON J. CALLAWAY** was involved in her most serious accident it has had during its career thus far. On August 21, 1955 the **CALLAWAY** was downbound on the St. Marys River with a load of iron ore when it collided head on with the **B. F. JONES (1)** near Lime Island. The **B. F. JONES (1)** was upbound light when the collision occurred and suffered major damages. The **CALLAWAY** also suffered major damage in this accident, and went under her own power to the Great Lakes Engineering Works at River Rouge for repairs following unloading. The value of damages to the Pittsburgh steamer was placed in excess of $250,000. Meanwhile, the **B. F. JONES (1)** was towed to Superior, Wisconsin where it was determined that the repair estimate of over $600,000 was in excess of what that vessel was worth and it was subsequently sold for scrap.

As with her sisters, the operations of the **CASON J. CALLAWAY** would be influenced by the opening of the St. Lawrence Seaway in 1959. United States Steel intended to place a number of their most efficient carriers into service through that system to carry ore back from the Labrador region of Canada and into its port facilities on Lakes Erie, and Michigan. On the outbound trip grain could be carried to eliminate a costly trip in ballast.

The **CALLAWAY**'s sister ship **ARTHUR M. ANDERSON** inaugurated this trade route when she arrived at Port Cartier, Quebec to load ore on August 17, 1962. Shortly thereafter, other members of the Pittsburgh Steamship fleet began to make the long Seaway voyages. Seaway trips would be somewhat common for the **CASON J. CALLAWAY** until the early 1970s.

In 1964, the Pittsburgh Steamship Division was directly integrated into the United States Steel Corporation becoming the Pittsburgh Fleet. This move was made to consolidate the operations of US Steel, and had no impact upon the duties of the **CASON J. CALLAWAY**. Three years later, in 1967, the operations of the Pittsburgh Fleet, and those of the Bradley Transportation fleet were combined becoming the United States Steel Great Lakes Fleet.

It was during this time period that winter operations were being promoted by the United States Steel Corporation to allow an extended navigational season, leading up to true year round shipping seasons on the Great Lakes. By the late 1960s the closing of the Soo Locks, which is directly tied to the ability to move ore from the upper lakes, was being pushed further into the winter. This began in 1968, and by 1974 the Soo Locks were in operation year round. These extended seasons remained in effect until 1979 when government funding for the project was ended and a fixed closing date for the Soo Locks was established.

During this decade long process US Steel operated its most efficient vessels in winter operations. All three ships of the "AAA" class, including the **CASON J. CALLAWAY**, were put into service during these winter runs. They were joined by the **JOHN G. MUNSON (2), BENJAMIN FAIRLESS, A. H. FERBERT (2), IRVING S. OLDS, LEON FRASER, ENDERS M. VOORHEES,** and later the **ROGER BLOUGH,** and **PRESQUE ISLE (2)**. Despite proving that winter navigation was possible on the Great Lakes, it was found to be costly to both the ships and their crews. During extreme winter conditions lake carriers commonly suffered significant delays. In some cases a distance covered in just a few hours during a normal season took days. Hull damages were common, and several minor collisions between both freighters, and icebreakers only compounded to illustrate the difficulties of operating during an extended season.

While on one of its winter runs on March 1, 1975, the **CASON J. CALLAWAY** was forced to use the MacArthur Lock at Sault Ste. Marie when the Poe Lock was closed for repairs. This lock is normally only used to handle ships with a length not exceeding 730 feet, but this passage was allowed by taking special precautions. Later that same month on the 21st, the **CASON J. CALLAWAY** went aground on Lansing Shoal in Lake Michigan suffering some hull damage. This occurred while the steamer was caught in drift ice. After freeing itself, the **CALLAWAY**, went to anchor to await a repair crew which was airlifted to the damaged vessel.

While passing downbound in the Poe Lock on February 26, 1976 with iron ore the **CASON J. CALLAWAY** struck the lock's safety boom, putting the lock out of operation. This forced the upbound **ARTHUR M. ANDERSON,** and **PHILIP R. CLARKE** to use the MacArthur Lock the following day on their upbound trip to Lake Superior. Shortly before this incident the **ROGER BLOUGH** had passed downbound, but went into lay-up shortly thereafter as it was unable to reenter Lake Superior with the Poe Lock being closed.

The opening of the new Poe Lock in 1968 would have a significant impact upon the **CASON J. CALLAWAY**. In 1974 when United States Steel sent this steamer to the Fraser Shipyards at Superior, Wisconsin to be lengthened by 120 feet to 767 feet in length. All three of the fleet's "AAA" class would receive this lengthening process at Fraser, with the **CALLAWAY** being the lead unit arriving there on April 13, 1974, and returning to service in early June of that year.

The **CALLAWAY** was now exempt from being able to operate any further east then Lake Erie as she was unable to pass through the Welland Canal. This was more then offset by the ability to carry an additional 6, 375 gross tons of iron ore. Additionally, the US Steel Seaway operations were winding down and were not to be a significant factor in the future operations of their fleet.

While transiting Lake Superior on July 23, 1981 the **EUGENE P. THOMAS** suffered a catastrophic engine failure. The **THOMAS** was located just west of the Apostle Islands in the western end of the lake, and was unable to proceed under her own power. At this time the **CASON J. CALLAWAY** was loading taconite at Two Harbors, Minnesota and she was contacted by the fleet operations office to proceed to the powerless **EUGENE P. THOMAS**. In the early afternoon of July 23rd, the **CALLAWAY** arrived on the scene and after taking the **THOMAS** into tow, headed for Duluth, Minnesota. Arriving off that port at 7:00PM that night, the **EUGENE P. THOMAS** was handed off to the tugs **NORTH DAKOTA,** and **VERMONT**. The **THOMAS** went into an immediate lay-up at Duluth, and was never to operate again, finally being sold for scrap in 1984.

By the early 1980s, the operation of the **CASON J. CALLAWAY** was becoming less efficient due to declining demand for raw materials along with the growing use of self-unloading vessels in the taconite trade. It was in these conditions that United States Steel decided to have this ship along with the **ANDERSON,** and **CLARKE** converted into self-unloaders at the end of the 1981 season. All three of these conversions were to take place at the Fraser Shipyards, where the lengthening program had been undertaken seven years previously. As with the lengthening, the **CALLAWAY** would be the lead unit in the reconstruction program. She was followed in turn by the **CLARKE,** and **ANDERSON** respectively. These conversions involved a complete rebuilding of the cargo hold, and the addition of an unloading structure on the deck just forward of the after cabins, and 262 foot unloading boom.

The self-unloading conversion not only allowed the **CASON J. CALLAWAY** to unload her cargo at a much faster rate than was possible by shore side equipment, it also allowed for the operation in trades outside of US Steel's demands. Thus, when the demand for taconite was depressed it was possible for the **CALLAWAY** to operate in the stone, and coal trades. Despite the added flexibility provided by the self-unloading conversion, the **CALLAWAY** did at times find herself idle during the dark days of the early to mid 1980s.

During this time the US Steel fleet went through some major changes. In 1980, the United States Steel Great Lakes Fleet owned 29 ships, by 1985 this was down to 23, and finally by 1990 it numbered only 11 ships. By 1990 all of the straight deckers had been disposed of, and the fleet was composed entirely of self-unloading vessels.

In 1987, the **CASON J. CALLAWAY** was upgraded again at the Fraser Shipyards when she was given a stern thruster to improve her maneuverability. This was completed by July 12th of that year, when she departed Duluth with iron ore for delivery to United States Steel's Lorain, Ohio facility.

In June of 1988 it was announced that United States Steel had sold its majority stake in their Great Lakes shipping operations to Blackstone Partners, Incorporated. This transaction had virtually no impact on the duties for the **CALLAWAY**, as all current contracts were fulfilled. The following year this steamer would receive the new color scheme implemented by Blackstone. This consisted of the placement of a gray, and black diagonal strip on the vessel's bow.

On September 6, 1988 the **CASON J. CALLAWAY** was downbound at Sault Ste. Marie, Michigan when a lubricating oil pump failed, causing damage to the steamer's engine. The **CALLAWAY** tied up at the Soo for repairs to the bearings holding the ships turbine rotor, which were not completed until September 18th, allowing a resumption of the trip to Lorain. A little over six years later while on a trip from Superior to Marquette, Michigan with coal on December 1, 1994 the **CASON J. CALLAWAY** lost power near Two Harbors, Minnesota requiring a tow to Duluth for repairs.

During the 2000-2001 lay-up period the **CASON J. CALLAWAY**'s engine room was automated at the Fraser Shipyards. This allowed for direct commands to be issued to the ship's propulsion system directly from the pilothouse. This engine room management technology allowed for a one person watch system to be implemented, additionally achieving a cost savings due to less fuel consumption during a typical shipping season. The **CALLAWAY** returned to service on May 15, 2001 when she departed the shipyard.

While entering the lower St. Clair River at 4:00 AM on May 21, 2003 the **CASON J. CALLAWAY** ran aground. This was a relatively minor stranding as she was pulled free by 11:00 AM the same day with the assistance of the tugs **MAINE**, and **WYOMING**. Following a inspection as St. Clair, Michigan, the **CALLAWAY** was allowed to proceed to Stoneport, Michigan with no damage being found.

In late 2003, it was announced that Canadian National was to purchase the Great Lakes Fleet, along with several other properties, from the Blackstone Group for a reported $380 million. United States Steel had sold their remaining interest in the Great Lakes Fleet in 2000. This transaction was not finalized until May of 2004, after which the ships of the fleet were placed under the management of Keystone Shipping of Pennsylvania.

A unique situation occurred in January of 2004 when **EDGAR B. SPEER** ran aground in the St. Marys River near the Rock Cut on January 18th. Following this the United States Coast Guard closed that channel down for the remainder of the season, forcing downbound vessels to use the Middle Neebish Channel. Four vessels delayed by the grounding of the **SPEER** were too deeply loaded to safely transit that channel, these being the **PRESQUE ISLE (2), CSL LAURENTIEN, JOSEPH H. THOMPSON,** and **STEWART J. CORT**. The **CASON J. CALLAWAY** which was upbound at the time was called upon to receive off-loaded cargo from each of these four ships. Each of the vessels unloaded enough taconite into the **CALLAWAY** via their own unloading gear to achieve a reduction of around one foot in draft. After receiving the cargo the **CALLAWAY** resumed her trip to the Twin Ports, where she arrived on January 24, 2004 and unloaded the pellets at the DM&IR dock prior to entering winter lay up at the Fraser Shipyards.

*The **CASON J. CALLAWAY** is shown while upbound on the St. Clair River bound for an upper lakes port in 1999. Clearly visible here are the gray, and black stripes added to the bow of the ship following the acquisition by Blackstone Partners from United States Steel in 1988. This color scheme which first appeared at the beginning of the 1989 shipping season remains current as of the end of the 2008 season despite the **CALLAWAY** now being owned by Canadian National following the 2003 season.*

*The **CASON J. CALLAWAY** shows her respectable 767 foot length in this view. The lengthening by 120 feet which occurred in 1974, restricts this ship to transit only the Poe Lock at Sault Ste. Marie, Michigan. However, this ship has been handled by the MacArthur Lock on at least one occasion since its rebuilding due to the Poe Lock being out of service.*

The start of the 2008 shipping season would be eventful for the **CASON J. CALLAWAY**. On March 25, 2008 this ship was the first commercial vessel to transit the Locks at Sault Ste. Marie, Michigan when it passed upbound to load taconite at Two Harbors for delivery to Gary, Indiana. On March 28th, while transiting the Straits of Mackinac the **CASON J. CALLAWAY** collided with the **AMERICAN REPUBLIC**. The **AMERICAN REPUBLIC** had been stopped by heavy ice about 15 miles west of the Mackinac Bridge when the **CALLAWAY** attempted to pass close by in attempt to free the **REPUBLIC** and in doing so collided. Both ships received damages to their starboard bow areas, with the **AMERICAN REPUBLIC** departing immediately for Sturgeon Bay, Wisconsin for repairs. The **CASON J. CALLAWAY** continued on her voyage to Gary, Indiana where it departed for Sturgeon Bay for repairs after unloading its cargo.

The **CASON J. CALLAWAY** is capable of carrying 25,300 gross tons of cargo at its mid-summer draft of 27 feet. This cargo is taken aboard through 23 hatches placed on 24 foot centers, with the cargo hold itself being subdivided into 7 separate sections. This steamer is still equipped with its original Westinghouse Electric steam turbine capable of generating 7,700 shaft horsepower.

This ship, along with others of her class, are among the most versatile US flagged ships currently sailing on the Great Lakes. The **CASON J. CALLAWAY** can be found in almost any corner of the inland seas west of the Welland Canal. Common ports of call include Two Harbors, Duluth, Superior, Gary, Conneaut, Green Bay, Lorain, Ashtabula, Toledo, Detroit, Calcite, Stoneport, Sandusky, and South Chicago. Less common ports served include Ashland, Huron, Gladstone, and Marathon, Ontario. Future plans for the **CALLAWAY** may include a conversion to diesel. If this occurs it is most likely that the **ANDERSON**, and **CLARKE** would undergo a similar conversion, but as of the end of the 2008 season there were no announced plans for this to occur. If such a conversion does take place it will surely increase the lifespan of this ship, enabling it to serve effectively in the transportation of bulk materials for many additional years.

*The **CASON J. CALLAWAY** is downbound on lower Lake Huron in the mid-1990s. As one of the most versatile ships on the Great Lakes the **CALLAWAY** can be found hard at work in every part of the Great Lakes west of the Welland Canal, which her 767 foot length prevents her from transiting.*

The MICHIPICOTEN (3)

As with several other operators, the Interlake Steamship Company found itself in need of new capacity at the beginning of the 1950s. As a massive building program began upon the Great Lakes during the Korean War, several shipyards began to be backlogged with orders. This prompted some companies to purchase surplus saltwater ships for quick conversions into Great Lakes bulk carriers. It also brought about the unique solution of building ships at shipyards not located upon the lakes themselves.

Interlake thus contracted the Bethlehem Steel Corporation to build a lake freighter at its Sparrows Point Shipbuilding Division. This facility was located at Sparrows Point, Maryland and it was here that hull# 4512 was launched as the **ELTON HOYT 2nd (2)** on March 7, 1952. This ship was the second of three ships built in this class, the others being the **JOHNSTOWN (2)**, and **SPARROWS POINT** which were also built at Sparrows Point, but for service in Bethlehem's Great Lakes fleet. As for Interlake, the **ELTON HOYT 2nd (2)** was the first ship built for the fleet since the Second World War, and one of four steamers built for that fleet during the 1950s.

After launching the **ELTON HOYT 2nd (2)** was towed into the Great Lakes via the Mississippi River, and Illinois Waterway. During this tow, the ship's cabins were lashed to the deck to undergo final assembly at American Ship Building's South Chicago yard. The **ELTON HOYT 2nd (2)** carried her first cargo on August 17, 1952, when it loaded iron ore at Superior, Wisconsin.

With a length of 626 feet, the **HOYT** was among the larger ships on the Great Lakes at the time of its entry into service. It was also designated as Interlake's flagship until 1958 when that honor was passed on to another ship. A large portion of Interlake's operations at the time was the movement of ore from the Lake Superior region to the lower lakes, and the **ELTON HOYT 2nd** was placed into this trading pattern.

Soon however, it was apparent that the **HOYT**'s original carrying capacity of 18,800 gross tons could be improved by lengthening the vessel. Following the end of the 1956 shipping season the **ELTON HOYT 2nd (2)** returned to American Ship Building's South Chicago yard where she was lengthened by 72 feet to 698 feet in length. This increased her cargo capacity to 21,100 gross tons. The **HOYT**'s two sister ships, **JOHNSTOWN (2)**, and **SPARROWS POINT** also received the same type of lengthening process in 1958.

While downbound approaching the Soo Locks on May 15, 1975 the **ELTON HOYT 2nd (2)** experienced some difficulties forcing the dropping of an anchor. While still in motion the steamer ran over the anchor holing its hull. Despite taking on some water during this incident, no major structural damages were reported.

As with many other ship owners during the 1970s, Interlake instituted a program of fleet modernization. While this involved the building of two 1,000 foot vessels, it also included the conversion to a self-unloader of the **HERBERT C. JACKSON** in 1975. The rebuilding of this ship proved the economic benefits of such a conversion could have on an existing vessel, rather then having to construct an entirely new ship.

In the late 1970s the Republic Steel Corporation starting accepting bids for their lucrative ore hauling contract. This contract involved a large amount of taconite being brought down to Lorain, Ohio from Lake Superior where it was to be unloaded for eventual transshipment to Cleveland. This required the building of a new pellet handling facility, which was only able to accept self-unloading vessels. Interlake was the successful bidder for this contract which was to begin in 1981.

*The **ELTON HOYT 2nd (2)** is entering the MacArthur Lock at Sault Ste. Marie, Michigan during the 1990s. The wake seen near the port bow indicates that the bow thruster is being used to keep the vessel against the lock wall.*

*The **ELTON HOYT 2nd (2)** is downbound on the St. Clair River during the Summer of 2000. She is in her last season as an active carrier for Interlake as she laid up on January 11, 2001, remaining idle until her sale to Lower Lakes Towing in 2003.*

The acquisition of this contract enabled Interlake to convert two of their existing steamers into self-unloaders, and build a third thousand foot vessel. In October of 1979 the **ELTON HOYT 2nd (2)** arrived at the American Ship Building's Toledo yard to be converted into a self-unloader. Following the successful completion of this reconstruction this ship reentered service during the 1980 season.

The early 1980s would be quiet for the **ELTON HOYT 2nd (2)** as she settled into her new role as a self-unloader. But as the downturn in the steel industry took hold during the same timeframe, this ship would find itself being idled from time to time. Statistics of this period illustrate the drop in the demand for ore movement. In 1980, 72,967,359 gross tons of ore were carried on the Great Lakes, by 1982 this had fallen to 38,512,74 gross tons, while by 1983 it had slightly increased to 52,085,008 gross tons. Throughout the 1980s, the movement of ore, lifeblood of the US fleet, would only exceed 60 million tons when it did very slightly, in 1988.

On December 22, 1983 the crew of the **ELTON HOYT 2nd (2)** discovered a crack in her hull following a storm on Lake Huron it had passed through while downbound from Escanaba, Michigan. Minor repairs were undertaken while anchored in the Detroit River, and the steamer was allowed to proceed to Ashtabula, Ohio, where her cargo was unloaded.

A later incident on September 21, 1985 occurred on the Calumet River, south of Chicago when the **ELTON HOYT 2nd (2)** struck the 95th Street Bridge. The accident put the bridge out of service for 5 hours, prompting the **HOYT** to proceed to Sturgeon Bay, Wisconsin for repairs at the Bay Shipbuilding yard.

The forward cabins of the ELTON HOYT 2nd (2) were virtually identical to those of her sister ships, SPARROWS POINT, and JOHNSTOWN (2). This trio of ships were easily identifiable from a distance with their stylish cabin profiles. Of these three ships, only this vessel remains as a self-powered vessel. The JOHNSTOWN (2) was sold for scrapping in 1985 following many years of idleness. The SPARROWS POINT was later sold to Oglebay Norton, becoming BUCKEYE (3). It operates today as the barge LEWIS J. KUBER.

Following her conversion to a self-unloader the **ELTON HOYT 2nd (2)** was utilized at times outside of the ore trade. On July 22, 1985 it arrived for the first time in its career at Fairport, Ohio when it carried a load of stone into that port. Later, on September 22, 1990 the **ELTON HOYT 2nd (2)** visited the port of Ashland, Wisconsin when it docked at the Reiss Coal Dock. This trip was not to be without incident however, as a crewmember would suffer a leg injury when a mooring line snapped during high winds.

The 1990s would see a continuance of the **ELTON HOYT 2nd (2)** being idle during certain periods. In one instance, this steamer was idle from January 9, 1991 to April 16, 1993 at Superior, Wisconsin. On July 14, 1994 the **ADAM E. CORNELIUS (4)** ran aground near the downbound approach of the Poe Lock at Sault Ste. Marie. The **CORNELIUS**, which was on charter to the Inland Steel Company at the time, was required to offload a portion of its cargo into the **ELTON HOYT 2nd (2)** the next day, before being pulled free.

The **ELTON HOYT 2nd (2)** is on her way to unload a cargo of taconite at the Rouge Steel mill at Dearborn, Michigan in this 2000 photo. On such trips this ship can carry 22,300 gross tons of cargo. Clearly evident in this photo are the lines of the classic Great Lakes freighter. This ship is one of a class of three built at an east coast shipyard in the early 1950s for service on the Inland Seas.

The **MICHIPICOTEN (3)** in Lower Lakes colors is shown downbound on the St. Clair River on April 7, 2007 in wintry conditions. Despite concentrating on Lake Superior for most of its season, this ship is a common sight on the St. Clair River.

While anchored off of Stoneport, Michigan on August 6, 1994 waiting to load stone the **ELTON HOYT 2nd (2)** responded to a distress call concerning a sinking cabin cruiser in Lake Huron. The **HOYT** rescued eight people from the stricken vessel which was located two miles offshore. On April 28, 1995 the **ELTON HOYT 2nd (2)** struck the seawall at Grand Haven, Michigan due to high winds. Though damages were reported to the seawall, no damages to the **HOYT** were indicated.

The Cuyahoga River at Cleveland is well known for its many tight twists and turns, thus limiting the size of ships able to transit that waterway. On May 11, 1997 the **ELTON HOYT 2nd (2)** became the largest ship to transit that river, arriving at the LTV Steel dock with a cargo of taconite. During the inbound transit this ship required the assistance of three tugs, and only one for the outbound leg.

The **ELTON HOYT 2nd (2)** suffered another hull fracture on December 17, 1999 while downbound on Lake Superior. Water was found entering the **HOYT** through a 12 inch crack in the number 5 starboard ballast tank. Following temporary repairs at Sault Ste. Marie, Michigan the **ELTON HOYT 2nd (2)** continued on her trip to Rouge Steel to unload her cargo of taconite, and effect permanent repairs.

During the late 1990s Interlake would engage this ship into trades outside of her normal movements of ore, stone, and coal. In December 1997 it carried a unique cargo when it carried a payload of 1,200 tons of sugar beets from Huron, Ohio to Marysville, Michigan. Later, in August 1999 the **ELTON HOYT 2nd (2)** loaded the first of several loads of grain at Superior, Wisconsin for delivery to Buffalo, New York.

The **ELTON HOYT 2nd (2)** would operate for Interlake Steamship until laying up at the Fraser Shipyards at Superior on January 11, 2001. This vessel never operated again for this fleet, remaining idle at that location until being sold in April of 2003 to Lower Lakes Towing. Following the sale, this steamer was renamed **MICHIPICOTEN (3)**, and placed under the Canadian flag.

Lower Lakes Towing was expanding their fleet operations at the time, and planned to place the **MICHIPICOTEN (3)** into service hauling taconite from Marquette to the Algoma Steel mill at Sault Ste. Marie, Ontario. Following a drydocking at Fraser, the **MICHIPICOTEN (3)** was towed to Sarnia, Ontario arriving there on May 7, 2003 under tow of the **ROGER STAHL**.

Formal dedication of this vessel took place on May 24, 2003 at Sarnia, with the first trip occurring on June 13, 2003 when it departed to load ore at Marquette. Shortly after entering service, the **MICHIPICOTEN (3)** suffered some bottom damages while in the St. Marys River, requiring a trip to Sturgeon Bay, Wisconsin for repairs, when she arrived there on September 3, 2003.

*The stern of the **MICHIPICOTEN (3)** is the location where the unloading boom and associated topside equipment was placed when this ship was converted into a self-unloader in 1980. The poor condition of the hull paint in this picture attests more to the busy activities of several dockings and lock transits this ship experiences during the season, rather than indicating the ship is in poor condition.*

As indicated earlier, the operation of this ship was to be primarily the movement of ore on Lake Superior, but other payloads are carried as the needs arise. This ship has been noted as carrying ore into Hamilton, Ontario on numerous occasions. In October of 2007 the **MICHIPICOTEN (3)** is recorded as transiting the Saginaw River with a load of stone for Bay City, Michigan for the first time under her new name and ownership.

The **MICHIPICOTEN (3)** can haul 22,300 gross tons of iron ore, this being transferred to shore with a 250 foot unloading boom. Motive power is provided with a 7,700 shaft horsepower rated steam turbine, providing a speed of 17.3 miles per hour. The repowering of the **SAGINAW (3)** from steam to diesel in 2008, leaves the **MICHIPICOTEN (3)** as the last steamer currently operated by Lower Lakes Towing.

This steamer has the distinction of closing the Soo Locks for the 2007 shipping season, when she was the last vessel to pass through on January 15, 2008. During the last two decades in the Interlake fleet this ship was usually one of the last to enter service, or first to enter lay up as cargo demands fluctuated, this is in sharp contrast as being one of the most active in the Lower Lakes Towing fleet. As of the end of the 2008 shipping season the **MICHIPICOTEN (3)** remains hard at work carrying ore between Marquette and the Canadian Soo. While on this shuttle run this steamer can make a round trip about every 36 hours. Despite this, she is no stranger to the lower lakes, and it is not an uncommon sight to see her working nearly anywhere on Great Lakes.

*The **MICHIPICOTEN (3)** passes upbound at St. Clair, Michigan on December 27, 2005 bound for the upper lakes where it will return to the ore shuttle run between Marquette, Michigan and Sault Sainte Marie, Ontario.*

The JOHN G. MUNSON (2)

In 1902 the wooden steamer **HENNEPIN (1)** was converted into a self-unloader at Sturgeon Bay, Wisconsin, thus making this wooden steamer the first such type of ship on the Great Lakes. This was followed in 1908 when the first vessel to be built from the keel up as a self-unloader, the **WYANDOTTE (1)**, was launched at Ecorse, Michigan by the Great Lakes Engineering Works. Though self-unloading vessels had many advantages over gearless bulk carriers, they were relegated for the most part to the stone, and coal trades during the first half of the twentieth century. This would slowly evolve until by the 1970s most every ship built was equipped with its own unloading gear, with the last straight deck freighter built for Great Lakes service being launched in 1985.

One of the early pioneers in the use of self-unloading vessels was the Bradley Steamship Company when it placed the steamer **CALCITE** into service in 1912 hauling stone products from Rogers City, Michigan. This fleet would continue to grow, adding five new ships to their fleet by 1927 when it commissioned the **CARL D. BRADLEY (2)**. This 638 foot steamer was the longest ship on the Great Lakes when it entered service, and would serve the Bradley fleet until sinking in Lake Michigan on November 18, 1958.

By the early 1950s, Bradley Transportation, a subsidiary of the United States Steel Corporation, decided that it would require the construction of a new carrier. On March 7, 1951 the keel for the **JOHN G. MUNSON (2)** was laid at Manitowoc, Wisconsin by Manitowoc Shipbuilding, Incorporated. This ship was to be one of the larger of her day at 666 feet 3 inches in length. This ship was to be the first of a trio of large self-unloaders built at Manitowoc, the others being the **JOHN J. BOLAND (3)**, and **DETROIT EDISON (2)**.

The **JOHN G. MUNSON (2)** was launched into an icy Manitowoc River on November 28, 1951. Over the winter months the ship's cabins, and self-unloading system were installed during final assembly, with sea trials beginning on August 12, 1952. Following the successful completion of these trials, and finishing touches the **JOHN G. MUNSON (2)** departed on her maiden trip on August 21, 1952 bound for Calcite, Michigan for a load of stone.

Early in her career this steamer set a cargo record when it loaded 21,101 tons of limestone in 1953 at Calcite, this record standing until 1966 when it was surpassed by Canada Steamship Lines' **MANITOULIN (5)**. To enhance its maneuverability and to ease docking operations the **JOHN G. MUNSON (2)** received a bow thruster in 1966.

In the late 1960s, the United States Steel Corporation was a staunch proponent for extended navigational shipping seasons on the Great Lakes. This fleet would place their most efficient vessels into service during the winter months which had normally shut down shipping operations by late December. The **JOHN G. MUNSON (2)** was chosen to participate in these winter runs. During the early years of the program this ship operated alongside the **ARTHUR M. ANDERSON, CASON J. CALLAWAY, PHILIP R. CLARKE, BENJAMIN FAIRLESS, A. H. FERBERT (2), LEON FRASER, ENDERS M. VOORHEES**, and **IRVING S. OLDS**. Later in the early 1970s, these vessels were joined by the **PRESQUE ISLE (2)**, and **ROGER BLOUGH**. Year-round navigation would continue until the late 1970s.

Extended seasons were hard on the ships, and crews while operating under extreme conditions, in which several collisions, and ice damages were suffered. Though the program demonstrated that ships could be kept in operation during the entire year, it was done at a heavy cost in fuel, and maintenance. Regardless, during the early 1980s a huge drop in the demand for the movement of iron ore had rendered the need for an extended shipping season academic.

*The **JOHN G. MUNSON (2)** is upbound on the St. Clair River during the mid 1990s. During a typical shipping season this ship will carry a variety of ore, coal, and stone cargoes to all corners of the upper lakes.*

*The **JOHN G. MUNSON (2)** is downbound on the St. Clair River on October 19, 2008. One of the largest ships on the Great Lakes when it was launched in 1952, this ship remains one of the longer vessels on the lakes today with a respectable length of 768 feet, 3 inches.*

In the early 1970s, United States Steel decided to lengthen it four steamers built during the 1950s to take advantage of the new Poe Lock at Sault Ste. Marie, Michigan, which had opened in 1968. All of these conversions took place at Superior, Wisconsin by the Fraser Shipyards, and along with the **JOHN G. MUNSON (2)** included the **ANDERSON, CALLAWAY,** and **CLARKE.** The **JOHN G. MUNSON (2)** arrived at this yard following the end of the 1975 shipping season to be lengthened by 102 feet to 768 feet, 3 inches in length. Upon re-entering service in 1976 this steamer became one of the longest ships owned by the United States Steel Corporation fleet, surpassed only by the **ROGER BLOUGH**, and the chartered **PRESQUE ISLE (2)**.

The **JOHN G. MUNSON (2)** is usually one of the earliest ships to leave winter lay-up at the beginning of the shipping season. During some of these early voyages ice damage has been suffered by this steamer. In March of 1978 this ship suffered rudder damage while in Whitefish Bay, which required a tow by the **USCG MACKINAW** back to Sault Saint Marie for repairs.

During the 1980s, the **JOHN G. MUNSON (2)** was involved in at least two incidents. The first of these occurred on February 2, 1983 when 3 persons received injuries following a fire in the ship's machine shop during winter lay-up at Milwaukee, Wisconsin. Later, on March 21, 1984 while entering Lorain, Ohio the **JOHN G. MUNSON (2)** struck the breakwall sustaining bow damages, including the loss of her port anchor. This anchor was later recovered, and was reinstalled on the steamer by late August of that year.

*The **JOHN G. MUNSON (2)** is downbound at Sault Ste. Marie, Michigan on September 19, 2008. This steamer had just cleared the Poe Lock and is headed to the lower lakes. As one of the busiest ships on the Great Lakes, this vessel carries cargoes of taconite, coal, and stone to a wide variety of ports on the inland seas. This ship was one of three large self-unloaders built at Manitowoc during the 1950s. The others were the **JOHN J. BOLAND (3)**, and **DETROIT EDISON (2)**. The former vessel sails today as the **SAGINAW (3)**, while the latter was sold for scrap in 1986.*

The **JOHN G. MUNSON (2)** is a regular visitor to a variety of ports. These include South Chicago, Toledo, Stoneport, Calcite, Duluth, Two Harbors, Gary, Conneaut, and Marquette. This ship is also a frequent caller to less common locations such as Ontonagon, Michigan. It was at this port that the **JOHN G. MUNSON (2)** ran aground on July 29, 1990. After being freed, this steamer went to Superior for drydocking and repairs at the Fraser Shipyards returning to service on August 9th.

As stated earlier the **JOHN G. MUNSON (2)** was the first of a trio of self-unloaders built at Manitowoc Shipbuilding during the 1950s sharing a similar design. Though this vessel shared the general appearance of the **JOHN J. BOLAND (3)**, and **DETROIT EDISON (2)**, the topside unloading gear of the **MUNSON (2)** differed in that it did not have a large A-frame structure common in with the other two vessels giving her a much more compact appearance. The fortunes of these three ships would also be markedly different. While the **MUNSON (2)** has remained active throughout her career, the **JOHN J. BOLAND (3)**, and **DETROIT EDISON (2)** were owned by the American Steamship Company, and had become some of the oldest vessels in that fleet by the early 1980s following a massive construction program undertaken by American Steamship during the 1970s. The **DETROIT EDISON (2)** was sold for scrapping in 1986 following being laid up since 1982. The **BOLAND (3)** would spend much of the 1980s idle, returning to service in the early 1990s, before being sold to Lower Lakes Towing and reflagged Canadian as **SAGINAW (3)** in 1999.

55

Since its construction this steamer has been constantly upgraded to maintain its efficiency. In 1986 a 1,000 horsepower stern thruster was installed, and in 2000 the ship's original steam whistles were replaced by electric whistles. Also over the years, new electronic navigational equipment has been installed as it became available.

While arriving at Corunna, Ontario on November 6, 2006 the **JOHN G. MUNSON (2)** struck the Shell fuel dock, knocking about 200 feet of the structure into the waters of the St. Clair River. No injuries were reported in this incident, but it did force the closing of the fuel dock for a significant period of time.

The **JOHN G. MUNSON (2)** is capable of carrying 25,550 gross tons of iron ore at her mid-summer draft of 27 feet, 4 inches. This ship's cargo hold is divided into 7 sections, with cargo being loaded through 22 hatches. Each of these hatches measure 45 feet, 9 inches by 11 feet and are removed for loading by a traveling hatch crane. Cargo is offloaded to shore via a 250 foot unloading boom. The **JOHN G. MUNSON (2)** is powered by a 7,700 shaft horsepower General Electric steam turbine, giving a rated speed of 17.3 miles per hour.

Since entering service the ownership, and management of this steamer has changed a number of times. In 1967, the operations of the Bradley fleet, and those of the Pittsburgh Steamship fleet were combined into the United States Steel Great Lakes Fleet. In 1988 this fleet was sold by United States Steel to Blackstone Partners, Incorporated. This transaction had little effect on the operation of the **JOHN G. MUNSON (2)**, although she was repainted into the standard colors of the fleet along with all of the other carriers of the old Bradley fleet. This included a red hull, with two diagonal strips at the bow, one of which was black, the other being gray. In 2003, Canadian National announced that it had acquired the Great Lakes Fleet, and other transportation properties, from Blackstone Partners. Following the completion of the sale in May of 2004 the **JOHN G. MUNSON (2)** was placed under the management of Keystone Shipping.

As of the 2009 shipping season, the **JOHN G. MUNSON (2)** continues to operate in the ore, stone, and coal trades. Thus far no repowering plans have been announced for this ship, therefore it can be assumed that this vessel will be serving as a steamer for many more seasons.

*In the late 1990s the **JOHN G. MUNSON (2)** is shown slowly passing Marysville, Michigan while preparing to dock at the Shell Fuel Dock across the St. Clair River. On November 6, 2006 this vessel struck this dock, severely damaging it.*

The JAMES NORRIS

The **JAMES NORRIS** was launched on September 10, 1951 at Midland, Ontario by the Midland Shipyards for the Upper Lakes & St. Lawrence Transportation Company. This was the third ship to be built in a class which can trace its roots back to the "Super" class built in American shipyards during the 1940s for the Pittsburgh Steamship Company. This class of ships would eventually consist of six vessels including this ship, and included the **HOCHELAGA, COVERDALE, SIR JAMES DUNN, THUNDER BAY (2),** and **GORDON C. LEITCH (1).** Of these the **GORDON C. LEITCH (1),** and **JAMES NORRIS** were built for Upper Lakes, with the other four ships being constructed for the Canada Steamship Lines fleet. The **JAMES NORRIS** was also the first ship to be built for the Upper Lakes fleet, although it had previously operated a number of vessels since being formed in 1932.

On May 14, 1952, the **JAMES NORRIS** loaded her first cargo when it loaded a cargo of wheat at Fort William, Ontario. This ship was placed into the ore, grain, and coal trades in its early career and was an active carrier for Upper Lakes despite being unable to pass through the pre-Seaway locks on the St. Lawrence River. This would change significantly in 1959 with the opening of the St. Lawrence Seaway, which allowed the **JAMES NORRIS** to operate from Lake Superior to the lower St. Lawrence River.

At 663 feet, 6 inches in length, the **JAMES NORRIS** was considered a large ship when it was launched in 1951, but it was soon to be outclassed when a large number of new Canadian ships were built during the 1960s of the 730 foot class. This was directly related to the new dimensions allowed by the then new waterway, fully transforming the Canadian flagged Great Lakes fleet. By 1959, the **JAMES NORRIS,** and **GORDON C. LEITCH (1)** had been joined by the **FRANK SHERMAN,** and **SEAWAY QUEEN**. The latter ship was significantly larger then the **NORRIS** at 717 feet, 3 inches in length.

During April of 1971 the **JAMES NORRIS** is noted to have sustained rudder damage while departing the Maple Leaf Elevator at Port Colborne, Ontario. Damages originating from this incident were serious enough to prompt a trip to the Port Weller Drydocks for repairs. The **JAMES NORRIS** arrived at this location on April 24th to receive repairs, under tow of the tugs **HERBERT A.,** and **G. W. ROGERS**.

A more significant accident occurred on June 27, 1978 when the **JAMES NORRIS** went aground at Kingston, Ontario. This stranding occurred near the harbor entrance, requiring the assistance of tugs from the McAllistar Towing and Salvage Company. Following being released, a survey of the hull determined that the **JAMES NORRIS** had sustained significant bottom damages, requiring a trip to the Port Weller Drydocks. The **NORRIS** was placed into the dry dock on July 9, 1978 for the necessary repairs.

During the 1970s ships like the **JAMES NORRIS** were becoming unprofitable to be operated as straight deck bulk carriers. The long haul trade route of grain from the upper lakes to the St. Lawrence River, with a return cargo of ore back into the lakes was dominated by ships of the 730 foot class.

In January of 1980 Upper Lakes announced that it had awarded a contract to the Port Weller Drydocks to convert the **JAMES NORRIS** into a self-unloader. This agreement was reported to be worth 4 million dollars. The conversion of a ship in the same class as the **JAMES NORRIS** was nothing new as Canada Steamship had both the **HOCHELAGA,** and **THUNDER BAY (2)** both converted to self-unloaders during the 1960s. The **THUNDER BAY (2)** was renamed **STADACONA (3)** in 1969.

*The **JAMES NORRIS** is upbound, without cargo on the St. Clair River during the late 1990s on the way to Lake Huron for another load of stone.*

*The **JAMES NORRIS** is upbound at Port Huron Michigan during a blustery summer day during the 2008 shipping season. This ship is the last member of her class, of which there were originally six, still in operation.*

The **JAMES NORRIS** spent the 1980-81 winter lay-up period at Port Weller undergoing the self-unloading conversion which was completed by the middle of March 1981. This steamer was now equipped with a 250 foot bow mounted unloading boom, enabling this ship to discharge its cargo virtually anywhere it could dock. This opened up several new trade routes, and ports for this ship to operate in which it had been unable to serve due to the previous reliance on shore side unloading facilities.

The first cargo this ship would carry as a self-unloader was consigned to Clarkson, Ontario where she arrived on April 1, 1981. The **JAMES NORRIS** soon settled into her new role as a self-unloader, with cargoes of stone becoming a large portion of this ship's seasonal tonnage commitments. Two years after being converted into a self-unloader the **JAMES NORRIS** struck a dock while arriving at Valleyfield, Quebec on December 1, 1983 resulting in minor damage.

The self-unloading conversion extended the life of this steamer as it is the only one of its class still in operation. In fact, the **GORDON C. LEITCH (1)**, a sister ship of the **JAMES NORRIS**, was sold by Upper Lakes for scrapping in 1985 after being idle since December of 1981. The **JAMES NORRIS** would itself be idled from time to time as cargoes became scarce. In November of 1992 the **JAMES NORRIS** arrived at Toronto, Ontario for lay-up which lasted until May 2, 1994 when enough cargoes in the aggregate trade became available to justify the reactivation of the classic steamer.

The most serious accident to befall the **JAMES NORRIS** so far in her career occurred on November 12, 1995 when this ship sank at Port Colborne, Ontario following being pushed in a dock during heavy weather. Despite its age at the time of the accident, the **JAMES NORRIS** was raised from the bottom and taken to Port Weller where extensive repairs were completed.

Another accident occurred on October 15, 1999 when the **JAMES NORRIS** ran aground while entering Ludington, Michigan. This stranding caused damages to a forward ballast tank, which required repairs at the Pascol Shipyard at Thunder Bay, Ontario. The **NORRIS** arrived at that shipyard on October 19, 1999, where repairs were completed on October 31st.

The **JAMES NORRIS** can carry 18,600 gross tons of cargo, which is loaded into the vessel's cargo hold through 17 hatches. This steamer is powered by a Canadian Vickers Uniflow steam engine with a rated 4,000 horsepower. This engine is equipped with five cylinders and allows the **JAMES NORRIS** to reach a rated speed of 16.1 miles per hour.

When the **JAMES NORRIS** entered service in 1952 it was the largest ship in the Upper Lakes fleet, but by the mid-1990s it had become both the smallest, and oldest in the fleet. This changed in 1998 when Upper Lakes commissioned the **CANADIAN TRANSFER**. This ship was the result of rebuilding the **HAMILTON TRANSFER**, with the stern section of the **CANADIAN EXPLORER**. The **HAMILTON TRANSFER** had been built in 1943 as the "Maritime" class vessel **J. H. HILLMAN, JR.**, and was later converted into a self-unloader, and renamed **CRISPIN OGLEBAY (2)** in 1974. This ship had been converted into a crane equipped self-unloading barge in 1995 to unload straight deck bulk carriers at the Defasco Steel facility in Hamilton following the collapse of one of their ore unloading towers. While operating in this capacity this vessel was give the name **HAMILTON TRANSFER**, with this role lasting until the building of a new unloading tower. Upper Lakes had this ship taken to Port Weller where the stern was removed and replaced with the stern section of the **CANADIAN EXPLORER**. The final result of this reconstruction was the **CANADIAN TRANSFER** which entered service in the stone trade in 1998. The **JAMES NORRIS** with a length of 663 feet, 6 inches became the second smallest ship in Upper Lakes colors, as she was 13 feet longer than the **CANADIAN TRANSFER**.

Since the early 1990s, ULS and Algoma Central Marine have had a close business relationship concerning the operation and management of their vessels. This began in 1990 with the formation of Seaway Bulk Carriers, which was a pooling agreement in which the operation of the gearless vessels in both of these fleets were managed as a whole to provide more efficient operations. In 1994, a similar arrangement was made concerning the self-unloading units of these two fleet, which was appropriately named Seaway Self-Unloaders.

In 2000, the operation of both the straight deckers, and self-unloaders in the Algoma, and ULS fleets were assumed by Seaway Marine Transport. This new entity was further evolution of the previous pooling agreements between the two companies to streamline operations for maximum efficiency and utilization of their vessels.

During a regular shipping season the **JAMES NORRIS** will visit a variety of ports around the Great Lakes. While her main trading pattern remains the clinker trade between Colborne, and Clarkson on Lake Ontario, trips to the upper lakes are common. While trading on the upper lakes this ship may visit ports such as Marquette, Saginaw, Bay City, Goderich, Sarnia, Grand Haven, and Drummond Island to name a few.

While operating in the stone trade on August 15, 2003 the **JAMES NORRIS** grounded in the St. Clair River near Marine City, Michigan. This grounding accident was not considered to be serious with the **JAMES NORRIS** being able to free herself shortly afterwards without suffering any damages.

Despite a dwindling number of steamers on the Great Lakes, and particularly under the Canadian flag, Upper Lakes is in possession of no less then five of this type of vessels as of the 2009 shipping season. Besides this ship, the steamers **CANADIAN LEADER**, **CANADIAN PROVIDER**, **MONTREALAIS**, and **QUEBECOIS** are also members of the Upper Lakes fleet.

During the 2008 shipping season the **JAMES NORRIS** remained actively servings its owners needs in the aggregate trades. During the summer of 2008, the **JAMES NORRIS** made several trips into Lake Huron to load stone destined for a number of ports along the St. Clair River. On December 24, 2008 this ship laid up at Port Colborne for the winter. During the winter lay up period this steamer received propeller work. The **JAMES NORRIS** was supposed to have been repowered during 2009 with two MaK type 6M25 diesel engines, but this was delayed due to a downturn in economic conditions during late 2008, and early 2009. It is currently planned that the **JAMES NORRIS** will operate as a steamer when it enters service during the 2009 season.

*The **JAMES NORRIS** is shown docked at Point Edward, Ontario in 1995. The fine curves of her stern are readily apparent in this view, as is the height of the aftermast compared to the steamer's stack.*

The AMERICAN FORTITUDE

This ship was one of two new vessels built for the National Steel Corporation during the 1950s, and the first to enter service. Built as hull # 869 at the American Ship Building Company in Lorain, Ohio it was launched on November 19, 1952 as the **ERNEST T. WEIR (2)**. This ship was built immediately following the **ARTHUR M. ANDERSON**, but the design of this ship had more in common with the **WILFRED SYKES** then those of Pittsburgh Steamship's "AAA" class. As with most other American steamers built during this time, the **ERNEST T. WEIR (2)** was built primarily to haul iron ore from the Lake Superior region to the lower lakes.

This ship departed Lorain on April 12, 1953 to load ore at Superior, Wisconsin for delivery to Cleveland, Ohio. This first payload was loaded two days later, and amounted to 18,198 gross tons. This began a pattern of service for National Steel which would continue for the next twenty-five years. With a length of the 690 feet this ship was the longest ever built at a Great Lakes shipyard at the time of its launching. It was eclipsed however by the **JOSEPH H. THOMPSON** which had a length of 714 feet, 3 inches, but this ship had been built on salt water as C-4 type troopship in 1944 prior to being rebuilt for Great Lakes service in 1952.

The most significant accident to befall this ship to date occurred on May 5, 1964 when it collided with the tanker **MERCURY (2)** in Lake St. Clair near the entrance of the St. Clair River. The **ERNEST T. WEIR (2)** suffered heavy damage to her port bow, with the **MERCURY (2)** also receiving bow damages, and running aground. At the time of this accident the 1912 built **MERCURY (2)** was owned by Cleveland Tankers, later being sold for scrap in 1975 following a long career on the Great Lakes.

In 1954, the **ERNEST T. WEIR (2)** was joined by the **GEORGE M. HUMPHREY (2)** which was similar in design but with enlarged dimensions. In 1961, the **PAUL H. CARNAHAN**, and **LEON FALK, JR.** were placed into service for National Steel. These two ships had been built in 1945 as salt water tankers, with their conversions into Great Lakes bulk carriers being undertaken at American Ship Building's Lorain yard.

As the 1970s began the **ERNEST T. WEIR (2)**, and ships of her class, began to be eclipsed by larger vessels then being built. National Steel placed a contract with the American Ship Building Company to build a 1,000 foot vessel based upon the design pioneered by Interlake's **JAMES R. BARKER**. This motor vessel would be built following the construction of the **MESABI MINER**, and entered service in 1978 as the **GEORGE A. STINSON**.

With the acquisition of the **STINSON**, the **ERNEST T. WEIR (2)** was deemed to be surplus tonnage and was sold to Oglebay Norton's Columbia Transportation Division in 1978, and renamed **COURTNEY BURTON**. In the early years of her career with Columbia Transportation this ship continued to concentrate on the movement of ore from the upper lakes, and also became that fleet's flagship.

By 1980, the need to convert this vessel to a self-unloader was determined to be necessary to provide for continued efficient operation in the changing material movement patterns on the Great Lakes of that timeframe. In all a total of 4 Oglebay Norton straight deckers would receive self-unloading conversions in the early 1980s, with all of these occurring at the Bay Shipbuilding Company at Sturgeon Bay, Wisconsin. Besides **COURTNEY BURTON**, the **ARMCO**, **RESERVE**, and **MIDDLETOWN** were also rebuilt. All of these conversions would involve the placement of the unloading boom at the stern, rather then the bow which had been common up to the mid-1970s.

On August 21, 1980 the **COURTNEY BURTON** is recorded as passing downbound at the Soo Locks carrying its last payload as a gearless straight decker. After unloading this cargo this ship arrived at Sturgeon Bay to undergo the reconstruction to a self-unloader. The following year this ship returned to service equipped with a 260 foot unloading boom.

Despite being a much more efficient carrier following the rebuilding this ship, along with many others, would be laid up several times during the early 1980s due to the dramatic drop in demand for raw materials. This ship would have undoubtedly spent even more time out of service had it not been able to effectively operate in the coal and aggregates trade.

The **COURTNEY BURTON** damaged her propeller following a grounding at Taconite Harbor, Minnesota on August 4, 1988. Following the incident this steamer went to the Fraser Shipyards at Superior, Wisconsin where one blade was removed, and two others given temporary repairs. The **COURTNEY BURTON** would later have these two blades replaced at Toledo, Ohio.

On May 25, 1990 the **COURTNEY BURTON** paid a rare visit at Ashland, Wisconsin when she brought in a cargo of coal to the Reiss Coal Dock. At the time, this was reported to have been her first visit since 1975. On July 27, 1994 the **COURTNEY BURTON** received hull plating repairs to her starboard side at amidships, by the Fraser Shipyards due to an unspecified cause.

While in the Columbia fleet ports such as Duluth, Superior, Ashtabula, Toledo, Marquette, Escanaba, and Stoneport were common stops for this steamer. The **COURTNEY BURTON** also served smaller and less well known locations such as Marine City, Marysville, and Munising.

The 1990s were relatively good years for Oglebay Norton as they were able to keep most of their vessels active, however the **COURTNEY BURTON**, along with her fleet mate **BUCKEYE (3)** would be idled from time to time during the 1990s. For instance, the **BURTON**'s 1993 season was cut short when she arrived in Toledo for lay-up in September of that year.

The **COURTNEY BURTON** arrived at Toledo, Ohio for winter lay up on December 30, 2002 and would remain inactive for the next two seasons. In March of 2005 the **COURTNEY BURTON** was moved into the dry dock at Toledo Shipbuilding for survey, minor repairs, and modifications to enable this ship to operate in the grain trade.

Upon reentering service in 2005, the **COURTNEY BURTON** was primarily engaged in the movement of grain into Buffalo, New York, with most of these cargoes originating at Superior. On September 7, 2005 the **COURTNEY BURTON** entered the Welland Canal, which was widely reported to be the first time since the mid-1960s when she transited as the **ERNEST T. WEIR (2)**. On this occasion this steamer was on her way to Hamilton, Ontario to load grain for delivery to Buffalo.

The design of the ERNEST T. WEIR (2) followed the same basic pattern established by the WILFRED SYKES in 1949. The forward cabin layout was very similar as can be seen when comparing this picture of the AMERICAN FORTITUDE with the picture of the WILFRED SYKES on page 22.

The **COURTNEY BURTON** is shown above while passing downbound on the St. Clair River with a load of ore during the 2000 shipping season.

The **AMERICAN FORTITUDE** is on lower Lake Huron with a partial cargo of grain on September 16, 2007. In recent seasons this type of cargo has become a large portion of this ship's seasonal tonnage commitments.

In the early 2000s Oglebay Norton started to experience significant financial difficulties and started to look at divesting themselves of their shipping operations in order to concentrate on their core aggregate business. In 2006, it was announced that the **COURTNEY BURTON**, along with the **ARMCO, COLUMBIA STAR, OGLEBAY NORTON, FRED R. WHITE, JR.,** and **MIDDLETOWN** were sold to the American Steamship Company. The **COURTNEY BURTON** was renamed **AMERICAN FORTITUDE**, remaining active in the grain trade and with other cargoes being carried as they became available.

This steamer is powered by a General Electric steam turbine which generates 7,700 shaft horsepower, providing a speed of 16 miles per hour. The **AMERICAN FORTITUDE** can carry a total of 22,300 gross tons of cargo at her maximum draft, and she is equipped with a bow thruster. This ship is also rated for service throughout the Great Lakes, and the gulf of the St. Lawrence River. This ships cargo hold is loaded through 19 hatches.

The **AMERICAN FORTITUDE** is one of the few ships built for the American fleet during the 1950s which has not undergone a lengthening reconstruction. The conversion into a self-unloader in 1981 has enabled this ship to survive the severe economic conditions of the 1980s. In fact this ship is the last remaining steamer active on the Great Lakes to have been built for the National Steel fleet, as well as being one of only two ships still in operation from that fleet. This other vessel, the **AMERICAN SPIRIT**, was originally the **GEORGE A. STINSON** and holds the distinction of not only being National Steel's only 1,000 footer, but also its sole self-unloader.

Today, the **AMERICAN FORTITUDE** remains active in the movement of grain into Buffalo. This ship arrived at Owen Sound, Ontario on September 15, 2007 to load a cargo of oats destined for delivery to Buffalo. This initial voyage was followed by several more similar trips between these two ports during the 2008 season. Economic conditions near the end of the 2008 season sent the **AMERICAN FORTITUDE** to an early lay-up at Toledo, Ohio on November 11, 2008. As a steamer in the American Steamship fleet, which is dominated by diesel powered ships, it is probable that this ship will be one of the last to be activated during seasons with poor tonnage demands. This is not to imply that the future of this ship is doubtful, as it remains a versatile carrier and should be utilized for several more years.

The AMERICAN FORTITUDE is shown downbound at Port Huron, Michigan on September 16, 2007 with a grain cargo. As of the end of the 2008 shipping season this ship's hull has not yet been repainted to American Steamship's color scheme, as she still retains the former Oglebay Norton colors. The stack was given the new color scheme shortly after her purchase from her former owners in 2006.

The AMERICAN VALOR

The 1953 season would see two new bulk carriers entering service for the Columbia Transportation fleet, these were the **ARMCO**, and **RESERVE**. The **ARMCO** was built at Lorain, Ohio by the American Ship Building Company, with launching occurring on January 24, 1953. This steamer departed Lorain on June 6, 1953 bound for Superior, Wisconsin where a cargo of iron ore was loaded on June 9th.

The **ARMCO**, and **RESERVE** both shared the dimensions of the "AAA" class, this being a length of 647 feet, 70 foot beam, and a 36 foot depth. The **ARMCO**'s forward cabins were a slightly modified version of the standard design given to the **RESERVE**, giving a noticeably different appearance. When these two ships joined the Columbia fleet, they would be the longest ships in this organization, until 1958 when the **EDMUND FITZGERALD** was built.

The operation of this ship during her early career concentrated on the movement of iron ore from Silver Bay, Wisconsin to Toledo, Ohio. The opening of the new Poe Lock created the opportunity for the lengthening of existing ships, taking advantage of the benefits offered by the new lock. In 1974, the **ARMCO** was lengthened by 120 feet at the Fraser Shipyards in Superior, Wisconsin, with the **RESERVE** receiving a similar reconstruction at the same shipyard the following year.

In her new lengthened state of 767 feet, the **ARMCO** was now able to haul 26,800 gross tons of iron ore. Since Oglebay Norton would not build any thousand footers during the 1970s, the **ARMCO**, and **RESERVE** were once again the longest in the fleet until the construction of the **COLUMBIA STAR** in 1981. Following reentering service, the movement of ore from Lake Superior to the lower lakes continued to be the mainstay of this ship's seasonal cargo commitments.

During the extended navigational season operations carried out during the 1970s, several shipping companies operated their more efficient vessels into the winter months. These operations were to prove to be more difficult than previously thought. Harsh ice conditions would take a heavy toll on the ships as ice damage was common. Also common during these operations were collisions which occurred often due to the operation of vessels in close quarters to one another. On January 4, 1978 the **ARMCO** was following the **IRVING S. OLDS** upbound in the Livingston Channel near Detroit, Michigan. These two steamers were following a track created by the United States Coast Guard cutter **MARIPOSA**. The **IRVING S. OLDS** ran into some heavy ice and ground to a halt, the **ARMCO** following close by was unable to stop, and collided with the stern of the United States Steel vessel. The **ARMCO** received damages amounting to three holes in the bow near the anchor pockets, all of which were above the waterline. These damages caused the **ARMCO** to divert from her upbound trip for repairs at Toledo, Ohio.

In the early 1980s the movement of domestic bulk cargoes on the Great Lakes was starting to be handled by self-unloading vessels. Self-unloading ships had been around for many decades by that time, but had been relegated to mainly the stone and coal trades whose customers in many cases did not maintain shore side unloading equipment. The development of taconite pellets had also demonstrated that this cargo could be handled easily by self-unloading equipment in contrast to natural ores which could not be handled as easily by self-unloaders. The unloading rates of self-unloaders were also much less then that by shore side unloading installations, thus translating in more trips per season.

The **ARMCO** is shown downbound at Port Huron, Michigan during the early 1990s. This steamer has been heavily modified since its construction in 1953. A lengthening during the 1970s, was followed by a self-unloading conversion during the early 1980s, thus enabling this ship to remain a viable member of the Great Lakes fleet. Without such reconstructions it is probable that this ship would have been scrapped during the late 1980s.

The **ARMCO** is upbound on the St. Marys River in the late 1990s on its way to Lake Superior. During most of her career this ship has been primarily engaged in the movement of ore from the upper lakes to Toledo, Ohio, making this steamer a common sight making passage through this waterway.

Oglebay Norton would have four steamers converted into self-unloaders during the 1981-83 time period. These were the **ARMCO, COURTNEY BURTON, MIDDLETOWN,** and **RESERVE.** The **ARMCO** arrived at the Bay Shipbuilding in Sturgeon Bay, Wisconsin following the end of the 1981 season to undergo a self-unloading conversion. This reconstruction was accomplished over the winter and the **ARMCO** reentered service in early 1982. Despite losing 1,300 tons in cargo capacity with the conversion, this ship was now able to unload at virtually any point it could dock at without any assistance from shore.

Following its conversion, the **ARMCO** could also be utilized in cargo routes in which it had been unable to previously operate. It was soon common to see the **ARMCO** engaged in carrying stone, and coal to smaller ports around the lakes. This was an added benefit as the demand for iron ore carriage dropped significantly during the early 1980s. Despite being able to operate in a wide array of trades, the **ARMCO** was not immune to periods of idleness during this timeframe. One of the most significant periods of inactivity for the **ARMCO** started October 6, 1984 when she arrived at the Fraser Shipyards for a lay-up which lasted until October 23, 1986.

This ship has been fortunate in not having been in any significant accidents in her career, with the exception of its collision with the **IRVING S. OLDS.** It has been involved in a few bumps and scrapes, none of which in its wide array of operation could be considered out of the ordinary.

In June of 2006, this ship along with the **COLUMBIA STAR, FRED R. WHITE, JR., COURTNEY BURTON, OGLEBAY NORTON,** and **MIDDLETOWN** were sold to the American Steamship Company. This had followed several years of financial hardship befalling Oglebay Norton prompting that company to divest itself of their shipping operations to raise cash to concentrate on its core aggregate operation.

Shortly following the sale this ship was renamed **AMERICAN VALOR,** and was slowly repainted in American Steamship's fleet colors. An interesting side note to the before mentioned purchase by American Steamship of the steamers **ARMCO, COURTNEY BURTON,** and **MIDDLETOWN** is the fact that this fleet had not operated a steamer since 1998 when it retired the **JOHN J. BOLAND (3).**

Meanwhile, the **RESERVE** which had a career similar to that of the **ARMCO** was converted into a self-unloading barge in 2007, and renamed **JAMES L. KUBER,** being operated by KK Integrated Logistics of Menominee, Michigan.

The design of the ***AMERICAN VALOR*** *was derived from the "AAA" class. However, the forward cabins of this ship are somewhat different in appearance then those installed on most other ships of this class. This is apparent when comparing this picture with the one of the* ***ARTHUR M. ANDERSON*** *on page 38.*

*The **ARMCO** is shown awaiting her turn to lock down through the Poe Lock at Sault Ste. Marie, Michigan in the late 1990s. The opening of this lock allowed this ship to be lengthened from 647 feet to 767 feet in 1974. This limits this ship's operation as no further then Lake Erie due to the size restrictions of the Welland Canal. During a normal shipping season this ship will transit the Soo Locks on several occasions.*

*The **AMERICAN VALOR** is shown downbound at Marysville, Michigan on April 27, 2008. As can be seen in this picture this steamer has received the color scheme of its current owner, the American Steamship Company.*

A 7,700 shaft horsepower Westinghouse steam turbine was installed in this ship when built in 1953, and this powerplant still provides the **AMERICAN VALOR** with motive power. This ship is rated to reach a speed of 19 miles per hour. This steamer is loaded through 23 hatches placed on 24 foot centers and is capable of carrying 25,500 gross tons of cargo at its mid-summer draft of 27 feet. The **AMERICAN VALOR** is equipped with a cargo hold which is subdivided into 5 sections. Cargo is unloaded by dropping through gates installed in the bottom of the cargo hold, which is ran topside via a series of conveyor belts which place the cargo onto a final conveyor belt installed on a 260 foot unloading boom mounted at the stern of the ship, just forward of the after cabins.

The **AMERICAN VALOR** continues to operate today thanks to both the lengthening, and self-unloading conversions accomplished earlier in her career. Without these rebuildings, in particular the self-unloading conversion, it is very doubtful that this ship would have survived the decade of the 1980s which had seen a number of contemporary vessels taken out of service and scrapped. In fact of the eight vessels built in the "AAA" class none operate today which have not been converted into a self-unloader. The one which was not, Ford Motor Company's **WILLIAM CLAY FORD**, was sold for scrapping in 1986 despite being lengthened to 767 feet in 1979.

The **AMERICAN VALOR** is a common sight around the lakes, with Toledo, Ohio being a common unloading destination. This ship is one of a dwindling number of steamers operating under the American flag, and a conversion to diesel is a possibility in the future, although no such plans have been announced as of the end of the 2008 shipping season. The **AMERICAN VALOR**, as with many other ships on the Great Lakes laid up early for the season when she arrived at Toledo for winter lay-up on November 13, 2008. This was due to the sudden drop in the demand for material movement on the inland seas in response to a global economic downturn which had caused the scaling back of steel production.

*The **AMERICAN VALOR** is downbound on the St. Marys River, just south of the Soo Locks on its way to the lower lakes on September 20, 2008. The long graceful lines of the 1950s era steamship are prominent in this view.*

The HERBERT C. JACKSON

This steamer was the last of four such ships built for the Interlake Steamship fleet during the 1950s. The other ships were the **ELTON HOYT 2nd (2)**, **J. L. MAUTHE**, and **JOHN SHERWIN (2)**. The **HERBERT C. JACKSON** was launched on February 20, 1959 at River Rouge, Michigan by the Great Lakes Engineering Works. This steamer was the second to last ship built by this shipyard, the final ship being the **ARTHUR B. HOMER** which was launched in November of 1959.

The **HERBERT C. JACKSON** was placed into service in May of 1959, carrying iron ore from the loading ports on the upper lakes to unloading points on the lower lakes. The **JACKSON** was one of the longer ships in service for Interlake when she began operation, surpassed only by the **JOHN SHERWIN (2)**, and **ELTON HOYT 2nd (2)**. She was also only the second ship to be operated by this fleet with a beam of 75 feet.

During the 1960s this steamer remained busy in the movement of bulk materials around the Great Lakes. In 1966 a bow thruster was installed on the **HERBERT C. JACKSON** to enhance her ability to operate in tight confines without tugboat assistance.

On August 12, 1970 the **HERBERT C. JACKSON** delivered a record cargo of 24,403 gross tons of iron ore to Huron, Ohio, this record would stand until May 16, 1971 when it was broken by the **CHARLES M. BEEGHLY**.

By the early 1970s, the **HERBERT C. JACKSON** which had been above average in size for service on the Great Lakes began to be surpassed by a significant degree by new ships being built to take advantage of the new Poe Lock at Sault Ste. Marie. Also at this time, the emergence of self-unloaders entering the taconite trades caused ship owners to consider upgrading their vessels.

To increase its efficiency, and to open up new trade routes the **HERBERT C. JACKSON** was sent to Bay City, Michigan in 1975 and converted into a self-unloader by the Defoe Shipbuilding Company. This marked the first time that Interlake had converted one of their 1950s era steamers, and was the second such unit under the American flag to be converted that year as the **WILFRED SYKES** received a similar conversion. The conversion of the **JACKSON**, and **WILFRED SYKES** sat the pattern of having the unloading boom placed at the stern of the ship extending forward, whereas the common practice up to that time for American conversions was to have the boom placed forward, just aft of the forward cabins. Prior to this, the Canada Steamship Lines' **FRONTENAC (3)** had received a self-unloading conversion with an aft mounted boom.

The **HERBERT C. JACKSON** was built to use coal as a fuel source, and by the early 1970s this was starting to lose favor on the Great Lakes. Thus, at the same time this ship received her self-unloading conversion she was converted to burn oil, along with having her boilers automated.

The work done to the **HERBERT C. JACKSON** was one of the last contracts handled by Defoe Shipbuilding as it ceased operations on December 31, 1976 due in large part to that firm being unable to secure any future US Navy contracts. By the middle of September of 1976 the **HERBERT C. JACKSON** had returned to service.

It was at this time that Interlake began to place the first of two new thousand foot vessels it would build during the 1970s into service. These new ships had a carrying capacity of 63,300 gross tons of ore, which was in stark contrast to the **JACKSON**'s capacity of 24,800 gross tons. Additionally, the **CHARLES M. BEEGHLY**, and **JOHN SHERWIN (2)** were lengthened to 806 feet, thus providing each of these vessels a cargo capacity of 31,500 gross tons. Despite such a contrast in payload capacity the **HERBERT C. JACKSON** continued to carry a large amount of ore following the commissioning, and lengthening of these vessels.

*The **HERBERT C. JACKSON** is upbound without cargo on the St. Clair River during the early 1990s.*

*The **HERBERT C. JACKSON** is downbound under the original Blue Water Bridge at Port Huron, Michigan following her conversion to a self-unloader. This ship carries a wide range of cargoes including ore, stone, coal, and grain.*

71

While departing Taconite Harbor, Minnesota on May 28, 1978 the **HERBERT C. JACKSON** ran aground causing serious rudder damage. This required a tow by the **CHARLES M. BEEGHLY** to the Twin Ports for repairs. Later that season this ship ran aground again, this time while entering Sheboygan, Wisconsin on October 15, 1978. This stranding occurred on a sandbar near the port's entrance, while this ship was inbound with a load of coal. The **HERBERT C. JACKSON** was able to free herself a short time later, with no damages being reported.

As the 1980s progressed the **HERBERT C. JACKSON** was tasked with carrying a wide variety of cargoes as the demand for ore transportation dropped. On one of these trips during the summer of 1981 this steamer delivered a cargo of stone to the Marblehead Lime dock on the Rouge River. This was believed to have been her first trip into that waterway, but this would change in years to come as she would later carry a significant amount of ore up the Rouge River into the Rouge Steel complex.

During the 1980s many ships in the Interlake Steamship fleet would be idled for significant periods of time. The **HERBERT C. JACKSON** however remained one of the most active ships in that fleet during the time period. In spite of difficult economic times during this decade, the **HERBERT C. JACKSON** was given an upgrade in 1986 when her cargo holds received polymer liners to aid in the unloading of difficult cargoes. In October of 1988, the **HERBERT C. JACKSON** developed problems with her bow thruster. This prompted a trip to the Fraser Shipyards at Superior were the engine for the bow thruster installed on the idle **JOHN SHERWIN (2)** was removed and placed into the **JACKSON**.

As stated earlier, the Rouge River would become a common destination for the **HERBERT C. JACKSON** in the late 1980s. This occurred primarily due to Interlake's purchase of the last three vessels in the Ford Fleet in March of 1989. As part of the transaction Interlake had signed a long term agreement to transport raw materials into the Rouge Steel plant at Dearborn, Michigan. One the first vessels to deliver ore under this arrangement was the **HERBERT C. JACKSON** when she arrived at Dearborn on March 22, 1989.

On May 18, 1993 the **HERBERT C. JACKSON** arrived at Duluth, Minnesota with a load of taconite pellets which had been loaded at Silver Bay, Wisconsin. This unusual movement was part of a test shipment involving a total of 100,000 tons of pellets for final delivery to a steel mill located at Geneva, Utah. For the balance of the 1990s the **HERBERT C. JACKSON** remained, as she had in the past, very active on the inland seas. The conversion to a self-unloader had enabled this ship to survive the 1980s when many other ships of her era had been dismantled. This ship is also one of the few steamers built during the 1950s which were not lengthened during the 1970s and 80s.

*A bow only view of the **HERBERT C. JACKSON** shows this ships unique forward cabins layout. The long curves produce a more modernistic appearance to the cabin installations on other steamers. This ship, along with the **KAYE E. BARKER**, are the last steamers to be part of the Interlake Steamship Company. This latter vessel is operated by Interlake's Lakes Shipping Company. In this photo the **HERBERT C. JACKSON** is downbound at Port Huron in the early 1990s in wavy conditions.*

*While the **HERBERT C. JACKSON** is a common sight in ports such as Marquette, and Toledo, it is also familiar with smaller ports, as is evidenced in this photo of this steamer unloading stone at Marine City, Michigan in the late 1990s.*

*The **HERBERT C. JACKSON** is shown downbound on the St. Marys River, just approaching Mission Point. On this occasion some work is being done on the forward cabins as can be ascertained by the workman on the ladder near one of the pilothouse windows.*

73

This ship serves a variety of ports around the Great Lakes. During her many travels around the lakes the **HERBERT C. JACKSON** usually quietly serves her owners needs, and will deliver her cargoes without any incident. On a few occasions however, this vessels has suffered some difficulties, none of which could be considered serious. One such occasion occurred on March 26, 2000 when the **HERBERT C. JACKSON** ran aground at Grand Haven, Michigan. The steamer was able to free herself a short time later without damages being reported.

On April 29, 2001 the **HERBERT C. JACKSON** arrived at Buffalo, New York with a load of grain which had been loaded at Superior, Wisconsin. Grain would become a significant portion of this steamer's seasonal tonnage commitments in the years to come, as she has remained active in this trade since that season.

The **HERBERT C. JACKSON** delivered the last cargo of coal to Port Washington, Wisconsin on June 26, 2004, following the local power plant being converted to burn natural gas. Following unloading this payload, this steamer was opened for tours at that city the following day to commemorate this final delivery.

The **HERBERT C. JACKSON** retains its original General Electric steam turbine with a rated shaft horsepower of 6,600. This power plant installation allows for a service speed of 16 miles per hour. This ship is capable of carrying a total of 24,800 gross tons of iron ore at a draft of 27 feet, 8 inches. The **HERBERT C. JACKSON** is equipped with both bow and stern thrusters, and is rated for operation on the St. Lawrence River, although this ship has not operated in the Seaway system in recent years and only on rare occasions prior to this.

During the 2008 shipping season the **HERBERT C. JACKSON** remained busy on the Great Lakes. Common ports served during this season were Marquette, Toledo, and Stoneport. An occasional load of sand and grain were loaded at Drummond Island, and Superior respectively. The **HERBERT C. JACKSON**, along with the **KAYE E. BARKER** are the last steamers operating in the Interlake Steamship fleet, and with this company's ongoing modernization program it is highly probable that the **HERBERT C. JACKSON** will be converted from steam to diesel within the next decade.

The **HERBERT C. JACKSON** is downbound on the St. Clair River on August 25, 2005. Highly evident in this view is the topside unloading housing installed just forward of the after cabins. This ship, along with Inland Steel's **WILFRED SYKES**, were the first ships given such an installation in the American fleet during the 1970s, setting a trend to be followed as other steamers were given similar conversions.

The EDWARD L. RYERSON

As the building of the St. Lawrence Seaway progressed during the 1950s, several improvements were made throughout the lakes which enabled the passage of larger vessels. The maximum permissible length to pass through the Soo Locks by 1959 was 730 feet, which was also the standard for the Welland, and St. Lawrence Seaway locks as well. This length was not to prove to be very popular with American ship owners with only two vessels to be built from the keel up to this length, these being the **ARTHUR B. HOMER**, and **EDWARD L. RYERSON**. In 1958, the **EDMUND FITZGERALD** entered service with a length of 729 feet, 3 inches, and can also be included in the 730 foot category.

While the Canadians went on to build dozens of ships with a 730 foot length, the only ships built to Seaway dimensions for the American flag after 1960 were the salt water conversions of the **WALTER A. STERLING, PIONEER CHALLENGER, LEON FALK, JR.,** and **PAUL H. CARNAHAN**. It can be ascertained from this that had the ship building boom which took place in the American fleet during the 1950s occurred a decade later, many operators would have opted to build ships to the maximum 730 foot length. By the 1970s, when the next phase of construction occurred in the American fleet, the new Poe Lock at Sault Ste. Marie had heralded an era of larger ships able to operate only on the upper lakes.

On April 20, 1959 the keel for the **EDWARD L. RYERSON** was laid by Manitowoc Shipbuilding, Incorporated at Manitowoc, Wisconsin. This was to be the second ship built for the Inland Steel fleet following the Second World War, and the second to last to be built for this fleet. This steamer was launched into an ice choked Manitowcc River on January 21, 1960, and beginning sea trials on August 1st of that year.

Following successful trials the **EDWARD L. RYERSON** departed Manitowoc on August 4, 1960. On this maiden trip the **RYERSON** was to load a cargo of ore at Escanaba, Michigan for delivery to Inland's steel manufacturing complex at Indiana Harbor, Indiana. This ship had been designed to operate almost exclusively in the transportation of iron ore, a design component which would have an impact on her later career. The **RYERSON**'s cargo hold has significantly smaller cubic capacity than most ships of her size, due to the specific gravity of iron ore which will bring a vessel to its maximum draft prior to filling the hold by volume. This is in contrast to coal and grain which can be filled into a ship's cargo hold up to the hatch coamings without achieving maximum draft.

A giant of her day, the **EDWARD L. RYERSON** remained one of the largest ships on the Great Lakes until the advent of the **STEWART J. CORT** in 1972. This steamer would set at least two cargo records in the early 1960s. Both of these occurred at Superior, Wisconsin the first being when she loaded 23,378 gross tons of ore in 1961, followed on August 28, 1962 when a total of 25,018 gross tons of iron ore was taken aboard. Both of these cargoes were destined to Indiana Harbor, with the latter record standing until 1965 when it was broken by a larger carrier.

In the late 1960s several ships were being fitted with bow thruster units. These installations consisted of a tunnel being placed at the bow of the vessel with a propeller placed inside. When activated this propeller will push the bow of the vessel in the desired direction, thus providing for easier docking operations. The **EDWARD L. RYERSON** was fitted with such an installation in 1969.

*The **EDWARD L. RYERSON** has always been a common sight on the St. Marys River, on this occasion she is just about to make the turn into the Rock Cut. The stylish curves of this ship are as evident in this picture, as they are unique with no other lake ship being built along these lines.*

*The **EDWARD L. RYERSON** is shown with the "Inland Steel" billboard lettering in 1998. After Inland Steel was purchased by Ispat this ship was placed into service with Central Marine Logistics, and all references to Inland Steel were removed. However the general color scheme was retained.*

Inland Steel had a reputation of maintaining their ships to high standards. With their eye catching color scheme, this fleet was one of the most popular on the lakes. In fact, it was widely rumored that the **EDWARD L. RYERSON** was often directed to lock through the MacArthur Lock at Sault Ste. Marie primarily due to her popularity with the tourists. This ship also seen a considerable amount of guests coming aboard for a trip on the inland seas. This often included members of Inland Steel's upper management, as well as guests from important customers. Onboard the **RYERSON** a stainless steel map of the Great Lakes had been installed with a magnetic representation of the steamer being placed at the location the ship was currently sailing to keep guests informed of the vessel's location.

Throughout the 1970s the **EDWARD L. RYERSON** remained busy in the transportation of ore into Indiana Harbor. In 1975, Inland Steel converted the **WILFRED SYKES** to a self-unloader, and the following year it commissioned its last new ship, the **JOSEPH L. BLOCK**. The **BLOCK** replaced the **RYERSON** as Inland Steel's largest ship, and with a carrying capacity of 37,200 gross tons was able to carry 9,700 tons more than the classic steamer. This ship was also able to unload its cargo at a much faster rate with its onboard unloading equipment than is possible with Inland's clamshell bucket unloading system at Indiana Harbor.

The forward cabins of the **EDWARD L. RYERSON** *demonstrate a unique style. There is no absence of curves in the design, being reminiscent of an era of streamlining popular during the early to mid twentieth century. The appearance of this ship is in stark contrast to those built since the 1970s which have been built with square lines. This ship is the only American ship built prior to 1972 to still be in operation without receiving some major modification in the form of lengthening, self-unloading conversion, cement carrying conversion or repowering.*

During the 1980s the American fleet suffered heavily from a drop in the demand for bulk cargo carriage. When the steel industry was effected by the importation of cheap foreign steel, along with a general nationwide recession the demand for ore dropped significantly following the 1981 season when it plummeted from 74,904,645 gross tons that year, to just slightly over half of that amount in 1982 when only 38,512,574 gross tons was transported. The **EDWARD L. RYERSON,** along with all of the other members of the Inland Steel fleet were effected by this change in demand. By the end of 1981 both the **PHILIP D. BLOCK**, and **L. E. BLOCK** had laid up for the final time, and the **E. J. BLOCK** remained active through 1984 primarily due to being able to serve one of Inland's constrained docking facilities. Meanwhile the **EDWARD L. RYERSON** was laid up on several occasions, primarily due to the lack of being a self-unloader. This steamer would be idle for some significant periods beginning during the 1980s and 1990s. For example, the **RYERSON** was idle at Indiana Harbor from the end of 1985 to the beginning of the 1988 season. This ship would also remain in lay-up starting at the start of the 1994 season when Inland Steel chartered American Steamship's **ADAM E. CORNEILIUS (4)**. This steamer returned to service in 1997, remaining active until December 10, 1998 when it laid up at Sturgeon Bay, Wisconsin.

The **EDWARD L. RYERSON** is upbound at Port Huron, Michigan on June 1, 2007. It is carrying a load of iron ore bound for Indiana Harbor which had been loaded during this vessel's first trip through the St. Lawrence Seaway. This ship was a rare sight on the St. Clair River prior to it being reactivated in 2006. Since then this, the **EDWARD L. RYERSON** has made numerous trips through this waterway with ore for Lorain, and Hamilton.

The **EDWARD L. RYERSON** is downbound with taconite in an ice filled St. Clair River on March 29, 2008 on its first trip of the season, bound for Hamilton, Ontario.

During its career the **EDWARD L. RYERSON** is not known to have been involved in any serious incident. Since being built this ship has concentrated on delivering cargoes into southern Lake Michigan, with a rare trip into Rogers City for stone being the furthest point south on Lake Huron she had traveled up to the late 1980s. In August of 1989 the **EDWARD L. RYERSON** made her first trip into Detroit, Michigan where she loaded mill scale at Great Lakes Steel destined for delivery to Indiana Harbor. This rare trip was followed up by a similar voyage later that season. While the appearance of the **EDWARD L. RYERSON** in the St. Clair, and Detroit Rivers was extremely rare at the time, events nearly twenty years later would see this ship regularly transiting these waterways.

On July 18, 1992 the **RYERSON** loaded the first cargo of crushed pellets to be shipped out of Escanaba, Michigan, with a final destination of Indiana Harbor. Until her laying up at the end of the 1998 season this ship was a regular caller to load taconite pellets at Escanaba, and Marquette during the 1990s. Escanaba was the most common loading port for all ships of the Inland Steel fleet during the early and late periods of the shipping season as it was located only 286 miles north of Indiana Harbor on Lake Michigan and did not require the transit of any river systems which are usually choked with ice during these time periods.

On April 12, 1997 the **EDWARD L. RYERSON** was recorded as being the first straight decker to load at Marquette since the **J. L. MAUTHE** had done so during the 1992 season. During this season the **RYERSON** concentrated on the movement of ore between Marquette and Indiana Harbor, and was the only gearless American ship on the Great Lakes to be committed solely to the transportation of iron ore.

In 1998 Ispat International purchased the Inland Steel Company, and due to restrictions of the Jones Act the ships of the fleet were sold to the Indiana Harbor Steamship Co. and placed under the management of Central Marine Logistics. Inland's fleet at the time of this transaction consisted of the **EDWARD L. RYERSON, JOSEPH L. BLOCK,** and **WILFRED SYKES.** Shortly following the sale all references to Inland Steel were removed from these vessels. This included the painting of the "Inland Steel" billboard lettering on the sides of the hull, and removal of the Inland "diamond" from the stacks. The general color scheme was retained however, giving these ships a sharp appearance for Great Lakes freighters.

As mentioned previously, the **EDWARD L. RYERSON** laid up at the end of the 1998 season at Sturgeon Bay. This ship would remain at this location, until being reactivated in 2006 when the demand for ore had increased to the point which justified this ship's operation. During the lay-up period this ship was opened on a few occasions for tours in cooperation with the Door County Maritime Museum. The first of these open houses occurred on July 20, 2002 and were a popular event due to the **RYERSON**'s popularity with the public.

*This photo of the stern of the **EDWARD L. RYERSON** shows this ship's unique stack and after mast. The stack, and mast is encased in stainless steel making for a very distinctive appearance. Noticeable in this view is the MITTAL logo placed on the stack over the location where the Inland Steel diamond logo had been placed, as can be barely seen behind the lettering. The stack has a light blue band painted at its top, as does the aftermast.*

Since the mid 1970s this ship has been the subject of speculation concerning a self-unloading conversion. For a variety of reasons this type of reconstruction has not been undertaken as of the 2009 season. As mentioned at the beginning of this section, the **EDWARD L. RYERSON** was built with a hold design which minimized cubic capacity. This has no impact on the ship while it is carrying taconite, and was a sound design feature at the time of its construction. However, a conventional self-unloading conversion would cause either a significant loss of capacity or require a total rebuilding of the cargo hold, and ballast tanks. To better illustrate the difference in the cubic feet designed into the cargo hold of the **EDWARD L. RYERSON**, an easy comparison can be made with that of the Canadian steamer **QUEBECOIS** which has the same length, beam, and depth. The **RYERSON**'s cargo hold has a volume equal to 761,000 cubic feet, while the **QUEBECOIS** has a volume of 1,162,185 cubic feet. This is primarily due to differing design philosophies between the two ships, with the **QUEBECOIS** having a higher cubic volume due to the expectation that this ship would be engaged in carrying grain in addition to other bulk cargoes.

While it has been widely reported Inland Steel had seriously considered a rebuilding of the **RYERSON** during the late 1970s, this type of reconstruction was not considered feasible by the early 1980s with the sudden drop in demand for ore carriage. This made the **EDWARD L. RYERSON** somewhat of a backup boat for Inland, only being activated when the demand for ore carriage warranted it. And as the turn of the century approached there were fears that this classic steamer would soon be decommissioned. Luckily this was not to be, and after sitting idle for nearly 8 years, new business opportunities arose which brought about an unlikely reactivation of this vessel.

During the summer of 2006 the **EDWARD L. RYERSON** was moved into the dry dock at Bay Shipbuilding where she was refitted to enter service. She left the shipyard on July 22, 2006 for a short trip to Escanaba where she loaded a cargo of ore for Indiana Harbor. Unlike her past operations, the **RYERSON** was utilized carrying ore into ports other than Indiana Harbor. On August 21, 2006 the **EDWARD L. RYERSON** arrived at the Jonick Dock in Lorain, Ohio carrying a cargo of taconite which had been loaded at Superior, Wisconsin. Since there are no permanent dockside unloading facilities at this location she was unloaded by gantry cranes. This process proved to be somewhat slow initially, but as the crane operators gained more experience in unloading this steamer, unloading times improved. The **RYERSON** would carry many loads into Lorain that season, and were followed up by repeat trips during the 2007 season.

In 2007, the **EDWARD L. RYERSON** transited the Welland Canal, and St. Lawrence Seaway for the first time in her career. This occurred in May of that season when this steamer went to the port of Quebec. While this transit was an extremely rare occurrence at the time, by the 2008 shipping season the **EDWARD L. RYERSON** was a common sight on the Welland Canal as she was primarily engaged in the movement of ore from Superior to Hamilton, Ontario. This route was interrupted at times with a trip up the Seaway to load for delivery to Indiana Harbor.

Near the end of the 2008 shipping season, the worldwide economic crisis caught up to the steel industry and the demand for ore movement once again dropped significantly. At this time, the **EDWARD L. RYERSON** had begun to carry ore from Superior into Lorain, following spending most of the season on the Hamilton run. On November 4, 2008 this steamer arrived for winter lay up at the Fraser Shipyards at Superior, thus ending her season early. This ship was not to be alone at the wall for long as many other Great Lakes freighters arrived early for the annual end of season lay up following an ongoing collapse in the demand of ore.

As the 2009 shipping season approached the economic crisis had not only continued but had worsened. At press time, several ships have not yet received sailing orders and their return to operation this season is highly questionable. The **EDWARD L. RYERSON**, the last straight deck bulk carrier in operation for an American fleet on the Great Lakes was actually one of the earliest vessels to fit out this season, and loaded her first cargo of ore at Duluth, Minnesota for Hamilton on April 2, 2009. This is a unique situation as she was in operation while many other newer, and self-unloading equipped vessels remained tied up awaiting a turnabout in the demand for raw material transport.

The **EDWARD L. RYERSON** was both the last steamer, and straight deck bulk carrier, built on the Great Lakes for an American shipping company. During the 1960s, several salt water conversions were undertaken to bolster the US flagged fleet, but these were rebuilds of existing steamers rather then completely new vessels. By the time the next round of ship building construction took place in American shipyards during the 1970s diesel powered engines had replaced steam as the desired choice for motive power. The only mention during this time period of building a steam powered freighter for Great Lakes service came from the Cleveland Cliffs Steamship fleet when they were considering the building of a steam powered ship of the thousand foot class. This plan never got beyond preliminary discussions, as this fleet was the losing bidder for both a major ore, and coal hauling contracts during the late 1970s, and early 1980s, thus causing the disbanding of this long standing fleet.

The **EDWARD L. RYERSON** is powered by its original General Electric steam turbine, rated at 9,900 shaft horsepower. This ship is capable of carrying 27,500 gross tons of taconite at a maximum draft of 28 feet, 4 inches. Cargo is loaded into the **RYERSON** through 18 hatches, placed on 24 foot centers. With a length of 730 feet this ship is easily able to transit the Welland Canal, and the St. Lawrence Seaway making it one of a handful of ships under the American flag to do so in the past five years.

Today the **EDWARD L. RYERSON** serves the needs of ArcelorMittal, which was formed in 2006 following a series of mergers of several steel corporations. It due to these business consolidations that this ship operates in the trade routes it does, as the **JOSEPH L. BLOCK**, and **WILFRED SYKES** continue to supply the needs of the ArcelorMittal's steel making operations at Indiana Harbor.

*The steamer **EDWARD L. RYERSON** is upbound on Lake Huron on April 3, 2008, bound for Superior, Wisconsin for a cargo of taconite. This ship, and others of her class, were the largest on the Great Lakes until 1972, when the thousand-footer **STEWART J. CORT** entered service. As can be seen in this photograph, the **EDWARD L. RYERSON** is equipped with forward and aft masts of a unique design.*

The AMERICAN VICTORY

This ship has one of the most interesting histories of ships currently sailing upon the Great Lakes, and was one of several salt-water conversions undertaken during the 1950s and 60s. While several of these conversions experienced short lived careers on the inland seas, this ship at 66 years old is still going strong.

During the Second World War the United States embarked upon a shipbuilding program which was unequalled before or since. Almost every category of vessel was necessary to ensure the successful outcome of that conflict. While warships garnered most of the attention with their exploits on the oceans, several auxiliary ships were required to ensure a rapid and constant flow of supplies to the areas of conflict. With this in mind, the United States Maritime Commission contracted the Bethlehem Shipyard at Sparrows Point, Maryland in 1942 to construct a T3-S-A1 tanker, which was assigned hull number 4381.

Originally named **MARQUETTE**, this was later changed to **NESHANIC** prior to launching which occurred on October 31, 1942. On February 20, 1943 this ship was commissioned into the United States Navy being assigned pennant number **AO-71**. With a length of 501 feet, 8 inches this ship was designed to fuel other naval vessels either while stationary, or underway. This ship had a carrying capacity of 133,800 barrels of petroleum products, and was able to obtain a speed of 15 knots.

On April 20, 1943 the **NESHANIC** departed Hampton Roads as part of a convoy bound for Aruba. Following the loading of cargo at that port, she set sail for the Pacific where she participated in supplying allied forces during the Solomons Campaign. The **NESHANIC** would shortly become involved in supply runs originating from San Pedro, California into the Hawaiian, and Aleutian Islands.

*The **MIDDLETOWN** betrays little of her extensive record on saltwater during World War II in this view of her unloading crushed stone at Marine City, Michigan in the late 1990s.*

On June 18, 1944 the **NESHANIC** was attacked by Japanese aircraft while off of Saipan. At 4:41 PM several bombs landed close to the tanker, and within a few minutes one bomb struck the vessel on the cargo deck, starting a fire. While damage was serious, it was not as catastrophic as it could have been since the bomb did not manage to penetrate into the vessel's interior spaces. Nevertheless, thirty-three of her crew were injured during the attack, and the damage control operations following it. During this incident the **NESHANIC**'s gunners were credited with the downing of two enemy planes. The damages suffered in this attack did not prevent this vessel from refueling American warships that night, which on the following day were involved in the Battle of the Philippine Sea.

The **NESHANIC** went on to be involved in several notable campaigns in the Pacific, including operations off of Guam, Iwo Jima, and Okinawa. Following the end of the Second World War, with the surrender of Japan the **NESHANIC** arrived in Tokyo Bay on the 26th of September 1945. Remaining there until late October, she arrived at Norfolk, Virginia on November 28, 1945 and was decommissioned on the 19th of December of that year.

In June of 1946, the **NESHANIC** was transferred to Maritime Commission, later being acquired by Gulf Oil in 1947. That same year she was renamed **GULFOIL**, and placed into service transporting petroleum products on deep sea routes. Operations in the Gulf Oil fleet continued until August 7, 1958 when this ship was in a collision the tanker **S. E. GRAHAM** off of Newport, Rhode Island.

The **GRAHAM** which was carrying five million gallons of gasoline at the time of the accident exploded, killing fifteen of the **GULFOIL**'s crew. After burning for several days, the flames were brought under control and the vessel was declared a total constructive loss and taken to Baltimore, Maryland following a sale to the Maryland Shipbuilding & Dry Dock Company.

It was at this time that the Pioneer Steamship Company was seeking to obtain some additional tonnage for its Great Lakes fleet. After securing financial arrangements in conjunction with the Northwestern Mutual Life Insurance company in 1959, the burnt out **GULFOIL** was purchased for conversion into a 730 foot lake freighter.

While the ship's mid-section had been damaged beyond economical repair, its stern section and its machinery spaces were in good shape. It was therefore decided to have a mid-section built at the Verholme-United Shipyards in the Netherlands at Rotterdam. Following completion, this hull section was towed across the Atlantic to Baltimore where it was joined to the bow and stern of the **GULFOIL**. The forward cabins, which included the pilot house, were moved from their mid-ships position to the bow, giving the vessel a traditional Great Lakes freighter profile.

By early summer of 1961 the conversion of this ship was nearly complete and it departed Baltimore in July bound for the Great Lakes under the name **PIONEER CHALLENGER**. This would be the largest vessel to be owned by Pioneer, but as will be seen her career in that fleet would be brief. Shortly after entering service, the **PIONEER CHALLENGER** struck bottom on July 31, 1961 near Buffalo, New York while carrying a cargo of iron ore. This accident required a trip to Superior, Wisconsin were repairs were completed at the Fraser Nelson Shipyard.

By the early 1960s, Pioneer Steamship began to wind down its shipping operations resulting from financial difficulties carried over from the late 1950s. After selling off a number of their other vessels, the **PIONEER CHALLENGER**, along with the **CLARENCE B. RANDALL (1)** were sold in 1962 to Oglebay Norton to be operated by its Columbia Transportation fleet.

Following this transaction, this ship was renamed **MIDDLETOWN**, while the **RANDALL (1)** became the **ASHLAND**. This latter ship was a "Maritime" class vessel built in 1943, and continued in operation with Columbia Transportation until laying up in 1979, later being sold for scrap in 1987. The **MIDDLETOWN** would be the only true 730 foot vessel to be operated by Columbia Transportation, although arguably she shares this title with the **EDMUND FITZGERALD** which came in 9 inches shorter and 729 feet, three inches. These same 9 inches also made the **MIDDLETOWN** the longest ship within the fleet until the lengthening of the **ARMCO** from 647 feet to 767 feet in 1974.

*The **MIDDLETOWN** is shown exiting the MacArthur Lock at Sault Ste. Marie, Michigan with a cargo of taconite ,during the late 1990s. With a usual trade route from the upper to lower lakes, such transits are common.*

*In July of 2000, the **MIDDLETOWN** is shown taking on fuel at the Imperial Fuel dock at Sarnia, Ontario.*

On September 6, 1975 the **MIDDLETOWN** ran aground in Lake St. Clair, around 4:30 in the morning. This grounding occurred near Light 2 of the St. Clair Cutoff Channel, with freeing of the ore carrier occurring with the assistance of the tugs **MAINE**, and **MARYLAND**. In December of 1978, the **MIDDLETOWN** required a tow into the Great Lakes Steel dock on the Detroit River following rudder damages in Lake Michigan. She arrived at that location on December 10th under tow of the **BARBARA ANN, LENNY B.,** and **WILLIAM SELVICK**. Two days later , after unloading, this ship departed under tow of the **BARBARA ANN,** and **JAMES A. HANNAH,** bound for repairs at Lorain, Ohio.

In August of 1979 the **MIDDLETOWN** suffered additional rudder problems, which required repairs at Port Colborne, Ontario. In this instance the freighter was towed to that location due to a labor strike which had occurred at the American Ship Building Company. Towing was provided by Great Lakes Towing's **SOUTH CAROLINA**, and **OHIO**.

While in operation for Columbia as a straight decker the **MIDDLETOWN** was engaged primarily in the movement of iron ore from the upper lakes to the lower lakes ports which served the steel industry. By the early 1980s, the operation of a US flagged straight decker in the ore trade was becoming less profitable. The economic benefits of a self-unloading Great Lakes freighter dictated less turnaround time while unloading, which equated to a greater number of trips per season. It also eliminated the need of shoreside unloading equipment, thus enabling a vessel to serve many unloading points which were previously inaccesible. Two notable drawbacks to a self-unloading vessel are higher maintenance costs, and a slight loss in carrying capacity when compared to similar sized gearless vessels.

In 1982, the **MIDDLETOWN** became the only American 730 foot ship to be converted into a self-unloader when it received such a conversion at the Bay Shipbuilding Company in Sturgeon Bay, Wisconsin. This involved the installation of a stern mounted 260 foot unloading boom, along with the associated unloading housing. Though the long haul ore trade remained the dominant cargo for this ship, the rebuilding opened up new trades for this ship, with cargoes of coal and stone becoming common. Also this ship was routinely used to service ports which had been impossible to serve due to the lack of unloading equipment.

*When this ship was converted into a Great Lakes steamer from an ocean going T-3 tanker, much of the original vessel was retained. One such item was the ship's forward cabins. These cabins were originally located at the middle of the vessel, as was the practice for tankers at the time of its construction. During the reconstruction, they were moved to the bow section, which was indicative of the standard layout of Great Lakes freighters up through the 1970s. In this view, the **MIDDLETOWN** is downbound at Port Huron, Michigan on April 14 2006.*

*The **AMERICAN VICTORY** is shown while downbound at St. Clair, Michigan on April 19, 2008. Immediately, following its sale to American Steamship the stack markings were changed to reflect the transaction. However, as of the 2008 season the ship's hull has not yet painted black, although the cabins had received a coat of white paint.*

The 1980s were a period of change within the United States Great Lakes shipping industry, with the downturn in the steel industry. As cargoes became scarce many operators were forced to lay up some of their ships due to a lack of demand. Many shipping companies, and ships, would not survive this decade. Additionally, many of the ships which survived the 1980s spent considerable amount of time tied up, with the **MIDDLETOWN** being idled for the entire 1984 season.

While nearing Port Washington, Wisconsin on September 15, 1986 with a cargo of coal loaded at Conneaut, Ohio a build up of methane gas caused an explosion in the engine room of this steamer. Though the explosion was brief, it was significant enough to burn both the Chief and Assistant Engineers, one fatally.

On April 19, 1990 the **MIDDLETOWN** loaded a cargo of taconite at the Cyprus North Shore Mining Company dock in Silver Bay, Wisconsin. Though this port had been a common port of call during her tenure in with Oglebay Norton in the past, this was the first cargo shipped from that port since the previous owners had closed the facility on July 31, 1986.

While downbound in the upper St. Marys River with a load of taconite on November 26, 1990, the **MIDDLETOWN** ran aground. After lightering around 4,500 tons into the **PML SALVAGER** the **MIDDLETOWN** was pulled free with the assistance of the tugs **SCOTT PURVIS, ANGLIAN LADY, MISSOURI, VERMONT,** and **WILFRED M. COHEN**. No significant damages were reported as having been caused by this grounding.

Three bent hull plates were reported on April 2, 1991 after this ship was struck by fleetmate **BUCKEYE (3)** during a windstorm at Toledo, Ohio. In early October of 2004 the **MIDDLETOWN** touched bottom while upbound in the St. Marys River, requiring drydocking for hull repairs at the Fraser Shipyard in Superior, Wisconsin. In this incident, the steamer suffered 400 feet worth of bottom damages, with repairs being completed by October 18th.

In June of 2006, the **MIDDLETOWN** was among six carriers sold by Oglebay Norton to the American Steamship Company in a move by that firm to abandon their Great Lakes shipping operations. Sold in this transaction along with this ship were the **OGLEBAY NORTON, COLUMBIA STAR, FRED R. WHITE, JR., ARMCO,** and **COURTNEY BURTON**. These last two ships, along with the **MIDDLETOWN** were the last steamers in operation for Oglebay Norton at the time of the sale, and were the first such vessels to be operated by American Steamship following their retirement of the **JOHN J. BOLAND** (3) in 1998. The **JOHN J. BOLAND** (3) was acquired in late 1999 by Lower Lakes Towing and renamed **SAGINAW** (3), remaining in operation as of 2008. After the sale was concluded the **MIDDLETOWN** was renamed **AMERICAN VICTORY**, remaining active in the ore, stone, and coal trades.

The **AMERICAN VICTORY** is capable of carrying 26,000 tons of cargo at a mid-summer draft of 29 feet, 1 and 1/2 inches. Motive power is provided by this ship's steam turbine capable of generating 7,700 shaft horsepower. This enables the vessel to obtain speeds of up to 16.1 miles per hour.

The **AMERICAN VICTORY** was one of four salt water tankers converted into Great Lakes bulk freighters for the American fleet in 1961, the others being **WALTER A. STERLING, PAUL H. CARNAHAN,** and **LEON FALK, JR.**. This ship was the only one of this group rebuilt off-lakes as the others were converted at Lorain, Ohio by the American Ship Building Company. The **STERLING** was converted for Cleveland Cliffs, while the **CARNAHAN,** and **FALK** became members of the National Steel fleet. The **STERLING** sails today for Interlake Steamship as the **LEE A. TREGURTHA**, being repowered from steam to diesel in 2006. The **PAUL H. CARNAHAN,** and **LEON FALK, JR.** were destined, like so many other salt-water conversions, to have short careers on the Great Lakes. The **FALK** was sold for scrapping in 1985, after being idle since 1980, while the **CARNAHAN** shared the same fate a year later after operating sporadically in the early 1980s.

On November 12, 2008, the **AMERICAN VICTORY** arrived at Toledo, Ohio for an early winter lay-up due to worsening economic conditions. In her 66 years of service, this ship has seen many parts of the world and serves in a capacity which could have never been envisioned at the time of her construction. It is likely that this ship may become a diesel repowering candidate in the future as the current trend of such conversions continues. In any case it is unlikely that the final chapter in this ship's history has been written.

A stern view of the
AMERICAN VICTORY
illustrates the curved lines of the vessel's stern which are traits of her salt water tanker origins. While many tanker conversions took place during the 1950s and 60s to obtain additional tonnage quickly, most did not enjoy a long tenure on the inland seas. At 66 years old, with 47 of those years in Great Lakes service, this ship is an exception.

The MONTREALAIS

This ship's construction was somewhat unique as both the bow, and stern sections were built at separate yards. The bow was constructed at Lauzon, Quebec by George T. Davie & Sons, while the stern was built at the Canadian Vickers Shipyard located in Montreal, Quebec. The stern section was launched first on October 19, 1961, with bow being launched the following week on October 25th. Both of these sections were joined at Lauzon and named **MONTREALER**. This name was changed to **MONTREALAIS** prior to it being christened at Montreal on April 12, 1962.

This 730 foot ship was the first ship to be built for the Papachristidis fleet, which was expanding their operations into the Great Lakes following having successful saltwater operations. Actual ownership of the **MONTREALAIS** was registered to Canadian Vickers with a bareboat charter agreement with Papachristidis.

The **MONTREALAIS** was built for the movement of raw materials throughout the Great Lakes, and St. Lawrence Seaway. This has remained the focus of her operations to this day. Early in her career, the **MONTREALAIS** was involved in a collision in Montreal harbor with the British saltwater tanker **ATHELTEMPLAR**. This collision, which occurred on August 3, 1962 resulted in minor damages to the **MONTREALAIS**.

A little over five years later, on November 21, 1967 the **MONTREALAIS** ran aground on the St. Lawrence River near Three Rivers, Quebec. This incident was a little more serious then the previous collision and resulted in 19 damaged hull plates.

Following a decade in operation on the Great Lakes, Papachristidis decided to abandon this portion of its activities to focus on saltwater operations. In 1972, the **MONTREALAIS** was sold to Upper Lakes Shipping along with the four other ships of the fleet. These were the **PETITE HERMINE, FEUX-FOLLETS, GRANDE HERMINE**, and **QUEBECOIS**. With the exception of the **MONTREALAIS**, and **QUEBECOIS** all of these ships received new names following this transaction.

The introduction of these bulk carriers, which were all less then ten years old along with being the maximum size allowed on the Seaway provided a sizable boost to Upper Lakes' seasonal carrying capacity. The operations of the **MONTREALAIS** remained similar to those it had already served in, namely the movement of grain down the Seaway with a return cargo of ore.

The most serious accident to befall this ship thus far occurred in the early morning hours of June 25, 1980. While downbound on the St. Clair River that date, the **MONTREALAIS** collided head-on with Algoma's **ALGOBAY** abreast of St. Clair Michigan. This collision occurred at 5:04 AM in heavy fog conditions, and resulted in major damages to the **MONTREALAIS**. The **ALGOBAY**, which was upbound for Sarnia, Ontario received relatively minor bow damages. The bow of the **MONTREALAIS** was pushed twenty feet inward, with some damages being done to the forward cabins. Following the collision both ships went to anchor by the stern, with their bows facing downstream. The **ALGOBAY**, suffered one large hole in the bow about twelve feet above the waterline, along with two eight foot rips in the same area. The **ALGOBAY** was able to leave the scene at around 10:00 AM, going to a stone dock at Mooretown, Ontario. The **MONTREALAIS** was towed by the Malcom tug **BARBARA ANN** later in the day to an anchorage below Recor's Point just north of Marine City, Michigan. The **MONTREALAIS** was later towed to Port Colborne. Following the unloading of cargo this steamer was taken to the Port Weller Dry Docks on July 1, 1980 for extensive repairs, reportedly costing in the neighborhood of $1 million dollars. Repairs proceeded quickly with the **MONTREALAIS** reentering service on September 25, 1980.

*A stern view of the **MONTREALAIS** illustrates the rounded cruiser type stern of this class of ships.*

*The **MONTREALAIS** is downbound on the St. Clair River during the 1990 season. This ship is a long haul vessel, commonly carrying grain from the western end of Lake Superior to the lower St. Lawrence. A return cargo of ore into the Great Lakes is common. This ship was built specifically for this purpose, and has remained active in such duties since 1962.*

The **MONTREALAIS** was involved in a much less serious collision on December 6, 1983 when she was struck by the **JEAN PARISIEN** while that vessel was docking at Quebec City, Quebec. Both vessels reported damages of a minor nature as a result of this incident. The **MONTREALAIS** is noted as to having carried a unique cargo in November of 1987 when it unloaded a 35 foot Christmas tree at Lock 1 of the Welland Canal destined for St. Catherines, Ontario following it being loaded at Baie Comeau, Quebec.

While transiting the Maumee River at Toledo on April 3, 1993 the **MONTREALAIS** struck the Conrail Bridge. Swift currents in the area due to high waters were blamed for the incident, with no significant damage being reported.

In 1990, Upper Lakes and Algoma Central Marine created a pooling arrangement for their gearless vessels. This new entity was named Seaway Bulk Carriers and involved the grouping of these ships under one management, to be utilized as effectively as possible as cargoes became available. This arrangement was successful, being followed in 1994 by the formation of Seaway Self-Unloaders, which was a similar arrangement to Seaway Bulk Carriers, but this time consisting of the self-unloading vessels of the two fleets.

In 2000, a further consolidation occurred with the creation of Seaway Marine Transport which replaced both of the previous pooling arrangements, replacing it with one management group controlling all of both Upper Lakes, and Algoma's straight deckers, and self-unloaders in service on the Great Lakes. Despite these pooling arrangements, each individual ship remains painted in its owning company's fleet colors.

The **MONTREALAIS** commonly carries iron ore on the Great Lakes and St. Lawrence Seaway system, however most of these movements involve it being carried from the St. Lawrence River and into the Great Lakes to be unloaded. In 2005, however, the **MONTREALAIS** arrived for a rare load of ore at Marquette, Michigan. This rare cargo was due to a high demand for ore carriage that season, prompting the loading of several Canadian straight deckers at Marquette, which do not usually serve that port. This included the **CANADIAN MINER, ALGOISLE, CANADIAN LEADER,** and **CEDARGLEN (2)**.

*The forward cabins of the **MONTREALAIS** represent a blend of traditional and modern styling. While mostly composed of straight lines, the cabins are clearly influenced by the traditional placement of the pilot house at the forward end of the vessel. This practice was common until the 1970s when new ships began to appear with an all cabins aft design. In 1974, the last ship built with both forward, and aft cabins, the **ALGOSOO (2)**, entered service. The **MONTREALAIS** was the third unit built by Canadian Vickers out of a class of six which were built during the 1960s. Of these only three remain, the others being scrapped in recent years.*

The **MONTREALAIS** is powered by a Canadian General Electric steam turbine, capable of generating 9,900 shaft horsepower. This engine gives this ship a respectable speed of 19 miles per hour. This steamer's cargo hold is divided into 5 sections, providing a carrying capacity of 27,800 gross tons of ore at its maximum draft of 27 feet, 8 inches.

This steamer is a common caller at Duluth, Superior, Toledo, Thunder Bay, and Hamilton. A common trade route for the **MONTREALAIS** is the carrying of cement into Duluth, and then loading a cargo of grain at either that port or Superior for return trip down the lakes. She is also a common hauler of iron ore into Hamilton, Ontario. In 2008, the **MONTREALAIS** is noted as making a very rare trip into Owen Sound, Ontario.

The **MONTREALAIS** is one of the older ships operating under the Canadian flag on the Great Lakes. Despite this, the **MONTREALAIS** was one of the earliest vessels to fit out for the 2009 season, being the recipient of the traditional Top Hat Award at St. Catherines, Ontario on March 31, 2009 when she became the first upbound ship to transit the Welland Canal that year. The start of the 2009 shipping season was significant in that it is the 50th anniversary of the opening of the St. Lawrence Seaway.

The **MONTREALAIS** would run into trouble on her return trip through the Welland Canal while she was approaching Bridge 11 on April 7, 2009. Difficulty was experienced while attempting to open the bridge in order to allow the passage of the **MONTREALAIS**, forcing the steamer to drop her anchors in an attempt to stop the vessel. The crew of the **MONTREALAIS** was able to avoid striking the bridge, but the vessel wound up sideways in the channel, suffering some hull damage upon striking shore.

The **MONTREALAIS** should remain active in the grain, ore, and cement trades for the foreseeable future. This ship is one of a dwindling number of 730 foot vessels built for the Seaway trade during the 1960s. Many ships of its class have been sold for scrap over the past ten years, and this trend will most likely continue. The recent downturn in the steel industry may have effects which have not yet been realized, which could in turn effect the future of this ship. However, a strong demand in grain movement at the beginning of the 2009 season may offset some of the tonnage lost due to the drop in ore demand.

*The **MONTREALAIS** is shown downbound at St. Clair, Michigan on November 1, 2008. It was at this location that she collided with the **ALGOBAY** on June 25, 1980.*

The CANADIAN PROVIDER

This ship was one of three steamers to enter service for the Canada Steamship Lines fleet during the 1963 shipping season. It had been built that year at Collingwood, Ontario by the Collingwood Shipyards as the **MURRAY BAY (3)**. When it loaded its initial cargo on July 18, 1963 at Taconite Harbor, Minnesota it became the last of the trio to be placed into operation. These other two vessels were the **BAIE ST. PAUL**, and **BLACK BAY**, these ships signaling the end of the building of steam powered straight deckers for Canada Steamship Lines. In fact, they were followed only by the self-unloading steamer **TARANTAU** built in 1965, entering fleet service that same year. All other ships built for Canada Steamship since have been diesel powered.

The **MURRAY BAY (3)** was built to the maximum allowable dimensions for operation on the St. Lawrence Seaway. This vessel was the second 730 foot vessel to carry this name for Canada Steamship Lines fleet as the **MURRAY BAY (2)** had been built at Collingwood in 1960. This steamer was sold in 1962 to the Paterson fleet being renamed **COMEAUDOC** in 1963.

The **MURRAY BAY (3)** was built for the movement of cargoes from the head of the Great Lakes, through the Seaway with a return cargo back into the lakes. It would be this role in which this ship would be engaged throughout her career. This ship would one of a number of similar vessels built during the 1960s for the Canadian fleet as their maritime operations adjusted to the new benefits allowed by the opening of the St. Lawrence Seaway. In fact, by the beginning of the 1970 shipping season the Canada Steamship Lines fleet had no less then eleven ships in operation which had been built during the 1960s, which were of the 730 foot class.

While part of the Canada Steamship fleet this ship was involved in a few minor incidents. On April 18, 1975 the **MURRAY BAY (3)** lost an anchor in the St. Marys River. While downbound on the St. Clair River on April 17, 1984 the **MURRAY BAY (3)** ran aground. This grounding occurred near the Canadian shore, with this steamer being released from its stranding shortly afterwards with no damages being reported.

The **MURRAY BAY (3)** was involved in a near collision with the **WILLIAM J. DELANCEY** while approaching Duluth on August 6, 1986. While nearing the **DELANCEY** as that vessel was outbound in the Duluth Ship Canal, winds pushed the **MURRAY BAY (3)** to within thirty feet of the Interlake vessel. Both ships were able to avoid making contact, but this incident surely caused some concern for the crews of the two lake vessels.

This steamer would come close to having another accident later in 1986, when Bridge 11 in Welland Canal failed to open in time to permit the passage of the **MURRAY BAY (3)** on October 18th. In this case, the **MURRAY BAY (3)** was able to avoid striking the bridge by dropping both anchors, and reversing its engine, but much like the previous incident in August it surely caused some anxious moments in the steamer's pilothouse.

November 14, 1992 would find the **MURRAY BAY (3)** docked at Anderson's Elevators' dock at Toledo, Ohio. While Algoma Central Marine's **ALGONORTH** was outbound on the Maumee River it ran aground with its bow coming in contact with the Conrail Bridge, while its stern came to rest in contact with the hull of the **MURRAY BAY (3)**. Damage was minor to both vessels, with the **ALGONORTH** being freed a short time later. The cause of this accident was contributed to strong currents in the Maumee River brought on by several days of rain.

*The **CANADIAN PROVIDER** is downbound on the St. Clair River on May 9, 2008. When built in 1963 this ship followed a traditional layout, then popular on the Great Lakes.*

*The classic stack design of the Upper Lakes fleet is visible in this view of the **CANADIAN PROVIDER**. The stack is painted red, with a black band circling the top 1/3 of the stack, with a large white diamond placed above where the red and black bands meet.*

In 1991, the **MURRAY BAY (3)** was transferred to Great Lakes Bulk Carriers, Incorporated, which was a pooling arrangement between Canada Steamship, Misener Holdings, and Pioneer Shipping. This firm was made up of all of the straight deckers in these fleets, and though ownership remained with their respective companies, the actual operation of these vessels was carried out through Great Lakes Bulk Carriers.

During this timeframe a decline in the transportation of exported grain thru the Seaway, caused an over capacity situation within the Canadian Great Lakes fleet. This was especially true for gearless ships as they were less flexible to operate in a variety of trades since they are dependent upon shore side unloading facilities. The drop in the demand for grain movement was also exaggerated by subsidies provided to railroad companies by the Canadian government which favored the shipment of grain through ports on the west coast.

In 1993, Canada Steamship placed their last remaining straight deck bulk carriers up for sale. The **MURRAY BAY (3)** was sold to Upper Lakes, and renamed **CANADIAN PROVIDER** in 1994. This brought this vessel under the management of Seaway Bulk Carriers, which was a pooling arrangement with Algoma Central Marine.

On April 20, 1998, the **CANADIAN PROVIDER** lost its anchor during an attempt to stop in the St. Marys River while losing engine power. The anchor, along with an estimated 200 feet of chain were lost during this occurrence, but no other damages were reported with the **CANADIAN PROVIDER** proceeding on its voyage shortly afterwards.

As is common with many other Canadian gearless ships engaged in the Seaway trade, the **CANADIAN PROVIDER** will often be idle during the summer months, being reactivated in time to participate in the late season grain rush.

On August 11, 2001 Paterson's motor vessel **WINDOC (2)** struck Welland Canal's Bridge #11 while passing. This occurred as the raised span of the bridge was lowered prior to the vessel clearing, causing serious damages to the **WINDOC (2)**. Following the accident, the stricken vessel continued in motion prior to grounding and catching on fire. The **WINDOC (2)** was declared a total loss, and towed to Hamilton, Ontario where its grain cargo was to be transferred to another vessel. To take on this cargo, the **CANADIAN PROVIDER** which was laid up at the time at Toronto, Ontario was towed to Hamilton, arriving there on September 9, 2001. By September 22nd, all but a small portion of the grain onboard the wrecked vessel had been transferred into the **CANADIAN PROVIDER**. The **CANADIAN PROVIDER** finally cleared Hamilton on October 13, 2001 to deliver the grain to Montreal, Quebec.

This steamer is powered by a 10,000 shaft horsepower steam turbine, which had been built by John Inglis Company, Ltd.. This firm is not well known as being a manufacturer of steam engines for Great Lakes freighters, although it produced the engine for Canada Steamship's passenger steamer **HURONIC**, which served on the Great Lakes from 1902 to 1950. This engine gives the **CANADIAN PROVIDER** a speed of 17.3 miles per hour.

This steamer can carry up to 27,450 gross tons of iron ore at a maximum draft of 27 feet, 5 inches. When operating in the St. Lawrence Seaway, the carrying capacity of this ship is slightly less at 25,600 gross tons due to draft restrictions. The **CANADIAN PROVIDER**'s cargo hold is sub-divided into 6 sections, with access to the hold being provided by 17 hatches.

As of April 15, 2009 the **CANADIAN PROVIDER** had not yet entered service for the 2009 shipping season. It is probable that this ship will operate during the season, but more questionable is the long term future of this steamer.

The HALIFAX

The opening of the St. Lawrence Seaway in 1959 prompted the Hall Corporation to build a 730 foot bulk carrier. This ship was the **LEECLIFFE HALL**, which was built at Glasgow, Scotland in 1961. A second 730 foot freighter was acquired in 1963 when this ship was built as the **FRANKCLIFFE HALL (2)**, at Lauzon, Quebec by Davie Shipbuilding. This ship was also to be the last steam powered bulk carrier to be built for the Hall fleet.

The building of this ship required the renaming of the original **FRANKCLIFFE HALL (1)** which was renamed **NORTHCLIFFE HALL** in 1962. This particular ship had been built as a canal sized freighter in 1952, remaining in active service for the Hall fleet until the end of the 1973 shipping season. This ship would later meet its end on May 27, 1982 when as the **ROLAND DESGAGNES** it sank in the St. Lawrence River following a grounding.

The **FRANKCLIFFE HALL (2)** departed Lauzon on May 26, 1963 bound for Duluth, Minnesota to load grain on its maiden trip. During the 1960s the Hall fleet would place four additional bulk carriers of the 730 foot class into service. These were, in the order of their construction: **LAWRENCECLIFFE HALL (2), BEAVERCLIFFE HALL, MAPLECLIFFE HALL**, and **OTTERCLIFFE HALL**. The career of the **LEECLIFFE HALL** proved to be short as she was lost on September 5, 1964 following a collision on the St. Lawrence River with the saltwater vessel **APOLLONIA**.

The **FRANKCLIFFE HALL (2)** also suffered a collision with a salt water vessel on the St. Lawrence River during the 1960s. This occurred on July 13, 1966 when the **FRANKCLIFFE HALL (2)** came into contact with the British flagged freighter **GLOXINIA** near Montreal, Quebec during a heavy rainstorm.

A grounding occurred the following year when the **FRANKCLIFFE HALL (2)** ran aground in Lake Superior on June 6, 1967. This stranding occurred in foggy conditions about two miles off of Thunder Cape, while the steamer was downbound with 600,000 bushels of wheat. The **FRANKCLIFFE HALL (2)** was released three days later, requiring the replacement of several hull plates.

The 1970s would see the **FRANKCLIFFE HALL (2)** continue to operate in the grain, and ore trades. This time period would also be a quiet one for this vessel, at least in the form of accidents. However, one incident is recorded as the **FRANKCLIFFE HALL (2)** ran aground near the Snell Lock in the St. Lawrence Seaway following a power failure on May 20, 1973. This incident was minor in nature, with the steamer being freed a short time later with no reported damages to the vessel.

The Hall Corporation did not have an extensive history of operating self-unloading vessels, but rather tankers, and gearless freighters. During the 1970s it operated only two vessels of this type, these being the **STONEFAX**, and **HALLFAX**. Both of these were small vessels with lengths of less then 450 feet. The **STONEFAX** was sold for scrap in 1971, while the **HALLFAX** operated into 1980 prior to being sold for off lakes use. It was therefore somewhat of a surprise when Hall announced in 1979 that it was going to have the **FRANKCLIFFE HALL (2)** converted into a self-unloader. This reconstruction was undertaken by the Port Arthur Shipbuilding Company at Thunder Bay, Ontario during the winter of 1979-80. The conversion also included deepening this ship by 6 feet, and additional stiffening was added to the hull to facilitate winter operations. In general appearance the topside unloading gear closely resembled that added to CSL's **FRONTENAC (5)**, which had been converted in 1973.

The **HALIFAX** is downbound at St. Clair, Michigan during the early 1990s. This vessel originally operated for Canada Steamship Lines with a fully black hull. This steamer is a member of a large class of ships built during the 1960s, of which many have been retired.

A stern view of the **HALIFAX** at Port Huron, Michigan illustrates this ship's unique stack. This stack was heightened in 1981 to solve updraft issues encountered following the conversion of this steamer into a self-unloader the previous year.

Upon resuming operations, the **FRANKCLIFFE HALL (2)** was able to operate in new trades with the flexibilities provided by the self-unloading conversion. Equipped with a 250 foot unloading boom it was now able to discharge its cargo without shore side assistance. Cargoes such as stone, coal, and potash became common cargoes, in addition to well established ore and grain payloads. During the winter lay-up of 1980-81 the stack of this steamer was heightened significantly to correct updraft issues.

On July 1, 1983 the **FRANKCLIFFE HALL (2)** made contact with the MacArthur Lock at Sault Ste. Marie, Michigan, requiring repairs to be made at the Port Weller Dry Docks. A little more then 3 years later on November 20, 1986, the **FRANKCLIFFE HALL (2)** was struck by the Yugoslavian freighter **SOLTA** while it was tied up at the St. Lambert Lock on the Seaway.

During the 1980s, the Hall Corporation experienced severe financial hardships forcing a restructuring during the mid-1980s. This was not successful, with the company's creditors eventually took control of their assets shortly afterwards. In 1987, the **FRANKCLIFFE HALL (2)** was chartered to the Canada Steamship Lines, being sold outright to this fleet the following year.

Following the sale, this ship was renamed **HALIFAX** and remained in service primarily on the upper lakes, with occasional voyages into the seaway. On April 7, 1988 the **HALIFAX** is recorded as making her first passage through the Welland Canal under her new name.

The **HALIFAX** suffered an explosion and fire in its unloading tunnel while upbound on the St. Marys River on April 6, 1993. Three crewmen had been working in the vicinity of the explosion at the time, killing one of them, while another received minor injuries. The **HALIFAX** was allowed to proceed to the Carbide Dock at Sault Ste. Marie, Michigan as quickly as possible, disregarding the speed restrictions for freight vessels on the St. Marys River. When arriving at the Carbide Dock, this steamer got caught in currents and overshot the dock, requiring the assistance of the tugs **MISSOURI**, and **AVENGER IV** to dock. Also assisting on scene were the United States Coast Guard cutters **KATMAI BAY**, and **MOBILE BAY**. The fire aboard the **HALIFAX** was extinguished by the ship's crew before it could spread to other parts of the vessel. Following a thorough investigation, it was determined that the explosion occurred as a result of mist of oil came into contact with an unprotected halogen light.

On April 9, 1993 the **HALIFAX** arrived at Thunder Bay, Ontario where she went into the Port Arthur Shipyard to receive repairs from the explosion and fire. The **HALIFAX** departed Thunder Bay on April 28th bound for Duluth following the completion of these repairs.

Christmas Day of 1999 would not be a joyous one for the **HALIFAX** as she ran aground in the St. Marys River, following a loss of power. The **HALIFAX** was able to free itself from the stranding, after which she proceeded to Sault Ste. Marie, Michigan. After arriving at that location, divers found an impression in this ship's hull measuring 10 feet wide, by 30 feet long.

On July 7, 2000 the tugs **OHIO**, and **IOWA** were called upon to tow the **HALIFAX** into Conneaut, Ohio following an engine failure in Lake Erie. The tugs brought the 730 foot steamer into harbor where she was secured for repairs.

In 2002, the **HALIFAX** was to suffer an onboard fire on at least two occasions. The first occurred during winter lay-up on February 27, 2002 while tied up at Thunder Bay. In this case a welder's torch set off a minor fire which was contained to a small storage room. This was followed in May by another fire which started in a exhaust header pipe while the **HALIFAX** was sailing on Lake Erie. Both of these fires resulted in minor damages, and no injuries.

On August 6, 2004 the **HALIFAX** ran aground in the St. Clair River near Fawn Island while carrying a stone cargo. The Great Lakes Towing tug **WYOMING** was called upon to assist in freeing this steamer from the soft bottom, which she successfully accomplished a short time later. Following being released the **HALIFAX** unloaded her cargo at a local stone dock, following which this ship went to Sarnia, Ontario for a damage survey.

The **HALIFAX** is powered by a John Inglis steam turbine rated at 10,000 horsepower which enables this ship to reach speed of up to 19.6 miles per hour making it one of the fastest on the Great Lakes. This steamer is capable of carrying a maximum cargo of 30,100 gross tons, although depth restrictions through some waterways force the carriage of smaller payloads. Cargo is loaded through 16 hatches, which are removed and re-installed by a traveling hatch crane installed on the vessel's deck. To unload cargo this ship is equipped with a 250 foot self-unloading boom which is mounted just forward of the aft cabins.

Although by no means the oldest Canadian flagged vessel on the Great Lakes, the **HALIFAX** is the second oldest in the Canada Steamship Lines fleet. In age, she is only exceeded by the **CEDARGLEN (2)** which originally dates back to 1959 when built for saltwater use, prior to being rebuilt for the Hall fleet for Great Lakes service in 1978. Regardless, the **HALIFAX** is the only steamer to be part of the Canada Steamship Lines fleet, and with the current trend in scrapping out older steamers sailing under the Canadian flag it will most likely be the last such type of ship to be operated by this fleet.

The **HALIFAX** operated throughout the 2008 shipping season, despite several years of rumors of an pending retirement. The onset of a severe recession at the end of the 2008 shipping season, which has thus far carried into the 2009 season places much doubt into the future operation of this ship.

*The **HALIFAX** is downbound on the St. Clair River on August 12, 2008 carrying a cargo of taconite loaded at Superior, Wisconsin bound for delivery to Hamilton, Ontario.*

The QUEBECOIS

During the 1960s several Canadian shipping companies modernized their fleets to take advantage of the St. Lawrence Seaway which had opened in 1959. Up to that time ships had been limited to 259 feet in length to transit the existing canals along the St. Lawrence River. The new locks built during the 1950s followed the dimensions set forth by the locks of the new Welland Canal which had opened in 1932. This allowed ships of 730 feet in length, and 75 feet in beam to pass through the newly opened waterway, creating a shipbuilding boom for Canada, much like had been seen in American Great Lakes fleet during the 1950s.

During the early to mid-1960s Canadian Vickers of Montreal, Quebec built a class of six vessels for service on the Great Lakes, and St. Lawrence Seaway. These ships would all be of the 730 foot class, and were all built in two sections to be joined together following individual launchings. The **QUEBECOIS** was the fourth vessel to be built in this class, with its stern section being launched on September 8, 1962 followed by the bow section which entered water for the first time on November 10, 1962. Both of these sections were later joined and the **QUEBECOIS** was christened on April 9, 1963.

The **QUEBECOIS** was built for Canada General Electric Corporation and chartered to the Papachristidis fleet. This fleet had just begun to operate a Great Lakes fleet of straight deck bulkers following having successful operations on salt-water. This ship, was a sister ship of the **MONTREALAIS**, and both have followed similar paths throughout their careers. In addition to these two ships, this class also included the **JOHN A. FRANCE (2), J. N. McWATTERS (2), DON-DE-DIEU**, and **MAPLECLIFFE HALL**.

The **QUEBECOIS** entered service in mid April of 1963, with its first cargo being iron ore from Sept Iles, Quebec for Cleveland, Ohio. As with other ships of this type, the **QUEBECOIS** would be engaged in the carrying of grain products from the upper lakes down the St. Lawrence with a return cargo of ore.

During the 1965, and 66 seasons the **QUEBECOIS**, and **MONTREALAIS** were joined by the **DON-DE-DIEU** which had been bareboat chartered to Papachristidis by its owner, the Distillers Corporation. This ship was purchased by the Labrador Steamship Company in 1967, and renamed **V. W. SCULLY**. Also occurring in 1965, the **QUEBECOIS** was purchased outright by Papachristidis.

During the winter lay-up of 1971-72 Papachristidis sold its fleet of five lakers to Upper Lakes Shipping, Limited. Besides this ship, the **MONTREALAIS, FEUX-FOLLETS, GRANDE HERMINE**, and **PETITE HERMINE** were also included in the $25 million dollar sale. While both the **QUEBECOIS**, and **MONTREALAIS** retained their original names, the other three ships were renamed following the sale. The **FEUX–FOLLETS, GRANDE HERMINE**, and **PETITE HERMINE** became the **CANADIAN LEADER, CANADIAN MARINER**, and **CANADIAN HUNTER** respectively. This sale enabled Upper Lakes to take possession of five relatively new and modern carriers for a fraction of what it would have cost to build a similar number of new vessels. Additionally, the carrying tonnage of the fleet grew significantly following this purchase as these ships had a collective single trip carrying capacity of 134,700 gross tons.

The **QUEBECOIS** would start the 1972 season in Upper Lakes colors, but for the most part her trade patterns remained the same as those prior to the transaction. On July 26, 1979 the **QUEBECOIS** lost power while upbound at the entrance to Lake St. Clair, and ran aground. This grounding caused no appreciable damage as it occurred in an area of soft mud. The **QUEBECOIS** was released about eight hours following the stranding, which was later blamed on an electronic malfunction.

*The **QUEBECOIS** is downbound at Marine City, Michigan on a sunny Summer afternoon during the early 1990s. This ship is a member of one of the more attractive classes of ships to have been built during the second half of the twentieth century.*

*The **QUEBECOIS** is upbound on the St. Clair River on October 29, 2005 bound for the upper lakes, and a load of grain. This ship has been active in the transport of grain down the seaway, usually with a return load of ore, since its construction in 1963.*

On October 5, 1990 the **QUEBECOIS** made its first delivery of cement into St. Lawrence Cement's dock at Duluth. After discharging the cargo, this steamer shifted over to the Harvest States Elevator to load grain. When engaged in the movement of cement into this facility, it is common for the **QUEBECOIS** to load grain at the Twin Ports for delivery on the lower St. Lawrence, and then from there a load of ore is usually carried into Hamilton, prior to loading cement at nearby Clarkson for a return trip to Duluth. While on this trade route, the **QUEBECOIS** only has to travel the short distance between Hamilton, and Clarkson without cargo making for a very efficient set of cargo movements.

As with many other straight deck bulk carriers serving under the Canadian flag, the **QUEBECOIS** is often idled for several weeks during summer. These lay-up periods usually come to an end by September, with the onset of the fall grain rush which creates enough demand to justify the reactivation of this ship.

The **QUEBECOIS** is powered by her original Canadian General Electric steam turbine, which generates 9,900 shaft horsepower. As with the **MONTREALAIS**, this power plant gives this ship a operating speed of 19 miles per hour. The **QUEBECOIS** is capable of carrying up to 27,800 gross tons, although this is effected by depth restrictions in place on many of the connecting channels to be transited during the voyage.

In 1990, Upper Lakes and Algoma Central Marine created a partnership named Seaway Bulk Carriers. This was a pooling arrangement in which the operation of both of these fleet's gearless vessels were managed as a group to maximize cargo movement. This was followed in 1994, by a similar arrangement for both fleet's self-unloaders. This firm was appropriately named Seaway Self-Unloaders. These arrangements were consolidated further in 2000 when Seaway Marine Transport was created to manage both the straight deckers, and self-unloaders of both fleets.

Of the six ships built in this class only half remain, with all three in Upper Lakes colors, the other three being scrapped during the early part of this century. Besides the **QUEBECOIS**, and **MONTREALAIS**, is the motor vessel **CANADIAN MINER**. The future of these ships is questionable, with the **CANADIAN MINER** entering an indefinite lay-up at the end of the 2008 shipping season. However, as of the 2009 shipping season, the **QUEBECOIS** is in operation.

*The **QUEBECOIS** has a respectable depth of 39 feet, which is apparent in this view of the steamer in ballast.*

The CANADIAN LEADER

This ship was built in 1967 by the Collingwood Shipyards at Collingwood, Ontario as the **FEUX-FOLLETS**. It had been constructed for the Papachristidis fleet, and was the largest vessel to ever have been built for that fleet. Following its launching on June 16, 1967 this ship was fitted out and departed Collingwood on October 12, 1967 on her maiden trip bound for Port Arthur to load grain. The **FEUX-FOLLETS** had been built to the maximum sized allowed for Seaway operation, with a length of 730 feet, beam of 75 feet, and a depth of 39 feet 8 inches. This ship was also the flagship of the small, but modern, Papachristidis fleet.

This ship would operate for Papachristidis until being sold on March 16, 1972 to the Upper Lakes fleet following its former owners abandoning freshwater operations. Shortly following the sale this ship was renamed **CANADIAN LEADER**. Since its commissioning this ship had concentrated in the movement of grain from the upper lakes to the St. Lawrence, with a return cargo of ore back into a Great Lakes port being common. After entering service for Upper Lakes this trade pattern continued to be the main focus of this ship's operations.

The **CANADIAN LEADER** was the last steamer to be built for Great Lakes service, and is one of the few left in the Canadian fleet. In recent years a number of similar vessels have been removed from service and sold for scrap. This is due in large part to a shift in the movement of grain from Lake Superior to the west coast of Canada, thereby creating excess capacity.

Since entering service this ship has been involved in a number of incidents. Shortly after becoming part of the Upper Lakes fleet this ship suffered bow damage at Thunder Bay, Ontario on August 5, 1972 when it struck a dock at Saskatchewan Pool #4.

The **CANADIAN LEADER** was damaged on April 5, 1989 after it was pushed by heavy ice into the Peavey Elevator at Superior, Wisconsin. This steamer received starboard bow damages in this accident, requiring repairs at the Fraser Shipyards.

*The forward cabins of the **CANADIAN LEADER** are among the most attractive built into a lake carrier. They are a blend of modern, and traditional styling consistent with a cabins fore and aft design. This profile was originally incorporated during the late 1800s into Great Lakes freighters enabling the navigating crew to have the best possible vantage point while navigating through the challenging waterways and weather conditions on the Great Lakes.*

*The prop wash, and a barely noticeable cloud of exhaust coming from its stack indicate the **CANADIAN LEADER** is bringing herself to full speed as it enters lower Lake Huron on June 23, 2007. At full power this ship can reach a speed of 19 miles per hour.*

*This steamer was originally part of the Papachristidis fleet as the **FEUX-FOLLETS**, and was the largest ship to be operated by that fleet. In this view of the **CANADIAN LEADER** shows her 75 foot beam as she approaches the Blue Water Bridge at the northernmost point of the St. Clair River.*

While carrying a grain cargo loaded at Thunder Bay the **CANADIAN LEADER** ran aground on August 21, 1998 in the St. Marys River near Drummond Island. This steamer remained firmly aground until August 23rd when it was finally pulled free by the tugs **WILFRED M. COHEN, AVENGER IV, NANCY K.,** and **ANGLIAN LADY.** After receiving temporary repairs the **CANADIAN LEADER** went to Montreal to unload its cargo, after being re-routed from its original destination of Baie Comeau, Quebec. The **CANADIAN LEADER** received permanent repairs at the Port Weller Dry Docks, where she arrived on August 28, 1998.

A little over a year later, on December 2, 1999, the **CANADIAN LEADER** ran aground again. This stranding occurred at Duluth, Minnesota, and although minor compared to the grounding the previous year, tug assistance was required in order to free the steamer. No damages were reported as having been suffered by the **CANADIAN LEADER** in this incident.

On September 26, 2005, this ship went aground in the St. Lawrence River while upbound with a cargo of iron ore for Hamilton, Ontario. An engine failure on the **CANADIAN LEADER** was cited as being the cause of this incident. This ship was released two days later, after which she continued her trip to Hamilton to unload the ore which had been loaded at Pointe Noire, Quebec. Following unloading, the **CANADIAN LEADER** went to the Port Weller Dry Docks yard for repairs.

During her time sailing for Upper Lakes the **CANADIAN LEADER** has carried a few noteworthy cargoes. On November 18, 1982 this steamer set a cargo record at Huron, Ohio when she loaded one million bushels of grain. On September 25, 1988, the **CANADIAN LEADER** departed Duluth with two 120 ton crusher shafts, which had been welded to the vessel's deck following being loaded at the Port Terminal. These two shafts had originated at the Reserve Mining Company in Babbit, Minnesota, and were destined for Quebec.

In 1990, the operation of the **CANADIAN LEADER** was assumed by Seaway Bulk Carriers, which was a pooling agreement between Upper Lakes, and the Algoma Central Marine fleet to manage the gearless vessels of both fleets as a whole. This was followed in 1993 with a similar entity being formed, Seaway Self-Unloaders, to manage the self-unloaders of these two fleets. The close business ties between these two organizations was continued in 2000 with the formation of Seaway Marine Transport, which was a further progression of the previous arrangements with the operations of both fleet's straight deckers, and self-unloaders being assumed by one organization.

The **CANADIAN LEADER** is powered by a Canadian General Electric steam turbine capable of generating 9,900 shaft horsepower. This allows this steamer to reach a operating speed of 19 miles per hour. The **CANADIAN LEADER** can carry a maximum payload of 28,300 gross tons of cargo. This ship's cargo hold is equipped with 17 hatches. To improve its maneuverability, and minimize reliance on tug assistance this ship is equipped with a bow thruster.

At the beginning of the 2009 shipping season, the **CANADIAN LEADER** is active in the movement of grain from the upper lakes to the St. Lawrence. During the 2007 and 2008 seasons this ship was utilized to move a number of cargoes of iron ore out of Marquette, Michigan. This was due to a strong demand for iron ore during these seasons, which dropped significantly as the 2008 season came to a close. As the 2009 season began, the continuing global economic recession has impacted the demand for cargo movement on the Great Lakes, and it will undoubtedly effect this ship's use in the movement of ore.

QUICK REFERENCE GUIDE

ST. MARYS CHALLENGER-Built:1906-Great Lakes Engineering Works, Ecorse, Michigan. Dimensions: 552'1" x 56' x 31'. Launched as WILLIAM P. SNYDER, renamed ELTON HOYT II (1) in 1926. Renamed ALEX D. CHISHOLM in 1952. Converted into a self-unloading cement carrier and renamed MEDUSA CHALLENGER in 1967. Renamed SOUTHDOWN CHALLENGER in 1999. Given current name in 2005. Operator: Central Marine Logistics. Official Number: 202859

ALPENA (2)-Built: 1942-Great Lakes Engineering Works, River Rouge, Michigan. Dimensions: 519'6" x 67' x 35'. Launched as LEON FRASER. Converted into a self-unloading cement carrier, shortened by 120 feet and renamed ALPENA (2) in 1991. Operator: Inland Lakes Management. Official Number: 241856

WILFRED SYKES-Built: 1949-American Ship Building Company, Lorain, Ohio. Dimensions: 678' x 70' x 37'. Converted into a self-unloader in 1975. Operator: Central Marine Logistics. Official Number: 259193

PHILIP R. CLARKE-Built: 1952-American Ship Building Company, Lorain, Ohio. Dimensions: 767' x 70' x 36'. Lengthened by 120 feet in 1974. Converted into a self-unloader in 1982. Operator: Great Lakes Fleet, Inc.. Official Number: 263699

KAYE E. BARKER-Built: 1952-American Ship Building Company, Toledo, Ohio. Dimensions: 767' x 70' x 36'. Launched as EDWARD B. GREENE. Lengthened by 120 feet in 1976. Converted into a self-unloader in 1981. Renamed BENSON FORD (3) in 1985. Renamed KAYE E. BARKER in 1989. Operator: Lakes Shipping. Official Number: 263980

ARTHUR M. ANDERSON-Built: 1952-American Ship Building Company, Lorain, Ohio. Dimensions: 767' x 70' x 36'. Lengthened by 120 feet in 1975. Converted into a self-unloader in 1982. Operator: Great Lakes Fleet, Inc.. Official Number: 264207

CASON J. CALLAWAY-Built: 1952-Great Lakes Engineering Works, River Rouge, Michigan. Dimensions: 767' x 70' x 36'. Lengthened by 120 feet in 1974. Converted into a self-unloader in 1982. Operator: Great Lakes Fleet, Inc.. Official Number: 264349

MICHIPICOTEN(3)-Built: 1952-Bethlehem Shipbuilding & Drydock, Sparrows Point, Maryland. Dimensions: 698'6" x 70' x 37'. Launched as ELTON HOYT 2nd (2). Lengthened 72 feet in 1957. Converted into a self-unloader in 1980. Renamed MICHIPICOTEN (3) and reflagged Canadian in 2003. Operator: Lower Lakes Towing. US Official Number: 264126   Can. Official Number: 825098

JOHN G. MUNSON (2)-Built: 1952-Manitowoc Shipbuilding, Manitowoc, Wisconsin. Dimensions: 768' 3" x 72' x 36'. Lengthened 102' in 1976. Operator: Great Lakes Fleet, Inc. Official Number: 264136

JAMES NORRIS-Built: 1952-Midland Shipyards, Midland, Ontario. Dimensions: 663' 6" x 67' x 35'. Converted into a self-unloader in 1981. Operator: Seaway Marine Transport. Official Number: 178247

AMERICAN FORTITUDE-Built: 1953-American Ship Building Company, Lorain, Ohio. Dimensions: 690' x 70' x 37'. Launched as ERNEST T. WEIR (2). Renamed COURTNEY BURTON in 1978. Converted into a self-unloader in 1981. Renamed AMERICAN FORTITUDE in 2006. Operator: American Steamship Company. Official Number: 265246

AMERICAN VALOR-Built: 1953-American Ship Building Company, Lorain, Ohio. Dimensions: 767' x 70' x 36'. Launched as ARMCO, renamed AMERICAN VALOR in 2006. Lengthened 120' in 1974. Converted into a self-unloader in 1982. Operator: American Steamship Company. Official Number: 265621

HERBERT C. JACKSON-Built: 1959-Great Lakes Engineering Works, River Rouge, Michigan. Dimensions: 690' x 75' x 37'6". Converted into a self-unloader in 1975. Operator: Interlake Steamship Company. Official Number: 278780

EDWARD L. RYERSON-Built: 1960-Manitowoc Shipbuilding, Incorporated, Manitowoc, Wisconsin. Dimensions: 730' x 75' x 39'. Operator: Central Marine Logistics. Official Number: 282106

AMERICAN VICTORY-Built: 1943-Bethlehem Shipbuilding & Drydock Company, Sparrows Point, Maryland. Dimensions: 730' x 75' x 39'3". Launched as tanker MARQUETTE. Renamed NESHANIC in 1943. Renamed GULFOIL in 1947. Converted into a Great Lakes bulk carrier, and renamed PIONEER CHALLENGER in 1961. Renamed MIDDLETOWN in 1962. Converted into a self-unloader in 1982. Renamed AMERICAN VICTORY in 2006. Operator: American Steamship Company. Official Number: 251093

MONTREALAIS-Built: 1962-(stern) Canadian Vickers, Montreal, Quebec & (bow) George T. Davie & Sons, Lauzon, Quebec. Dimensions: 730' x 75' x 39'. Built as MONTREALER, renamed MONTREALAIS in 1962. Operator: Seaway Marine Transport. Official Number: 314394

CANADIAN PROVIDER-Built 1963-Collingwoods Shipyards, Collingwood, Ontario. Dimensions: 730' x 75' 3" x 39'2". Launched as MURRAY BAY (3). Renamed CANADIAN PROVIDER in 1994. Operator: Seaway Marine Transport. Official Number: 318684

HALIFAX-Built: 1963-Davie Shipbuilding, Lauzon, Quebec. Dimensions: 730' x 75' x 39' 3". Launched as FRANKCLIFFE HALL (2), renamed HALIFAX in 1988. Converted into a self-unloader and deepened by 6' in 1980. Operator: Canada Steamship Lines. Official Number: 313963

QUEBECOIS-Built: 1963-Canadian Vickers, Montreal, Quebec. Dimensions: 730' x 75' x 39'. Operator: Seaway Marine Transport. Official Number: 319265

CANADIAN LEADER-Built: 1967-Collingwood Shipyards, Collingwood, Ontario. Dimensions: 730' x 75' x 39'8". Launched as FEUX-FOLLETS, renamed CANADIAN LEADER in 1972. Operator: Seaway Marine Transport. Official Number: 325746

VESSEL INDEX

VESSEL INDEX

VESSEL INDEX

*This photo illustrates the size differential between the 552 foot **ST. MARYS CHALLENGER**, and the 1004 foot **MESABI MINER**, while both are tied up at Bay Shipbuilding, Sturgeon Bay, Wisconsin.*

Answers:

A complex number is in the form of $a + bi$, where a is the real part and bi is the imaginary part.

(A) $20 = 20 + 0i$ **The real part is 20, and there is no imaginary part.**

(B) $10 - i = 10 - 1i$ **The real part is 10, and $-1i$ is the imaginary part.**

(C) $15i = 0 + 15i$ **The real part is 0, and the imaginary part is 15i.**

POSITIVE AND NEGATIVE NUMBERS

POSITIVE NUMBERS are greater than 0, and **NEGATIVE NUMBERS** are less than 0. Both positive and negative numbers can be shown on a **NUMBER LINE**.

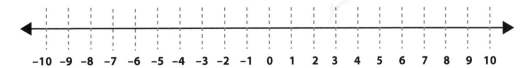

Figure 6.2. Number Line

The **ABSOLUTE VALUE** of a number is the distance the number is from 0. Since distance is always positive, the absolute value of a number is always positive. The absolute value of a is denoted $|a|$. For example, $|-2| = 2$ since -2 is two units away from 0.

Positive and negative numbers can be added, subtracted, multiplied, and divided. The sign of the resulting number is governed by a specific set of rules shown in the table below.

Table 6.1. Operations with Positive and Negative Numbers

ADDING REAL NUMBERS		SUBTRACTING REAL NUMBERS*	
Positive + Positive = Positive	$7 + 8 = 15$	Negative – Positive = Negative	$-7 - 8 =$ $-7 + (-8) =$ -15
Negative + Negative = Negative	$-7 + (-8) =$ -15	Positive – Negative = Positive	$7 - (-8) =$ $7 + 8 = 15$

ADDING REAL NUMBERS		SUBTRACTING REAL NUMBERS*	
Negative + Positive OR Positive + Negative = Keep the sign of the number with larger absolute value	$-7 + 8 = 1$ $7 + -8 = -1$	Negative – Negative = Keep the sign of the number with larger absolute value	$-7 - (-8) =$ $-7 + 8 = 1$ $-8 - (-7) = -8$ $+ 7 = -1$

MULTIPLYING REAL NUMBERS		DIVIDING REAL NUMBERS	
Positive × Positive = Positive	$8 \times 4 = 32$	Positive ÷ Positive = Positive	$8 \div 4 = 2$
Negative × Negative = Positive	$-8 \times (-4) = 32$	Negative ÷ Negative = Positive	$-8 \div (-4) = 2$
Positive × Negative OR Negative × Positive = Negative	$8 \times (-4) = -32$ $-8 \times 4 = -32$	Positive ÷ Negative OR Negative ÷ Positive = Negative	$8 \div (-4) = -2$ $-8 \div 4 = -2$

*Always change the subtraction to addition and change the sign of the second number; then use addition rules.

Examples

1. Add or subtract the following real numbers:

(A) $-18 + 12$

(B) $-3.64 + (-2.18)$

(C) $9.37 - 4.25$

(D) $86 - (-20)$

Answers:

(A) Since $|-18| > |12|$, the answer is negative: $|-18| - |12| = 6$. So the answer is **−6**.

(B) Adding two negative numbers results in a negative number. Add the values: **−5.82**.

(C) The first number is larger than the second, so the final answer is positive: **5.12**.

(D) Change the subtraction to addition, change the sign of the second number, and then add: $86 - (-20) = 86 + (+20) = $ **106**.

2. Multiply or divide the following real numbers:

(A) $\left(\frac{10}{3}\right)\left(-\frac{9}{5}\right)$

(B) $\frac{-64}{-10}$

(C) $(2.2)(3.3)$

(D) $-52 \div 13$

Answers:

(A) Multiply the numerators, multiply the denominators, and simplify: $\frac{-90}{15} = $ **−6**.

(B) A negative divided by a negative is a positive number: **6.4**.

(C) Multiplying positive numbers gives a positive answer: **7.26**.

(D) Dividing a negative by a positive number gives a negative answer: **−4**.

ORDER OF OPERATIONS

The ORDER OF OPERATIONS is simply the order in which operations are performed. **PEMDAS** is a common way to remember the order of operations:

1.	Parentheses	4.	Division
2.	Exponents	5.	Addition
3.	Multiplication	6.	Subtraction

Multiplication and division, and addition and subtraction, are performed together from left to right. So, performing multiple operations on a set of numbers is a four-step process:

1. P: Calculate expressions inside parentheses, brackets, braces, etc.

2. **E**: Calculate exponents and square roots.

3. **MD**: Calculate any remaining multiplication and division in order from left to right.

4. **AS**: Calculate any remaining addition and subtraction in order from left to right.

Always work from left to right within each step when simplifying expressions.

Examples

1. Simplify: $2(21 - 14) + 6 \div (-2) \times 3 - 10$

Answer:

$2(21 - 14) + 6 \div (-2) \times 3 - 10$	
$= 2(7) + 6 \div (-2) \times 3 - 10$	Calculate expressions inside parentheses.
$= 14 + 6 \div (-2) \times 3 - 10$ $= 14 + (-3) \times 3 - 10$ $= 14 + (-9) - 10$	There are no exponents or radicals, so perform multiplication and division from left to right.
$= 5 - 10$ $= \mathbf{-5}$	Perform addition and subtraction from left to right.

2. Simplify: $-(3)^2 + 4(5) + (5 - 6)^2 - 8$

Answer:

$-(3)^2 + 4(5) + (5 - 6)^2 - 8$	
$= -(3)^2 + 4(5) + (-1)^2 - 8$	Calculate expressions inside parentheses.
$= -9 + 4(5) + 1 - 8$	Simplify exponents and radicals.
$= -9 + 20 + 1 - 8$	Perform multiplication and division from left to right.
$= 11 + 1 - 8$ $= 12 - 8$ $= \mathbf{4}$	Perform addition and subtraction from left to right.

3. Simplify: $\dfrac{(7 - 9)^3 + 8(10 - 12)}{4^2 - 5^2}$

Answer:

$\dfrac{(7 - 9)^3 + 8(10 - 12)}{4^2 - 5^2}$	
$= \dfrac{(-2)^3 + 8(-2)}{4^2 - 5^2}$	Calculate expressions inside parentheses.
$= \dfrac{-8 + (-16)}{16 - 25}$	Simplify exponents and radicals.
$= \dfrac{-24}{-9}$	Perform addition and subtraction from left to right.
$= \mathbf{\dfrac{8}{3}}$	Simplify.

UNITS OF MEASUREMENT

The standard units for the metric and American systems are shown below, along with the prefixes used to express metric units.

Table 6.2. Units and Conversion Factors

DIMENSION	AMERICAN	SI
length	inch/foot/yard/mile	meter
mass	ounce/pound/ton	gram
volume	cup/pint/quart/gallon	liter
force	pound-force	newton
pressure	pound-force per square inch	pascal
work and energy	cal/British thermal unit	joule
temperature	Fahrenheit	kelvin
charge	faraday	coulomb

Table 6.3. Metric Prefixes

PREFIX	SYMBOL	MULTIPLICATION FACTOR
tera	T	1,000,000,000,000
giga	G	1,000,000,000
mega	M	1,000,000
kilo	k	1,000
hecto	h	100
deca	da	10
base unit	--	--
deci	d	0.1
centi	c	0.01
milli	m	0.001
micro	μ	0.0000001
nano	n	0.0000000001
pico	p	0.0000000000001

A mnemonic device to help remember the metric system is *King Henry Drinks Under Dark Chocolate Moon* (KHDUDCM).

Units can be converted within a single system or between systems. When converting from one unit to another unit, a conversion factor (a numeric multiplier used to convert a value with a unit to another unit) is used. The process of converting between units using a conversion factor is sometimes known as dimensional analysis.

Table 6.4. Conversion Factors

1 in. = 2.54 cm	1 lb. = 0.454 kg
1 yd. = 0.914 m	1 cal = 4.19 J
1 mi. = 1.61 km	$1°F = \frac{5}{9}(°F - 32°C)$
1 gal. = 3.785 L	$1 cm^3 = 1 mL$
1 oz. = 28.35 g	1 hr = 3600 s

Examples

1. Convert the following measurements in the metric system.

   (A) 4.25 kilometers to meters

   (B) 8 m² to mm²

   Answers:

   (A) $4.25 \text{ km} \left(\frac{1000 \text{ m}}{1 \text{ km}}\right) = \textbf{4250 m}$

   (B) $\frac{8 \text{ m}^2}{1} \times \frac{1000 \text{ mm}}{1 \text{ m}} \times \frac{1000 \text{ mm}}{1 \text{ m}} = \textbf{8,000,000 mm}^2$

   Since the units are square units (m²), multiply by the conversion factor twice, so that both meters cancel.

2. Convert the following measurements in the American system.

   (A) 12 feet to inches

   (B) 7 yd² to ft²

   Answers:

   (A) $12 \text{ ft} \left(\frac{12 \text{ in}}{1 \text{ ft}}\right) = \textbf{144 in}$

   (B) $7 \text{ yd}^2 \left(\frac{3 \text{ft}}{1 \text{yd}}\right)\left(\frac{3 \text{ft}}{1 \text{yd}}\right) = \textbf{63 ft}^2$

   Since the units are square units (yd²), multiply by the conversion factor twice.

3. Convert the following measurements in the metric system to the American system.

   (A) 23 meters to feet

   (B) 10 m² to yd²

   Answers:

   (A) $23 \text{ m} \left(\frac{3.28 \text{ ft}}{1 \text{ m}}\right) = \textbf{75.44 ft}$

   (B) $\frac{10 \text{ m}^2}{1} \times \frac{1.094 \text{ yd}}{1 \text{ m}} \times \frac{1.094 \text{ yd}}{1 \text{ m}} = \textbf{11.97 yd}^2$

4. Convert the following measurements in the American system to the metric system.

   (A) 8 in³ to milliliters

   (B) 16 kilograms to pounds

Answers:

(A) $8 \text{ in}^3 \left(\frac{16.39 \text{ ml}}{1 \text{ in}^3}\right) = \mathbf{131.12 \text{ mL}}$

(B) $16 \text{ kg}\left(\frac{2.2 \text{ lb}}{1 \text{ kg}}\right) = \mathbf{35.2 \text{ lb}}$

DECIMALS AND FRACTIONS

Decimals

A **DECIMAL** is a number that contains a decimal point. A decimal number is an alternative way of writing a fraction. The place value for a decimal includes **TENTHS** (one place after the decimal), **HUNDREDTHS** (two places after the decimal), **THOUSANDTHS** (three places after the decimal), etc.

Table 6.5. Place Values

1,000,000	10^6	millions
100,000	10^5	hundred thousands
10,000	10^4	ten thousands
1,000	10^3	thousands
100	10^2	hundreds
10	10^1	tens
1	10^0	ones
.		decimal
$\frac{1}{10}$	10^{-1}	tenths
$\frac{1}{100}$	10^{-2}	hundredths
$\frac{1}{1000}$	10^{-3}	thousandths

Decimals can be added, subtracted, multiplied, and divided:

- To add or subtract decimals, line up the decimal point and perform the operation, keeping the decimal point in the same place in the answer.
- To multiply decimals, first multiply the numbers without the decimal points. Then, sum the number of decimal places to the right of the decimal point in the original numbers and place the decimal point in the answer so that there are that many places to the right of the decimal.
- When dividing decimals move the decimal point to the right in order to make the divisor a whole number and move the decimal the same number of places in the dividend. Divide the numbers without regard to the decimal. Then, place the decimal point of the quotient directly above the decimal point of the dividend.

4.2 ← quotient
2.5)10.5 ← dividend
↑
divisor

Figure 6.3. Division Terms

Examples

1. Simplify: 24.38 + 16.51 − 29.87

Answer:

24.38 + 16.51 − 29.87	
24.38 + 16.51 = 40.89	Align the decimals and apply the order of operations left to right.
40.89 − 29.87 = **11.02**	

2. Simplify: (10.4)(18.2)

Answer:

(10.4)(18.2)	
104 × 182 = 18,928	Multiply the numbers ignoring the decimals.
18,928 → 189.28	The original problem includes two decimal places (one in each number), so move the decimal point in the answer so that there are two places after the decimal point.

Estimating is a good way to check the answer: $10.4 \approx 10$, $18.2 \approx 18$, and $10 \times 18 = 180$.

3. Simplify: 80 ÷ 2.5

Answer:

80 ÷ 2.5	
80 → 800 2.5 → 25	Move both decimals one place to the right (multiply by 10) so that the divisor is a whole number.
800 ÷ 25 = 32	Divide normally.

Fractions

A **FRACTION** is a number that can be written in the form $\frac{a}{b}$, where b is not equal to 0. The a part of the fraction is the **NUMERATOR** (top number) and the b part of the fraction is the **DENOMINATOR** (bottom number).

If the denominator of a fraction is greater than the numerator, the value of the fraction is less than 1 and it is called a **PROPER FRACTION** (for example, $\frac{3}{5}$ is a proper fraction). In an **IMPROPER FRACTION**, the denominator is less than the numerator and the value of the fraction is greater than 1 ($\frac{8}{3}$ is an improper fraction). An improper fraction can be written as a **MIXED NUMBER**, which has a whole number part and a proper fraction part. Improper fractions can be converted to mixed numbers by dividing the numerator by the denominator, which gives the whole number part, and the remainder becomes the numerator of the proper fraction part. (For example, the improper fraction $\frac{25}{9}$ is equal to mixed number $2\frac{7}{9}$ because 9 divides into 25 two times, with a remainder of 7.)

Conversely, mixed numbers can be converted to improper fractions. To do so, determine the numerator of the improper fraction by multiplying the denominator by the whole number, and then adding the numerator. The final number is written as the (now larger) numerator over the original denominator.

To convert mixed numbers to improper fractions:
$$a\frac{m}{n} = \frac{n \times a + m}{n}$$

Fractions with the same denominator can be added or subtracted by simply adding or subtracting the numerators; the denominator will remain unchanged. To add or subtract fractions with different denominators, find the **LEAST COMMON DENOMINATOR (LCD)** of all the fractions. The LCD is the smallest number exactly divisible by each denominator. (For example, the least common denominator of the numbers 2, 3, and 8 is 24.) Once the LCD has been found, each fraction should be written in an equivalent form with the LCD as the denominator.

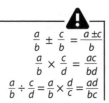

$$\frac{a}{b} \pm \frac{c}{b} = \frac{a \pm c}{b}$$
$$\frac{a}{b} \times \frac{c}{d} = \frac{ac}{bd}$$
$$\frac{a}{b} \div \frac{c}{d} = \frac{a}{b} \times \frac{d}{c} = \frac{ad}{bc}$$

To multiply fractions, the numerators are multiplied together and denominators are multiplied together. If there are any mixed numbers, they should first be changed to improper fractions. Then, the numerators are multiplied together and the denominators are multiplied together. The fraction can then be reduced if necessary. To divide fractions, multiply the first fraction by the reciprocal of the second.

Any common denominator can be used to add or subtract fractions. The quickest way to find a common denominator of a set of values is simply to multiply all the values together. The result might not be the least common denominator, but it will allow the problem to be worked.

Examples

1. Simplify: $2\frac{3}{5} + 3\frac{1}{4} - 1\frac{1}{2}$

Answer:

$2\frac{3}{5} + 3\frac{1}{4} - 1\frac{1}{2}$	
$= 2\frac{12}{20} + 3\frac{5}{20} - 1\frac{10}{20}$	Change each fraction so it has a denominator of 20, which is the LCD of 5, 4, and 2.
$2 + 3 - 1 = 4$ $\frac{12}{20} + \frac{5}{20} - \frac{10}{20} = \frac{7}{20}$	Add and subtract the whole numbers together and the fractions together.
$4\frac{7}{20}$	Combine to get the final answer (a mixed number).

2. Simplify: $\frac{7}{8} \times 3\frac{1}{3}$

Answer:

$\frac{7}{8} \times 3\frac{1}{3}$

$3\frac{1}{3} = \frac{10}{3}$	Change the mixed number to an improper fraction.
$\frac{7}{8}\left(\frac{10}{3}\right) = \frac{7 \times 10}{8 \times 3}$ $= \frac{70}{24}$	Multiply the numerators together and the denominators together.
$= \frac{35}{12}$ $= 2\frac{11}{12}$	Reduce the fraction.

3. Simplify: $4\frac{1}{2} \div \frac{2}{3}$

Answer:

$4\frac{1}{2} \div \frac{2}{3}$	
$4\frac{1}{2} = \frac{9}{2}$	Change the mixed number to an improper fraction.
$\frac{9}{2} \div \frac{2}{3}$ $= \frac{9}{2} \times \frac{3}{2}$ $= \frac{27}{4}$	Multiply the first fraction by the reciprocal of the second fraction.
$= 6\frac{3}{4}$	Simplify.

Converting Between Fractions and Decimals

A fraction is converted to a decimal by using long division until there is no remainder and no pattern of repeating numbers occurs.

A decimal is converted to a fraction using the following steps:

- Place the decimal value as the numerator in a fraction with a denominator of 1.
- Multiply the fraction by $\frac{10}{10}$ for every digit in the decimal value, so that there is no longer a decimal in the numerator.
- Reduce the fraction.

Examples

1. Write the fraction $\frac{7}{8}$ as a decimal.

Answer:

$$\begin{array}{r} 0.875 \\ 8{\overline{\smash{\big)}\,7000}} \\ \underline{-64} \\ 60 \\ \underline{-56} \\ 40 \end{array}$$	Divide the denominator into the numerator using long division.

2. Write the fraction $\frac{5}{11}$ as a decimal.

Answer:

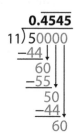

Dividing using long division yields a repeating decimal.

3. Write the decimal 0.125 as a fraction.

Answer:

0.125

$= \dfrac{0.125}{1}$

Create a fraction with 0.125 as the numerator and 1 as the denominator.

$\dfrac{0.125}{1} \times \dfrac{10}{10} \times \dfrac{10}{10} \times \dfrac{10}{10} = \dfrac{125}{1000}$

Multiply by $\dfrac{10}{10}$ three times (one for each numeral after the decimal).

$= \dfrac{1}{8}$

Simplify.

Alternatively, recognize that 0.125 is read "one hundred twenty-five thousandths" and can therefore be written in fraction form as $\dfrac{125}{1000}$.

RATIOS

A **RATIO** is a comparison of two numbers and can be represented as $\dfrac{a}{b}$, $a{:}b$, or a to b. The two numbers represent a constant relationship, not a specific value: for every a number of items in the first group, there will be b number of items in the second. For example, if the ratio of blue to red candies in a bag is 3:5, the bag will contain 3 blue candies for every 5 red candies. So, the bag might contain 3 blue candies and 5 red candies, or it might contain 30 blue candies and 50 red candies, or 36 blue candies and 60 red candies. All of these values are representative of the ratio 3:5 (which is the ratio in its lowest, or simplest, terms).

To find the "whole" when working with ratios, simply add the values in the ratio. For example, if the ratio of boys to girls in a class is 2:3, the "whole" is five: 2 out of every 5 students are boys, and 3 out of every 5 students are girls.

Examples

1. There are 10 boys and 12 girls in a first-grade class. What is the ratio of boys to the total number of students? What is the ratio of girls to boys?

Answer:

number of boys: 10
number of girls: 12
number of students: 22

Identify the variables.

number of boys : number of students $= 10 : 22$ $= \dfrac{10}{22}$ $= \dfrac{5}{11}$	Write out and simplify the ratio of boys to total students.
number of girls : number of boys $= 12 : 10$ $= \dfrac{12}{10}$ $= \dfrac{6}{5}$	Write out and simplify the ratio of girls to boys.

2. A family spends $600 a month on rent, $400 on utilities, $750 on groceries, and $550 on miscellaneous expenses. What is the ratio of the family's rent to their total expenses?

Answer:

rent = 600 utilities = 400 groceries = 750 miscellaneous = 550 total expenses = 600 + 400 + 750 + 550 = 2300	Identify the variables.
rent : total expenses $= 600 : 2300$ $= \dfrac{600}{2300}$ $= \dfrac{6}{23}$	Write out and simplify the ratio of rent to total expenses.

PROPORTIONS

A **PROPORTION** is an equation which states that two ratios are equal. A proportion is given in the form $\frac{a}{b} = \frac{c}{d}$, where the a and d terms are the extremes and the b and c terms are the means. A proportion is solved using cross-multiplication ($ad = bc$) to create an equation with no fractional components. A proportion must have the same units in both numerators and both denominators.

Examples

1. Solve the proportion for x: $\frac{3x-5}{2} = \frac{x-8}{3}$.

Answer:

$\dfrac{(3x-5)}{2} = \dfrac{(x-8)}{3}$	
$3(3x-5) = 2(x-8)$	Cross-multiply.

$$9x - 15 = 2x - 16$$
$$7x - 15 = -16$$
$$7x = -1$$
$$x = -\frac{1}{7}$$

Solve the equation for x.

2. A map is drawn such that 2.5 inches on the map equates to an actual distance of 40 miles. If the distance measured on the map between two cities is 17.25 inches, what is the actual distance between them in miles?

Answer:

$\frac{2.5}{40} = \frac{17.25}{x}$	Write a proportion where x equals the actual distance and each ratio is written as inches : miles.
$2.5x = 690$ $x = 276$ The two cities are **276 miles apart**.	Cross-multiply and divide to solve for x.

3. A factory knows that 4 out of 1000 parts made will be defective. If in a month there are 125,000 parts made, how many of these parts will be defective?

Answer:

$\frac{4}{1000} = \frac{x}{125,000}$	Write a proportion where x is the number of defective parts made and both ratios are written as defective : total.
$1000x = 500,000$ $x = 500$ There are **500 defective parts** for the month.	Cross-multiply and divide to solve for x.

PERCENTAGES

A **PERCENT** (or percentage) means per hundred and is expressed with a percent symbol (%). For example, 54% means 54 out of every 100. A percent can be converted to a decimal by removing the % symbol and moving the decimal point two places to the left, while a decimal can be converted to a percent by moving the decimal point two places to the right and attaching the % sign. A percent can be converted to a fraction by writing the percent as a fraction with 100 as the denominator and reducing. A fraction can be converted to a percent by performing the indicated division, multiplying the result by 100, and attaching the % sign.

The equation for finding percentages has three variables: the part, the whole, and the percent (which is expressed in the equation as a decimal). The equation, as shown below, can be rearranged to solve for any of these variables.

- part = whole × percent
- percent = $\frac{\text{part}}{\text{whole}}$
- whole = $\frac{\text{part}}{\text{percent}}$

This set of equations can be used to solve percent word problems. All that's needed is to identify the part, whole, and/or percent, and then to plug those values into the appropriate equation and solve.

Examples

1. Change the following values to the indicated form:

(A) 18% to a fraction

(B) $\frac{3}{5}$ to a percent

(C) 1.125 to a percent

(D) 84% to a decimal

Answers:

(A) The percent is written as a fraction over 100 and reduced: $\frac{18}{100} = \frac{9}{50}$.

(B) Dividing 5 by 3 gives the value 0.6, which is then multiplied by 100: **60%**.

(C) The decimal point is moved two places to the right:
$1.125 \times 100 = \textbf{112.5\%}$.

D. The decimal point is moved two places to the left: $84 \div 100 = \textbf{0.84}$.

2. In a school of 650 students, 54% of the students are boys. How many students are girls?

Answer:

Percent of students who are girls = 100% − 54% = 46% percent = 46% = 0.46 whole = 650 students part = ?	Identify the variables.
part = whole × percent = 0.46 × 650 = 299 **There are 299 girls.**	Plug the variables into the appropriate equation.

Percent Change

Percent change problems involve a change from an original amount. Often percent change problems appear as word problems that include discounts, growth, or markups. In order to solve percent change problems, it's necessary to identify the percent change (as a decimal), the amount of change, and the original amount. (Keep in mind that one of these will be the value being solved for.) These values can then be plugged into the equations below:

Key terms associated with percent change problems include discount, sales tax, and markup.

- amount of change = original amount × percent change
- percent change = $\dfrac{\text{amount of change}}{\text{original amount}}$
- original amount = $\dfrac{\text{amount of change}}{\text{percent change}}$

Examples

1. An HDTV that originally cost $1,500 is on sale for 45% off. What is the sale price for the item?

   Answer:

original amount = $1,500 percent change = 45% = 0.45 amount of change = ?	Identify the variables.
amount of change = original amount × percent change = 1500 × 0.45 = 675	Plug the variables into the appropriate equation.
1500 − 675 = 825 **The final price is $825.**	To find the new price, subtract the amount of change from the original price.

2. A house was bought in 2000 for $100,000 and sold in 2015 for $120,000. What was the percent growth in the value of the house from 2000 to 2015?

   Answer:

original amount = $100,000 amount of change = 120,000 − 100,000 = 20,000 percent change = ?	Identify the variables.
$\text{percent change} = \dfrac{\text{amount of change}}{\text{original amount}}$ $= \dfrac{20,000}{100,000}$ $= 0.20$	Plug the variables into the appropriate equation.
0.20 × 100 = **20%**	To find the percent growth, multiply by 100.

EXPONENTS AND RADICALS

Exponents

An expression in the form b^n is in an exponential notation where b is the BASE and n is an EXPONENT. To perform the operation, multiply the base by itself the number of times indicated by the exponent. For example, 2^3 is equal to $2 \times 2 \times 2$ or 8.

Table 6.6. Operations with Exponents

RULE	EXAMPLE	EXPLANATION
$a^0 = 1$	$5^0 = 1$	Any base (except 0) to the 0 power is 1.
$a^{-n} = \dfrac{1}{a^n}$	$5^3 = \dfrac{1}{5^3}$	A negative exponent becomes positive when moved from numerator to denominator (or vice versa).
$a^m a^n = a^{m+n}$	$5^3 5^4 = 5^{3+4} = 5^7$	Add the exponents to multiply two powers with the same base.

RULE	EXAMPLE	EXPLANATION
$(a^m)^n = a^{mn}$	$(5^3)^4 = 5^{3(4)} = 5^{12}$	Multiply the exponents to raise a power to a power.
$\dfrac{a^m}{a^n} = a^{m-n}$	$\dfrac{5^4}{5^3} = 5^{4-3} = 5^1$	Subtract the exponents to divide two powers with the same base.
$(ab)^n = a^n b^n$	$(5 \times 6)^3 = 5^3 6^3$	Apply the exponent to each base to raise a product to a power.
$\left(\dfrac{a}{b}\right)^n = \dfrac{a^n}{b^n}$	$\left(\dfrac{5}{6}\right)^3 = \dfrac{5^3}{6^3}$	Apply the exponent to each base to raise a quotient to a power.
$\left(\dfrac{a}{b}\right)^{-n} = \left(\dfrac{b}{a}\right)^n$	$\left(\dfrac{5}{6}\right)^{-3} = \left(\dfrac{6}{5}\right)^3$	Invert the fraction and change the sign of the exponent to raise a fraction to a negative power.
$\dfrac{a^m}{b^n} = \dfrac{b^{-n}}{a^{-m}}$	$\dfrac{5^3}{6^4} = \dfrac{6^{-4}}{5^{-3}}$	Change the sign of the exponent when moving a number from the numerator to denominator (or vice versa).

Examples

1. Simplify: $\dfrac{(10^2)^3}{(10^2)^{-2}}$

Answer:

$\dfrac{(10^2)^3}{(10^2)^{-2}}$	
$= \dfrac{10^6}{10^{-4}}$	Multiply the exponents raised to a power.
$= 10^{6 - (-4)}$	Subtract the exponent in the denominator from the one in the numerator.
$= 10^{10}$ $= \mathbf{10{,}000{,}000{,}000}$	Simplify.

2. Simplify: $\dfrac{(x^{-2}y^2)^2}{x^3 y}$

Answer:

$\dfrac{(x^{-2}y^2)^2}{x^3 y}$	
$= \dfrac{x^{-4}y^4}{x^3 y}$	Multiply the exponents raised to a power.
$= x^{-4-3}y^{4-1}$ $= x^{-7}y^3$	Subtract the exponent in the denominator from the one in the numerator.
$= \dfrac{\mathbf{y^3}}{\mathbf{x^7}}$	Move negative exponents to the denominator.

Radicals

RADICALS are expressed as $\sqrt[b]{a}$, where b is called the **INDEX** and a is the **RADICAND**. A radical is used to indicate the inverse operation of an exponent: finding the base which can be raised to b to yield a. For example, $\sqrt[3]{125}$ is equal to 5 because $5 \times 5 \times 5$ equals 125. The same operation can be expressed using a fraction exponent, so $\sqrt[b]{a} = \frac{1}{a^b}$. Note that when no value is indicated for b, it is assumed to be 2 (square root).

When b is even and a is positive, $\sqrt[b]{a}$ is defined to be the positive real value n such that $n^b = a$ (example: $\sqrt{16} = 4$ only, and not –4, even though $(-4)(-4) = 16$). If b is even and a is negative, $\sqrt[b]{a}$ will be a complex number (example: $\sqrt{-9} = 3i$). Finally if b is odd, $\sqrt[b]{a}$ will always be a real number regardless of the sign of a. If a is negative, $\sqrt[b]{a}$ will be negative since a number to an odd power is negative (example: $\sqrt[5]{-32} = -2$ since $(-2)^5 = -32$).

$\sqrt[n]{x}$ is referred to as the nth root of x.

- $n = 2$ is the square root
- $n = 3$ is the cube root
- $n = 4$ is the fourth root
- $n = 5$ is the fifth root

The following table of operations with radicals holds for all cases EXCEPT the case where b is even and a is negative (the complex case).

Table 6.7. Operations with Radicals

RULE	EXAMPLE	EXPLANATION
$\sqrt[b]{ac} = \sqrt[b]{a}\sqrt[b]{c}$	$\sqrt[3]{81} = \sqrt[3]{27}\sqrt[3]{3} = 3\sqrt[3]{3}$	The values under the radical sign can be separated into values that multiply to the original value.
$\sqrt[b]{\frac{a}{c}} = \frac{\sqrt[b]{a}}{\sqrt[b]{c}}$	$\sqrt{\frac{4}{81}} = \frac{\sqrt{4}}{\sqrt{81}} = \frac{2}{9}$	The b-root of the numerator and denominator can be calculated when there is a fraction under a radical sign.
$\sqrt[b]{a^c} = (\sqrt[b]{a})^c = a^{\frac{c}{b}}$	$\sqrt[3]{6^2} = (\sqrt[3]{6})^2 = 6^{\frac{2}{3}}$	The b-root can be written as a fractional exponent. If there is a power under the radical sign, it will be the numerator of the fraction.
$\frac{c}{\sqrt[b]{a}} \times \frac{\sqrt[b]{a}}{\sqrt[b]{a}} = \frac{c\sqrt[b]{a}}{a}$	$\frac{5}{\sqrt{2}} \frac{\sqrt{2}}{\sqrt{2}} = \frac{5\sqrt{2}}{2}$	To rationalize the denominator, multiply the numerator and denominator by the radical in the denominator until the radical has been canceled out.
$\frac{c}{b-\sqrt{a}} \times \frac{b+\sqrt{a}}{b+\sqrt{a}}$ $= \frac{c(b+\sqrt{a})}{b^2-a}$	$\frac{4}{3-\sqrt{2}} \frac{3+\sqrt{2}}{3+\sqrt{2}}$ $= \frac{4(3+\sqrt{2})}{9-2} = \frac{12+4\sqrt{2}}{7}$	To rationalize the denominator, the numerator and denominator are multiplied by the conjugate of the denominator.

Examples

1. Simplify: $\sqrt{48}$

    Answer:

$\sqrt{48}$	
$= \sqrt{16 \times 3}$	Determine the largest square number that is a factor of the radicand (48) and write the radicand as a product using that square number as a factor.

$= \sqrt{16}\sqrt{3}$ $= 4\sqrt{3}$	Apply the rules of radicals to simplify.

2. Simplify: $\frac{6}{\sqrt{8}}$

Answer:

$\frac{6}{\sqrt{8}}$	
$= \frac{6}{\sqrt{4}\sqrt{2}}$ $= \frac{6}{2\sqrt{2}}$	Apply the rules of radicals to simplify.
$= \frac{6}{2\sqrt{2}}\left(\frac{\sqrt{2}}{\sqrt{2}}\right)$ $= \frac{3\sqrt{2}}{2}$	Multiply by $\frac{\sqrt{2}}{\sqrt{2}}$ to rationalize the denominator.

ALGEBRAIC EXPRESSIONS

The foundation of algebra is the **VARIABLE**, an unknown number represented by a symbol (usually a letter such as x or a). Variables can be preceded by a **COEFFICIENT**, which is a constant (i.e., a real number) in front of the variable, such as $4x$ or $-2a$. An **ALGEBRAIC EXPRESSION** is any sum, difference, product, or quotient of variables and numbers (for example $3x^2$, $2x + 7y - 1$, and $\frac{5}{x}$ are algebraic expressions). **TERMS** are any quantities that are added or subtracted (for example, the terms of the expression $x^2 - 3x + 5$ are x^2, $3x$, and 5). A **POLYNOMIAL EXPRESSION** is an algebraic expression where all the exponents on the variables are whole numbers. A polynomial with only two terms is known as a **BINOMIAL**, and one with three terms is a **TRINOMIAL**. A **MONOMIAL** has only one term.

EVALUATING EXPRESSIONS is another way of saying "find the numeric value of an expression if the variable is equal to a certain number." To evaluate the expression, simply plug the given value(s) for the variable(s) into the equation and simplify. Remember to use the order of operations when simplifying:

1.	**P**arentheses		**4.**	**D**ivision
2.	**E**xponents		**5.**	**A**ddition
3.	**M**ultiplication		**6.**	**S**ubtraction

Example

If $m = 4$, find the value of the following expression:

$5(m - 2)^3 + 3m^2 - \frac{m}{4} - 1$

Answer:

$5(m - 2)^3 + 3m^2 - \frac{m}{4} - 1$	
$= 5(4 - 2)^3 + 3(4)^2 - \frac{4}{4} - 1$	Plug the value 4 in for m in the expression.
$= 5(2)^3 + 3(4)^2 - \frac{4}{4} - 1$	Calculate all the expressions inside the parentheses.

$= 5(8) + 3(16) - \frac{4}{4} - 1$	Simplify all exponents.
$= 40 + 48 - 1 - 1$	Perform multiplication and division from left to right.
= 86	Perform addition and subtraction from left to right.

OPERATIONS WITH EXPRESSIONS

Adding and Subtracting

Expressions can be added or subtracted by simply adding and subtracting LIKE TERMS, which are terms with the same variable part (the variables must be the same, with the same exponents on each variable). For example, in the expressions $2x + 3xy - 2z$ and $6y + 2xy$, the like terms are $3xy$ and $2xy$. Adding the two expressions yields the new expression $2x + 5xy - 2z + 6y$. Note that the other terms did not change; they cannot be combined because they have different variables.

Example
If $a = 12x + 7xy - 9y$ and $b = 8x - 9xz + 7z$, what is $a + b$?

Answer:

$a + b = (12x + 8x) + 7xy - 9y - 9xz + 7z =$ **$20x + 7xy - 9y - 9xz + 7z$**	The only like terms in both expressions are $12x$ and $8x$, so these two terms will be added, and all other terms will remain the same.

Distributing and Factoring

Distributing and factoring can be seen as two sides of the same coin. **DISTRIBUTION** multiplies each term in the first factor by each term in the second factor to get rid of parentheses. **FACTORING** reverses this process, taking a polynomial in standard form and writing it as a product of two or more factors.

Operations with polynomials can always be checked by evaluating equivalent expressions for the same value.

When distributing a monomial through a polynomial, the expression outside the parentheses is multiplied by each term inside the parentheses. Using the rules of exponents, coefficients are multiplied and exponents are added.

When simplifying two polynomials, each term in the first polynomial must multiply each term in the second polynomial. A binomial (two terms) multiplied by a binomial, will require 2 × 2 or 4 multiplications. For the binomial × binomial case, this process is sometimes called **FOIL**, which stands for first, outside, inside, and last. These terms refer to the placement of each term of the expression: multiply the first term in each expression, then the outside terms, then the inside terms, and finally the last terms. A binomial (two terms) multiplied by a trinomial (three terms), will require 2 × 3 or 6 products to simplify. The first

Distribute

$3x(7xy - z^3)$ → $21x^2y - 3xz^3$

Factor

Figure 6.4. Distribution and Factoring

term in the first polynomial multiplies each of the three terms in the second polynomial, then the second term in the first polynomial multiplies each of the three terms in the second polynomial. A trinomial (three terms) by a trinomial will require 3×3 or 9 products, and so on.

Factoring is the reverse of distributing: the first step is always to remove ("undistribute") the GCF of all the terms, if there is a GCF (besides 1). The GCF is the product of any constants and/or variables that <u>every</u> term shares. (For example, the GCF of $12x^3$, $15x^2$ and $6xy^2$ is $3x$ because $3x$ evenly divides all three terms.) This shared factor can be taken out of each term and moved to the outside of the parentheses, leaving behind a polynomial where each term is the original term divided by the GCF. (The remaining terms for the terms in the example would be $4x^2$, $5x$, and $2y^2$.) It may be possible to factor the polynomial in the parentheses further, depending on the problem.

Example

1. Expand the following expression: $5x(x^2 - 2c + 10)$

Answer:

$5x(x^2 - 2c + 10)$	
$(5x)(x^2) = 5x^3$ $(5x)(-2c) = -10xc$ $(5x)(10) = 50x$	Distribute and multiply the term outside the parentheses to all three terms inside the parentheses.
$= 5x^3 - 10xc + 50x$	

2. Expand the following expression: $(x^2 - 5)(2x - x^3)$

Answer:

$(x^2 - 5)(2x - x^3)$	
$(x^2)(2x) = 2x^3$ $(x^2)(-x^3) = -x^5$ $(-5)(2x) = -10x$ $(-5)(-x^3) = 5x^3$	Apply FOIL: first, outside, inside, and last.
$= 2x^3 - x^5 - 10x + 5x^3$	Combine like terms and put them in order.
$= -x^5 + 7x^3 - 10x$	

3. Factor the expression $16z^2 + 48z$

Answer:

$16z^2 + 48z$ $= 16z(z + 3)$	Both terms have a z, and 16 is a common factor of both 16 and 48. So the greatest common factor is $16z$. Factor out the GCF.

4. Factor the expression $6m^3 + 12m^3n - 9m^2$

→ CONTINUE

Answer:

$6m^3 + 12m^3n - 9m^2$
$= 3m^2(2m + 4mn - 3)$

All the terms share the factor m^2, and 3 is the greatest common factor of 6, 12, and 9. So, the GCF is $3m^2$.

LINEAR EQUATIONS

An **EQUATION** states that two expressions are equal to each other. Polynomial equations are categorized by the highest power of the variables they contain: the highest power of any exponent of a linear equation is 1, a quadratic equation has a variable raised to the second power, a cubic equation has a variable raised to the third power, and so on.

Solving Linear Equations

Solving an equation means finding the value or values of the variable that make the equation true. To solve a linear equation, it is necessary to manipulate the terms so that the variable being solved for appears alone on one side of the equal sign while everything else in the equation is on the other side.

The way to solve linear equations is to "undo" all the operations that connect numbers to the variable of interest. Follow these steps:

On multiple choice tests, it is often easier to plug the possible values into the equation and determine which solution makes the equation true than to solve the equation.

1. Eliminate fractions by multiplying each side by the least common multiple of any denominators.

2. Distribute to eliminate parentheses, braces, and brackets.

3. Combine like terms.

4. Use addition or subtraction to collect all terms containing the variable of interest to one side, and all terms not containing the variable to the other side.

5. Use multiplication or division to remove coefficients from the variable of interest.

Sometimes there are no numeric values in the equation or there are a mix of numerous variables and constants. The goal is to solve the equation for one of the variables in terms of the other variables. In this case, the answer will be an expression involving numbers and letters instead of a numeric value.

Examples

1. Solve for x: $\frac{100(x + 5)}{20} = 1$

Answer:

$\frac{100(x + 5)}{20} = 1$	
$(20)\left(\frac{100(x + 5)}{20}\right) = (1)(20)$ $100(x + 5) = 20$	Multiply both sides by 20 to cancel out the denominator.
$100x + 500 = 20$	Distribute 100 through the parentheses.

$100x = -480$	"Undo" the +500 by subtracting 500 on both sides of the equation to isolate the variable term.
$x = \dfrac{-480}{100}$	"Undo" the multiplication by 100 by dividing by 100 on both sides to solve for x.
$x = -4.8$	

2. Solve for x: $2(x + 2)^2 - 2x^2 + 10 = 42$

Answer:

$2(x + 2)^2 - 2x^2 + 10 = 42$	
$2(x + 2)(x + 2) - 2x^2 + 10 = 42$	Eliminate the exponents on the left side.
$2(x^2 + 4x + 4) - 2x^2 + 10 = 42$	Apply FOIL.
$2x^2 + 8x + 8 - 2x^2 + 10 = 42$	Distribute the 2.
$8x + 18 = 42$	Combine like terms on the left-hand side.
$8x = 24$	Isolate the variable. "Undo" +18 by subtracting 18 on both sides.
$x = 3$	"Undo" multiplication by 8 by dividing both sides by 8.

3. Solve the equation for D: $\dfrac{A(3B + 2D)}{2N} = 5M - 6$

Answer:

$\dfrac{A(3B + 2D)}{2N} = 5M - 6$	
$3AB + 2AD = 10MN - 12N$	Multiply both sides by 2N to clear the fraction, and distribute the A through the parentheses.
$2AD = 10MN - 12N - 3AB$	Isolate the term with the D in it by moving 3AB to the other side of the equation.
$D = \dfrac{(10MN - 12N - 3AB)}{2A}$	Divide both sides by 2A to get D alone on the right-hand side.

Graphs of Linear Equations

The most common way to write a linear equation is **SLOPE-INTERCEPT FORM**, $y = mx + b$. In this equation, m is the slope, which describes how steep the line is, and b is the y-intercept. Slope is often described as "rise over run" because it is calculated as the difference in y-values (rise) over the difference in x-values (run). The slope of the line is also the rate of change of the dependent variable y with respect to the independent variable x. The y-intercept is the point where the line crosses the y-axis, or where x equals zero.

To graph a linear equation, identify the y-intercept and place that point on the y-axis. If the slope is not written as a fraction,

Use the phrase "Begin, Move" to remember that b is the y-intercept (where to begin) and m is the slope (how the line moves).

make it a fraction by writing it over 1 $\left(\frac{m}{1}\right)$. Then use the slope to count up (or down, if negative) the "rise" part of the slope and over the "run" part of the slope to find a second point. These points can then be connected to draw the line.

To find the equation of a line, identify the y-intercept, if possible, on the graph and use two easily identifiable points to find the slope. If the y-intercept is not easily identified, identify the slope by choosing easily identifiable points; then choose one point on the graph, plug the point and the slope values into the equation, and solve for the missing value b.

slope-intercept form:
$y = mx + b$
slope: $m = \frac{y_2 - y_1}{x_2 - x_1}$

- standard form: $Ax + By = C$
- $m = -\frac{A}{B}$
- x-intercept $= \frac{C}{A}$
- y-intercept $= \frac{C}{B}$

Another way to express a linear equation is standard form: $Ax + By = C$. In order to graph equations in this form, it is often easiest to convert them to point-slope form. Alternately, it is easy to find the x- or y-intercept from this form, and once these two points are known, a line can be drawn through them. To find the x-intercept, simply make $y = 0$ and solve for x. Similarly, to find the y-intercept, make $x = 0$ and solve for y.

Examples

1. What is the slope of the line whose equation is $6x - 2y - 8 = 0$?

Answer:

$6x - 2y - 8 = 0$	
$-2y = -6x + 8$ $y = \frac{-6x + 8}{-2}$ $y = 3x - 4$	Rearrange the equation into slope-intercept form by solving the equation for y.
$m = 3$	The slope is 3, the value attached to x.

2. What is the equation of the following line?

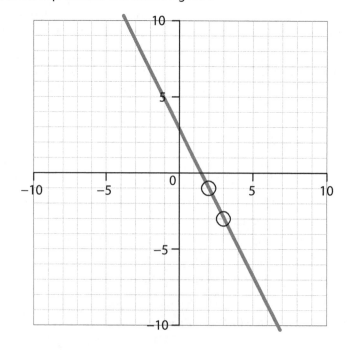

Answer:

$b = 3$	The *y*-intercept can be identified on the graph as $(0, 3)$.
$m = \dfrac{(-3) - (-1)}{3 - 2} = \dfrac{-2}{1} = -2$	To find the slope, choose any two points and plug the values into the slope equation. The two points chosen here are $(2, -1)$ and $(3, -3)$.
$y = -2x + 3$	Replace *m* with -2 and *b* with 3 in $y = mx + b$.

3. Write the equation of the line which passes through the points $(-2, 5)$ and $(-5, 3)$.

Answer:

$(-2, 5)$ and $(-5, 3)$	
$m = \dfrac{3 - 5}{(-5) - (-2)}$ $\quad = \dfrac{-2}{-3}$ $\quad = \dfrac{2}{3}$	Calculate the slope.
$5 = \dfrac{2}{3}(-2) + b$ $5 = \dfrac{-4}{3} + b$ $b = \dfrac{19}{3}$	To find *b*, plug into the equation $y = mx + b$ the slope for *m* and a set of points for *x* and *y*.
$y = \dfrac{2}{3}x + \dfrac{19}{3}$	Replace *m* and *b* to find the equation of the line.

4. What is the equation of the following graph?

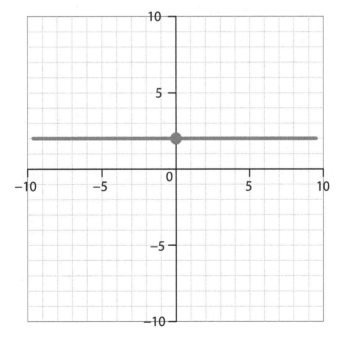

CONTINUE

Answer:

$y = 0x + 2$, or $y = 2$

The line has a rise of 0 and a run of 1, so the slope is $\frac{0}{1} = 0$. There is no x-intercept. The y-intercept is $(0, 2)$, meaning that the b-value in the slope-intercept form is 2.

PROPERTIES OF SHAPES

Basic Definitions

The basic figures from which many other geometric shapes are built are points, lines, and planes. A **POINT** is a location in a plane. It has no size or shape, but is represented by a dot. It is labeled using a capital letter.

A **LINE** is a one-dimensional collection of points that extends infinitely in both directions. At least two points are needed to define a line, and any points that lie on the same line are **COLINEAR**. Lines are represented by two points, such as A and B, and the line symbol: ($\overleftrightarrow{AB}$). Two lines on the same plane will intersect unless they are **PARALLEL**, meaning they have the same slope. Lines that intersect at a 90-degree angle are **PERPENDICULAR**.

A **LINE SEGMENT** has two endpoints and a finite length. The length of a segment, called the measure of the segment, is the distance from A to B. A line segment is a subset of a line, and is also denoted with two points, but with a segment symbol: ($\overline{AB}$). The **MIDPOINT** of a line segment is the point at which the segment is divided into two equal parts. A line, segment, or plane that passes through the midpoint of a segment is called a **BISECTOR** of the segment, since it cuts the segment into two equal segments.

A **RAY** has one endpoint and extends indefinitely in one direction. It is defined by its endpoint, followed by any other point on the ray: $\overrightarrow{AB}$. It is important that the first letter represents the endpoint. A ray is sometimes called a half line.

Table 6.8. Basic Geometric Figures

TERM	DIMENSIONS	GRAPHIC	SYMBOL
point	zero	●	$\cdot A$
line segment	one	A ———— B	$\overline{AB}$
ray	one	A ——→ B	$\overrightarrow{AB}$
line	one	←——→	$\overleftrightarrow{AB}$
plane	two	▱	Plane M

A **PLANE** is a flat sheet that extends indefinitely in two directions (like an infinite sheet of paper). A plane is a two-dimensional (2D) figure. A plane can always be defined through any three noncollinear points in three-dimensional (3D) space. A plane is named using any three points that are in the plane (for example, plane **ABC**). Any points lying in the same plane are said to be **COPLANAR**. When two planes intersect, the intersection is a line.

Example

1) Which points and lines are not contained in plane *M* in the diagram below?

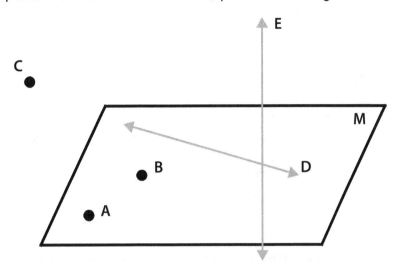

Answer:

Points *A* and *B* and line *D* are all on plane *M*. Point *C* is above the plane, and line *E* cuts through the plane and thus does not lie on plane *M*. The point at which line *E* intersects plane *M* is on plane *M* but the line as a whole is not.

Angles

ANGLES are formed when two rays share a common endpoint. They are named using three letters, with the vertex point in the middle (for example ∠*ABC*, where *B* is the vertex). They can also be labeled with a number or named by their vertex alone (if it is clear to do so). Angles are also classified based on their angle measure. A **right angle** has a measure of exactly 90°. **Acute angles** have measures that are less than 90°, and **obtuse angles** have measures that are greater than 90°.

Any two angles that add to make 90° are called **COMPLEMENTARY ANGLES**. A 30° angle would be complementary to a 60° angle. **SUPPLEMENTARY ANGLES** add up to 180°. A supplementary angle to a 60° angle would be a 120° angle; likewise, 60° is the **SUPPLEMENT** of 120°. Angles that are next to each other and share a common ray are called **ADJACENT ANGLES**. Angles that are adjacent and supplementary are called a **LINEAR PAIR** of angles. Their nonshared rays form a line (thus the *linear* pair). Note that angles that are supplementary do not need to be adjacent; their measures simply need to add to 180°.

 Angles can be measured in degrees or radians. Use the conversion factor 1 rad = 57.3 degrees to convert between them.

VERTICAL ANGLES are formed when two lines intersect. Four angles will be formed; the vertex of each angle is at the intersection point of the lines. The vertical angles across from each other will be equal in measure. The angles adjacent to each other will be linear pairs and therefore supplementary.

A ray, line, or segment that divides an angle into two equal angles is called an **ANGLE BISECTOR**.

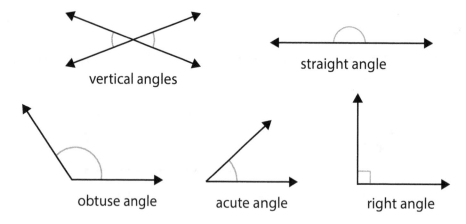

Figure 6.5. Types of Angles

Examples

1. If angles *M* and *N* are supplementary and ∠*M* is 30° less than twice ∠*N*, what is the degree measurement of each angle?

Answer:

∠*M* + ∠*N* = 180° ∠*M* = 2∠*N* − 30°	Set up a system of equations.
∠*M* + ∠*N* = 180° (2∠*N* − 30°) + ∠*N* = 180° 3∠*N* − 30° = 180° 3∠*N* = 210° **∠*N* = 70°**	Use substitution to solve for ∠*N*.
∠*M* + ∠*N* = 180° ∠*M* + 70° = 180° **∠*M* = 110°**	Solve for ∠*M* using the original equation.

2. How many linear pairs of angles are there in the following figure?

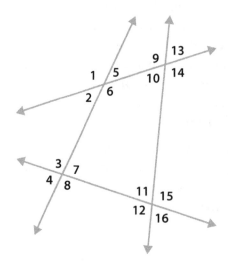

Circles

A **CIRCLE** is the set of all the points in a plane that are the same distance from a fixed point called the **CENTER**. The distance from the center to any point on the circle is the **RADIUS** of the circle. The distance around the circle (the perimeter) is called the **CIRCUMFERENCE**.

The ratio of a circle's circumference to its diameter is a constant value called pi (π), an irrational number which is commonly rounded to 3.14. The formula to find a circle's circumference is $C = 2\pi r$. The formula to find the enclosed area of a circle is $A = \pi r^2$.

Circles have a number of unique parts and properties:

Trying to square a circle means attempting to create a square that has the same area as a circle. Because the area of a circle depends on π, which is an irrational number, this task is impossible. The phrase is often used to describe trying to do something that can't be done.

- The **DIAMETER** is the largest measurement across a circle. It passes through the circle's center, extending from one side of the circle to the other. The measure of the diameter is twice the measure of the radius.

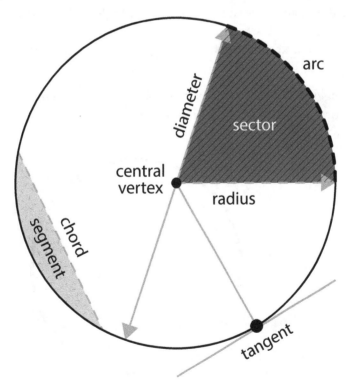

Figure 6.6. Parts of a Circle

- A line that cuts across a circle and touches it twice is called a **SECANT** line. The part of a secant line that lies within a circle is called a **CHORD**. Two chords within a circle are of equal length if they are are the same distance from the center.

- A line that touches a circle or any curve at one point is **TANGENT** to the circle or the curve. These lines are always exterior to the circle. A line tangent to a circle and a radius drawn to the point of tangency meet at a right angle (90°).

- An **ARC** is any portion of a circle between two points on the circle. The **MEASURE** of an arc is in degrees, whereas the **LENGTH OF THE ARC** will be in linear measurement (such as centimeters or inches). A **MINOR ARC** is the small arc between the two points (it measures less than 180°), whereas a **MAJOR ARC** is the large arc between the two points (it measures greater than 180°).

- An angle with its vertex at the center of a circle is called a **CENTRAL ANGLE**. For a central angle, the measure of the arc intercepted by the sides of the angle (in degrees) is the same as the measure of the angle.

- A **SECTOR** is the part of a circle *and* its interior that is inside the rays of a central angle (its shape is like a slice of pie).

	Area of Sector	Length of an Arc
Degrees	$A = \frac{\theta}{360°} \times \pi r^2$	$s = \frac{\theta}{360°} \times 2\pi r$
Radians	$A = \frac{1}{2}\, r^2 \theta$	$s = r\theta$

- An **INSCRIBED ANGLE** has a vertex on the circle and is formed by two chords that share that vertex point. The angle measure of an inscribed angle is one-half the angle measure of the central angle with the same endpoints on the circle.

- A **CIRCUMSCRIBED ANGLE** has rays tangent to the circle. The angle lies outside of the circle.

- Any angle outside the circle, whether formed by two tangent lines, two secant lines, or a tangent line and a secant line, is equal to half the difference of the intercepted arcs.

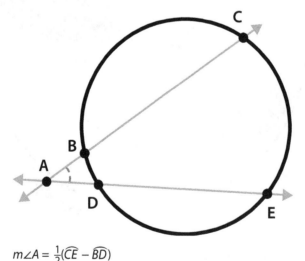

$m\angle A = \frac{1}{2}(\overset{\frown}{CE} - \overset{\frown}{BD})$

Figure 6.7. Angles Outside a Circle

- Angles are formed within a circle when two chords intersect in the circle. The measure of the smaller angle formed is half the sum of the two smaller arc measures (in degrees). Likewise, the larger angle is half the sum of the two larger arc measures.

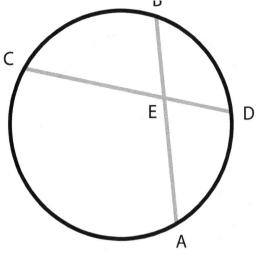

$$m\angle E = \tfrac{1}{2}(\overset{\frown}{AC} + \overset{\frown}{BD})$$

Figure 6.8. Intersecting Chords

- If a chord intersects a line tangent to the circle, the angle formed by this intersection measures one half the measurement of the intercepted arc (in degrees).

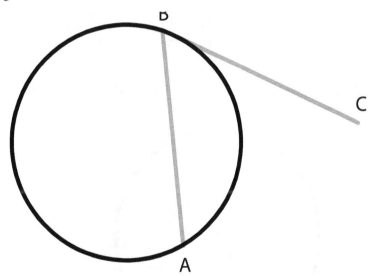

$$m\angle ABC = \tfrac{1}{2}m\overset{\frown}{AB}$$

Figure 6.9. Intersecting Chord and Tangent

CONTINUE

Examples

1. Find the area of the sector *NHS* of the circle below with center at *H*:

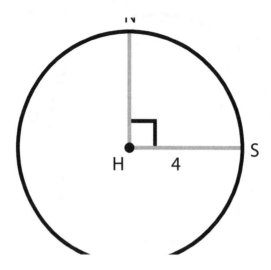

Answer:

$r = 4$ $\angle NHS = 90°$	Identify the important parts of the circle.
$A = \dfrac{\theta}{360°} \times \pi r^2$ $= \dfrac{90}{360} \times \pi (4)^2$	Plug these values into the formula for the area of a sector.
$= \dfrac{1}{4} \times 16\pi$ $\mathbf{= 4\pi}$	Plug these values into the formula for the area of a sector (continued).

2. In the circle below with center *O*, the minor arc *ACB* measures 5 feet. What is the measurement of *m∠AOB*?

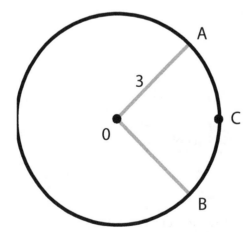

Answer:

$r = 3$ length of $\overset{\frown}{ACB} = 5$	Identify the important parts of the circle.

$$s = \frac{\theta}{360°} \times 2\pi r$$

$$5 = \frac{\theta}{360} \times 2\pi(3)$$

$$\frac{5}{6\pi} = \frac{\theta}{360}$$

$$\theta = 95.5°$$

$$m\angle AOB = 95.5°$$

Plug these values into the formula for the length of an arc and solve for θ.

Triangles

Much of geometry is concerned with triangles as they are commonly used shapes. A good understanding of triangles allows decomposition of other shapes (specifically polygons) into triangles for study.

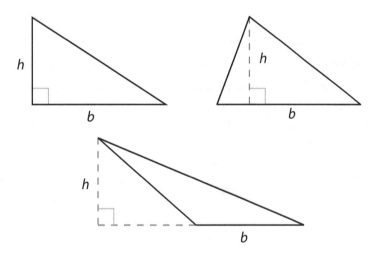

Figure 6.10. Finding the Base and Height of Triangles

Triangles have three sides, and the three interior angles always sum to 180°. The formula for the area of a triangle is $A = \frac{1}{2}bh$ or one-half the product of the base and height (or altitude) of the triangle.

Some important segments in a triangle include the angle bisector, the altitude, and the median. The **ANGLE BISECTOR** extends from the side opposite an angle to bisect that angle. The **ALTITUDE** is the shortest distance from a vertex of the triangle to the line containing the base side opposite that vertex. It is perpendicular to that line and can occur on the outside of the triangle. The **MEDIAN** extends from an angle to bisect the opposite side.

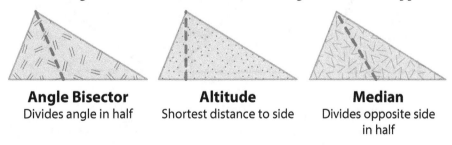

| **Angle Bisector** | **Altitude** | **Median** |
| Divides angle in half | Shortest distance to side | Divides opposite side in half |

Figure 6.11. Important Segments in a Triangle

Triangles have two "centers." The CENTROID is where a triangle's three medians meet. The ORTHOCENTER is formed by the intersection of a triangle's three altitudes.

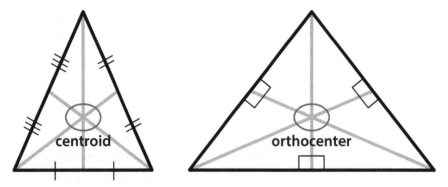

Figure 6.12. Centroid and Orthocenter of a Triangle

Triangles can be classified in two ways: by sides and by angles.

A SCALENE TRIANGLE has no equal sides or angles. An ISOSCELES TRIANGLE has two equal sides and two equal angles, often called BASE ANGLES. In an EQUILATERAL TRIANGLE, all three sides are equal as are all three angles. Moreover, because the sum of the angles of a triangle is always 180°, each angle of an equilateral triangle must be 60°.

Triangles Based on Sides

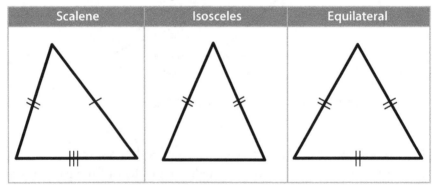

Triangles Based on Angles

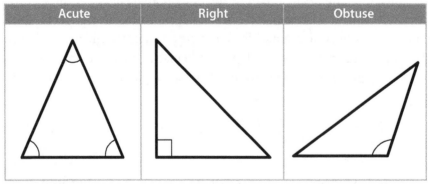

Figure 6.13. Types of Triangles

A RIGHT TRIANGLE has one right angle (90°) and two acute angles. An ACUTE TRIANGLE has three acute angles (all angles are less than 90°). An OBTUSE TRIANGLE has one obtuse angle (more than 90°) and two acute angles.

For any triangle, the side opposite the largest angle will have the longest length, while the side opposite the smallest angle will have the shortest length. The TRIANGLE INEQUALITY THEOREM states that the sum of any two sides of a triangle must be greater than the third side. If this inequality does not hold, then a triangle cannot be formed. A consequence of this theorem is the THIRD-SIDE RULE: if b and c are two sides of a triangle, then the measure of the third side a must be between the sum of the other two sides and the difference of the other two sides: $c - b < a < c + b$.

 Trigonometric functions can be employed to find missing sides and angles of a triangle.

Solving for missing angles or sides of a triangle is a common type of triangle problem. Often a right triangle will come up on its own or within another triangle. The relationship among a right triangle's sides is known as the PYTHAGOREAN THEOREM: $a^2 + b^2 = c^2$, where c is the hypotenuse and is across from the 90° angle. Right triangles with angle measurements of 90° – 45° – 45° and 90° – 60° – 30° are known as "special" right triangles and have specific relationships between their sides and angles.

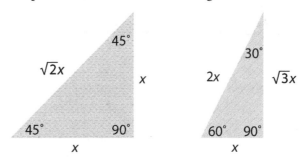

Figure 6.14. Special Right Triangles

Examples

1. Examine and classify each of the following triangles:

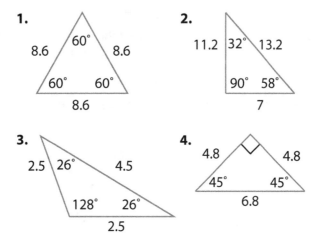

Answers:

Triangle 1 is an equilateral triangle (all 3 sides are equal, and all 3 angles are equal)

Triangle 2 is a scalene, right triangle (all 3 sides are different, and there is a 90° angle)

Triangle 3 is an isosceles triangle (there are 2 equal sides and, consequently, 2 equal angles)

Triangle 4 is a right, isosceles triangle (there are 2 equal sides and a 90° angle)

2. Given the diagram, if $XZ = 100$, $WZ = 80$, and $XU = 70$, then $WY = ?$

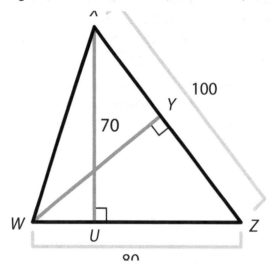

Answer:

$WZ = b_1 = 80$
$XU = h_1 = 70$
$XZ = b_2 = 100$
$WY = h_2 = ?$

$A = \frac{1}{2}bh$ $A_1 = \frac{1}{2}(80)(70) = 2800$ $A_2 = \frac{1}{2}(100)(h_2)$	The given values can be used to write two equation for the area of $\triangle WXZ$ with two sets of bases and heights.
$2800 = \frac{1}{2}(100)(h_2)$ $h_2 = 56$ **$WY = 56$**	Set the two equations equal to each other and solve for WY.

3. What are the minimum and maximum values of x to the nearest hundredth?

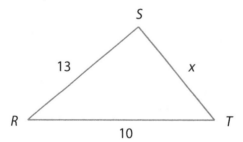

Answers:

The sum of two sides is 23 and their difference is 3. To connect the two other sides and enclose a space, x must be less than the sum and greater than the difference (that is, $3 < x < 23$). Therefore, **x's minimum value to the nearest hundredth is 3.01 and its maximum value is 22.99.**

Quadrilaterals

All closed, four-sided shapes are **QUADRILATERALS**. The sum of all internal angles in a quadrilateral is always 360°. (Think of drawing a diagonal to create two triangles. Since each triangle contains 180°, two triangles, and therefore the quadrilateral, must contain 360°.) The **AREA OF ANY QUADRILATERAL** is $A = bh$, where b is the base and h is the height (or altitude).

A **PARALLELOGRAM** is a quadrilateral with two pairs of parallel sides. A rectangle is a parallelogram with two pairs of equal sides and four right angles. A **KITE** also has two pairs of equal sides, but its equal sides are consecutive. Both a **SQUARE** and a **RHOMBUS** have four equal sides. A square has four right angles, while a rhombus has a pair of acute opposite angles and a pair of obtuse opposite angles. A **TRAPEZOID** has exactly one pair of parallel sides.

> ⚠ All squares are rectangles and all rectangles are parallelograms; however, not all parallelograms are rectangles and not all rectangles are squares.

Table 6.9. Properties of Parallelograms

TERM	SHAPE	PROPERTIES
Parallelogram		Opposite sides are parallel. Consecutive angles are supplementary. Opposite angles are equal. Opposite sides are equal. Diagonals bisect each other.
Rectangle		All parallelogram properties hold. Diagonals are congruent *and* bisect each other. All angles are right angles.
Square		All rectangle properties hold. All four sides are equal. Diagonals bisect angles. Diagonals intersect at right angles and bisect each other.
Kite		One pair of opposite angles is equal. Two pairs of consecutive sides are equal. Diagonals meet at right angles.
Rhombus		All four sides are equal. Diagonals bisect angles. Diagonals intersect at right angles and bisect each other.
Trapezoid		One pair of sides is parallel. Bases have different lengths. Isosceles trapezoids have a pair of equal sides (and base angles).

CONTINUE →

Examples

1. In parallelogram *ABCD*, the measure of angle *m* is is $m° = 260°$. What is the measure of *n*°?

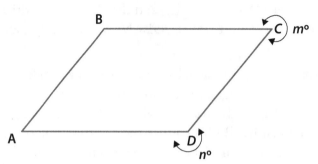

Answers:

$260° + m\angle C = 360°$ $m\angle C = 100°$	Find $\angle C$ using the fact that the sum of $\angle C$ and *m* is 360°.
$m\angle C + m\angle D = 180°$ $100° + m\angle D = 180°$ $m\angle D = 80°$	Solve for $\angle D$ using the fact that consecutive interior angles in a quadrilateral are supplementary.
$m\angle D + n = 360°$ **n = 280°**	Solve for *n* by subtracting $m\angle D$ from 360°.

2. A rectangular section of a football field has dimensions of *x* and *y* and an area of 1000 square feet. Three additional lines drawn vertically divide the section into four smaller rectangular areas as seen in the diagram below. If all the lines shown need to be painted, calculate the total number of linear feet, in terms of *x*, to be painted.

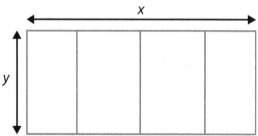

Answer:

$A = 1000 = xy$ $L = 2x + 5y$	Find equations for the area of the field and length of the lines to be painted (*L*) in terms of *x* and *y*.
$y = \frac{1000}{x}$ $L = 2x + 5y$ $L = 2x + 5\left(\frac{1000}{x}\right)$ **$L = 2x + \frac{5000}{x}$**	Substitute to find *L* in terms of *x*.

Polygons

Any closed shape made up of three or more line segments is a polygon. In addition to triangles and quadrilaterals, **OCTAGONS** and **HEXAGONS** are two common polygons.

The two polygons depicted below are **REGULAR POLYGONS**, meaning that they are equilateral (all sides having equal lengths) and equiangular (all angles having equal measurements). Angles inside a polygon are **INTERIOR ANGLES**, whereas those formed by one side of the polygon and a line extending outside the polygon are **EXTERIOR ANGLES**.

Breaking an irregular polygon down into triangles and quadrilaterals helps in finding its area.

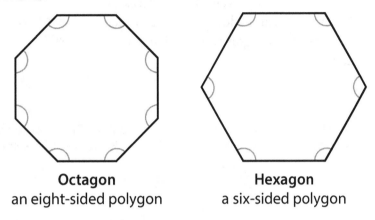

Octagon
an eight-sided polygon

Hexagon
a six-sided polygon

Figure 6.15. Common Polygons

The sum of all the exterior angles of a polygon is always 360°. Dividing 360° by the number of a polygon's sides finds the measure of the polygon's exterior angles.

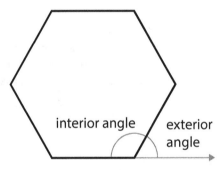

Figure 6.16. Interior and Exterior Angles

To determine the sum of a polygon's interior angles, choose one vertex and draw diagonals from that vertex to each of the other vertices, decomposing the polygon into multiple triangles. For example, an octagon has six triangles within it, and therefore the sum of the interior angles is 6 × 180° = 1080°. In general, the formula for finding the sum of the angles in a polygon is *sum of angles* = $(n - 2) \times 180°$, where n is the number of sides of the polygon.

To find the measure of a single interior angle, simply divide the sum of the interior angles by the number of angles (which is the same as the number of sides). So, in the octagon example, each angle is $\frac{1080}{8}$ = 135°.

In general, the formula to find the measure of a regular polygon's interior angles is: *interior angle* = $\frac{(n-2)}{n} \times 180°$ where n is the number of sides of the polygon.

To find the area of a polygon, it is helpful to know the perimeter of the polygon (p), and the **APOTHEM** (a). The apothem is the shortest (perpendicular) distance from the polygon's center to one of the sides of the polygon. The formula for the area is: $area = \frac{ap}{2}$.

Finally, there is no universal way to find the perimeter of a polygon (when the side length is not given). Often, breaking the polygon down into triangles and adding the base of each triangle all the way around the polygon is the easiest way to calculate the perimeter.

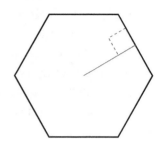

Figure 6.17. Apothem in a Hexagon

Examples

1. The circle and hexagon below both share center point T. The hexagon is entirely inscribed in the circle. The circle's radius is 5. What is the area of the shaded area?

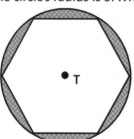

Answer:

$A_C = \pi r^2$ $= \pi(5)^2$ $= 25\pi$	The area of the shaded region will be the area of the circle minus the area of the hexagon. Use the radius to find the area of the circle.
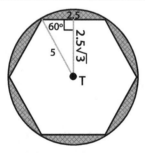 $a = 2.5\sqrt{3}$ $A_H = \frac{ap}{2}$ $= \frac{(2.5\sqrt{3})(30)}{2}$ $= 64.95$	To find the area of the hexagon, draw a right triangle from the vertex, and use special right triangles to find the hexagon's apothem. Then, use the apothem to calculate the area.
$= A_C - A_H$ $= 25\pi - 64.95$ $\approx \mathbf{13.59}$	Subtract the area of the hexagon from the circle to find the area of the shaded region.

2. What is the measure of an exterior angle and an interior angle of a regular 400-gon?

Answer:

The sum of the exterior angles is 360°. Dividing this sum by 400 gives $\frac{360°}{400}$ = **0.9°**. Since an interior angle is supplementary to an exterior angle, all the interior angles have measure 180 − 0.9 = **179.1°**. Alternately, using the formula for calculating the interior angle gives the same result:

$$interior\ angle = \frac{400 - 2}{400} \times 180° = 179.1°$$

THREE-DIMENSIONAL SHAPES

THREE-DIMENSIONAL SHAPES have depth in addition to width and length. VOLUME is expressed as the number of cubic units any shape can hold—that is, what it takes to fill it up. SURFACE AREA is the sum of the areas of the two-dimensional figures that are found on its surface. Some three-dimensional shapes also have a unique property called a slant height (ℓ), which is the distance from the base to the apex along a lateral face.

Table 6.10. Three-Dimensional Shapes and Formulas

TERM	SHAPE	FORMULA	
Prism		$V = Bh$ $SA = 2lw + 2wh + 2lh$ $d^2 = a^2 + b^2 + c^2$	B = area of base h = height l = length w = width d = longest diagonal
Cube	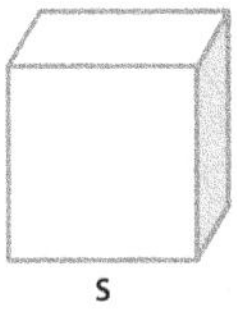	$V = s^3$ $SA = 6s^2$	s = cube edge
Sphere	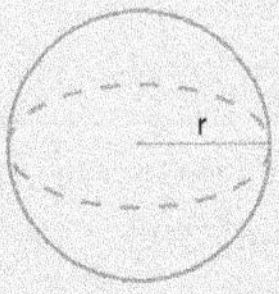	$V = \frac{4}{3}\pi r^3$ $SA = 4\pi r^2$	r = radius
Cylinder	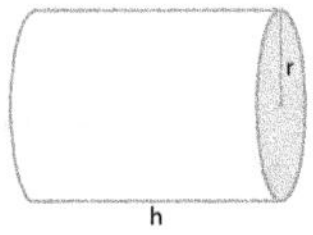	$V = Bh = \pi r^2 h$ $SA = 2\pi r^2 + 2\pi rh$	B = area of base h = height r = radius
Cone	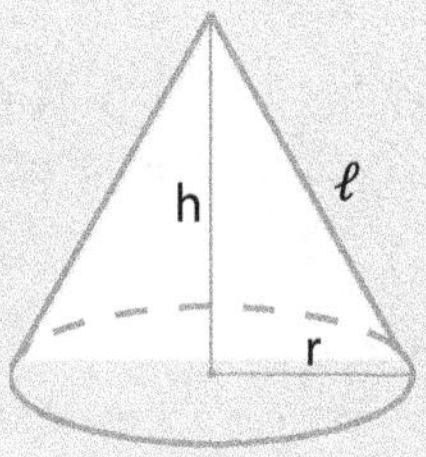	$V = \frac{1}{3}\pi r^2 h$	r = radius h = height

Table 6.10. Three-Dimensional Shapes and Formulas (continued)

TERM   **SHAPE**   **FORMULA**

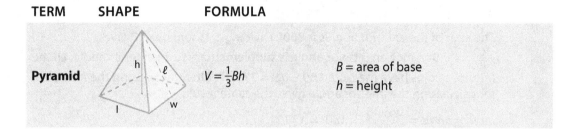

| Pyramid | | $V = \frac{1}{3}Bh$ | B = area of base
h = height |

Finding the surface area of a three-dimensional solid can be made easier by using a **net**. This two-dimensional "flattened" version of a three-dimensional shape shows the component parts that comprise the surface of the solid.

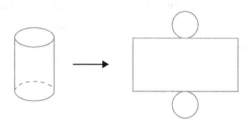

Figure 6.18. Net of a Cylinder

Examples

1. A sphere has a radius z. If that radius is increased by t, by how much is the surface area increased? Write the answer in terms of z and t.

Answer:

$SA_1 = 4\pi z^2$	Write the equation for the area of the original sphere.
$SA_2 = 4\pi(z + t)^2$ $= 4\pi(z^2 + 2zt + t^2)$ $= 4\pi z^2 + 8\pi zt + 4\pi t^2$	Write the equation for the area of the new sphere.
$A_2 - A_1 = 4\pi z^2 + 8\pi zt + 4\pi t^2 - 4\pi z^2$ $= \mathbf{4\pi t^2 + 8\pi zt}$	To find the difference between the two, subtract the original from the increased surface area.

2. A cube with volume 27 cubic meters is inscribed within a sphere such that all of the cube's vertices touch the sphere. What is the length of the sphere's radius?

Answer:

Since the cube's volume is 27, each side length is equal to $\sqrt[3]{27} = 3$. The long diagonal distance from one of the cube's vertices to its opposite vertex will provide the sphere's diameter:

$$d = \sqrt{3^2 + 3^2 + 3^2} = \sqrt{27} = 5.2$$

Half of this length is the radius, which is **2.6 meters**.

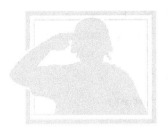

2

READING COMPREHENSION

The Reading Skills test includes short reading passages followed by questions about those passages. The paper test will have 20 questions, and the computer adaptive test will have between 20 and 30 questions. The passages will cover simple, easy-to-understand topics, and no outside knowledge will be needed to answer the questions. The sections below will introduce the types of questions that are included on the test and explain how to answer them.

THE MAIN IDEA

The **MAIN IDEA** of a text describes the author's main topic and general concept; it also generalizes the author's point of view about a subject. It is contained within and throughout the text. The reader can easily find the main idea by considering how the main topic is addressed throughout a passage. In the reading test, the expectation is not only to identify the main idea but also to differentiate it from a text's theme and to summarize the main idea clearly and concisely.

The main idea is closely connected to topic sentences and how they are supported in a text. Questions may deal with finding topic sentences, summarizing a text's ideas, or locating supporting details. The sections and practice examples that follow detail the distinctions between these aspects of text.

Identifying the Main Idea

To identify the main idea, first identify the topic. The difference between these two things is simple: the **TOPIC** is the overall subject matter of a passage; the main idea is what the author wants to say about that topic. The main idea covers the author's direct perspective about a topic, as distinct from the **THEME**, which is a generally true idea that the reader might derive from a text. Most of the time, fiction has a theme, whereas nonfiction has a main idea. This is the case because in a nonfiction text, the author speaks more directly

The author's perspective on the subject of the text and how he or she has framed the argument or story hints at the main idea. For example, if the author framed the story with a description, image, or short anecdote, this suggests a particular idea or point of view.

to the audience about a topic—his or her perspective is more visible. For example, the following passage conveys the topic as well as what the author wants to communicate about that topic.

The "shark mania" of recent years can be largely pinned on the sensationalistic media surrounding the animals: from the release of *Jaws* in 1975 to the week of ultra-hyped shark feeding frenzies and "worst shark attacks" countdowns known as Shark Week, popular culture both demonizes and fetishizes sharks until the public cannot get enough. Swimmers and beachgoers may look nervously for the telltale fin skimming the surface, but the reality is that shark bites are extremely rare and they are almost never unprovoked. Sharks attack people at very predictable times and for very predictable reasons. Rough surf, poor visibility, or a swimmer sending visual and physical signals that mimic a shark's normal prey are just a few examples.

Of course, some places are just more dangerous to swim. Shark attack "hot spots," such as the coasts of Florida, South Africa, and New Zealand try a variety of solutions to protect tourists and surfers. Some beaches employ "shark nets," meant to keep sharks away from the beach, though these are controversial because they frequently trap other forms of marine life as well. Other beaches use spotters in helicopters and boats to alert beach officials when there are sharks in the area. In addition, there is an array of products that claim to offer personal protection from sharks, ranging from wetsuits in different colors to devices that broadcast electrical signals in an attempt to confuse the sharks' sensory organs. At the end of the day, though, beaches like these remain dangerous, and swimmers must assume the risk every time they paddle out from shore.

The author of this passage has a clear topic: sharks and the relationship between humans and sharks. In order to identify the main idea of the passage, the reader must ask what the author wants to say about this topic, what the reader is meant to think or understand. The author makes sure to provide information about several different aspects of the relationship between sharks and humans, and points out that humans must respect sharks as dangerous marine animals, without sensationalizing the risk of attack. This conclusion results from looking at the various pieces of information the author includes as well as the similarities between them. The passage describes sensationalistic media, then talks about how officials and governments try to protect beaches, and ends with the observation that people must take personal responsibility. These details clarify what the author's main idea is. Summarizing that main idea by focusing on the connection between the different details helps the reader draw a conclusion.

Readers should identify the topic of a text and pay attention to how the details about it relate to one another. A passage may discuss, for example, topic similarities, characteristics, causes, and/ or effects.

Examples

The art of the twentieth and twenty-first centuries demonstrates several aspects of modern societal advancement. A primary example is the advent and ascendancy of technology: New technologies have developed new avenues for art making, and the globalization brought about by the Internet has both diversified the art world and brought it together simultaneously. Even as artists are able to engage in a global conversation about the categories and characteristics of art, creating a more uniform understanding, they can now express themselves in a diversity of ways for a diversity of audiences. The result has been a rapid change in how art is made and consumed.

1. This passage is primarily concerned with

   (A) the importance of art in the twenty-first century.

   (B) the use of art to communicate overarching ideals to diverse communities.

   (C) the importance of technology to art criticism.

   (D) the change in understanding and creation of art in the modern period.

   (E) artists' desires to diversify the media with which art is created.

   Answers:

   (A) is incorrect. The focus of the passage is what the art of the twentieth and twenty-first centuries demonstrates.

   (B) is incorrect. Although the passage mentions a diversity of audiences, it discusses the artists expressing themselves, not attempting to communicate overarching ideals.

   (C) is incorrect. The passage discusses how new technologies have "developed new avenues for art making," but nothing about criticism.

   (D) is correct. The art of the modern period reflects the new technologies and globalization possible through the Internet.

   (E) is incorrect. The passage mentions the diversity of ways artists express themselves, not the media specifically.

2. Which of the following best describes the main idea of the passage?

   (A) Modern advances in technology have diversified art making and connected artists to distant places and ideas.

   (B) Diversity in modern art is making it harder for art viewers to understand and talk about that art.

   (C) The use of technology to discuss art allows us to create standards for what art should be.

   (D) Art making before the invention of technology such as the Internet was disorganized and poorly understood.

   (E) Art making in the twenty-first century is dependent on the use of technology in order to meet current standards.

   Answers:

   (A) is correct. According to the text, technology and the Internet have "diversified the art world and brought it together simultaneously."

   (B) is incorrect. The passage explains that the global conversation about art has created a more uniform understanding.

   (C) is incorrect. The passage indicates that artists now engage in a global conversation about art, but this is one detail in the passage. The main idea of the passage concerns the advances in art in the twentieth and twenty-first centuries.

   (D) is incorrect. The invention of technology and the Internet have diversified art; however, that does not mean it was disorganized previously.

   (E) is incorrect. Technology is a means to an end; art is not dependent on it.

Topic and Summary Sentences

Identifying the main idea requires understanding the structure of a piece of writing. In a short passage of one or two paragraphs, the topic and summary sentences quickly relate what the paragraphs are about and what conclusions the author wants the reader to draw. These sentences function as bookends to a paragraph or passage, telling readers what to think and keeping the passage tied tightly together.

Generally, the TOPIC SENTENCE is the first, or very near the first, sentence in a paragraph. It is a general statement that introduces the topic, clearly and specifically directing the reader to access any previous experience with that topic.

A **summary** is a very brief restatement of the most important parts of an argument or text. Building a summary begins with the most important idea in a text. A longer summary also includes supporting details. The text of a summary should be much shorter than the original.

The SUMMARY SENTENCE, on the other hand, frequently—but not always!—comes at the end of a paragraph or passage, because it wraps up all the ideas presented. This sentence provides an understanding of what the author wants to say about the topic and what conclusions to draw about it. While a topic sentence acts as an introduction to a topic, allowing the reader to activate his or her own ideas and experiences, the summary statement asks the reader to accept the author's ideas about that topic. Because of this, a summary sentence helps the reader quickly identify a piece's main idea.

Examples

Altogether, Egypt is a land of tranquil monotony. The eye commonly travels either over a waste of waters, or over a green plain unbroken by elevations. The hills which inclose (*sic*) the Nile valley have level tops, and sides that are bare of trees, or shrubs, or flowers, or even mosses. The sky is generally cloudless. No fog or mist enwraps the distance in mystery; no rainstorm sweeps across the scene; no rainbow spans the empyrean; no shadows chase each other over the landscape. There is an entire absence of picturesque scenery. A single broad river, unbroken within the limits of Egypt even by a rapid, two flat strips of green plain at its side, two low lines of straight-topped hills beyond them, and a boundless open space where the river divides itself into half a dozen sluggish branches before reaching the sea, constitute Egypt, which is by nature a southern Holland—"weary, stale, flat and unprofitable."

—from *Ancient Egypt* by George Rawlinson

1. Which of the following best explains the general idea and focus indicated by the topic sentence?

   (A) Egypt is a boring place without much to do.

   (B) The land of Egypt is undisturbed; the reader will read on to find out what makes it so dull.

   (C) Egypt is a peaceful place; its people live with a sense of predictability.

   (D) The land of Egypt is quiet; the reader wants to know what is missing.

   (E) The reader is curious about how people survive in an area of worn-out uniformity.

Answers:

(A) is incorrect. The word *monotony* does suggest the idea of being bored; however, the focus is the land of Egypt, not what people have to do. In addition, tranquility is part of the general idea.

(B) is correct. This option indicates both the main idea and what the reader will focus on while reading.

(C) is incorrect. This option leaves out what the focus will be.

(D) is incorrect. This option leaves out the general idea of monotony.

(E) is incorrect. This option is inaccurate; the topic sentence does not suggest anything about survival.

2. Which of the following best states what the author wants the reader to understand after reading the summary sentence?

   (A) There is not much to get excited about while visiting Egypt.

   (B) Egypt is a poverty-stricken wasteland.

   (C) The land of Egypt is worn out from overuse.

   (D) The land of Egypt is quiet, but not worth visiting.

   (E) The land of Egypt lacks anything fresh or inspiring.

   Answers:

   (A) is incorrect. The summary describes the place, not a visit to the place.

   (B) is incorrect. The word *unprofitable* suggests that the land of Egypt is unrewarding, not poverty stricken.

   (C) is incorrect. The reason the land is stale and weary may not be due to overuse. This summary describes; it does not explain the reasons the land is worn.

   (D) is incorrect. The first part of the sentence is correct, but the summary sentence does not indicate that Egypt is not worth visiting.

   (E) is correct. The words *weary*, *stale*, and *unprofitable* suggest a lack of freshness or anything that stimulates enthusiasm.

SUPPORTING DETAILS

Between a topic sentence and a summary sentence, the rest of a paragraph is built with SUPPORTING DETAILS. Supporting details come in many forms; the purpose of the passage dictates the type of details that will support the main idea. A persuasive passage may use facts and data or detail specific reasons for the author's opinion. An informative passage will primarily use facts about the topic to support the main idea. Even a narrative passage will have supporting details—specific things the author says to develop the story and characters.

The most important aspect of supporting details is exactly what the term states: They support the main idea. Examining the various supporting details and how they work with one another will solidify how the author views a topic and what the main idea of the passage is. Supporting details are key to understanding a passage.

Identifying Supporting Details

How can the reader identify the most important pieces of information in a passage? Supporting details build an argument and contain the concepts upon which the main idea rests. While supporting details will help the reader determine the main idea, it is actually easier to find the most important supporting details by first understanding the main idea; the pieces that make up the main argument then become clear.

SIGNAL WORDS—transitions and conjunctions—explain to the reader how one sentence or idea is connected to another. These words and phrases can be anywhere in a sentence, and it is important to understand what each signal word means. Signal words can add information, provide counterarguments, create organization in a passage, or draw conclusions. Some common signal words include *in particular*, *in addition*, *besides*, *contrastingly*, *therefore*, and *because*.

Examples

The war is inevitable—and let it come! I repeat it, sir, let it come! It is in vain, sir, to extenuate the matter. Gentlemen may cry, "Peace! Peace!"—but there is no peace. The war is actually begun! The next gale that sweeps from the north will bring to our ears the clash of resounding arms! Our brethren are already in the field! Why stand we here idle? What is it that gentlemen wish? What would they have? Is life so dear, or peace so sweet, as to be purchased at the price of chains and slavery? Forbid it, Almighty God! I know not what course others may take; but as for me, give me liberty or give me death!

—from "Give Me Liberty or Give Me Death"
speech by Patrick Henry

1. In the fourth sentence of the text, the word *but* signals

(A) an example.

(B) a consequence.

(C) an exception.

(D) a counterargument.

(E) a reason

Answers:

(A) is incorrect. The author includes an example that the war has begun when he says "Our brethren are already in the field!" The word *but* does not signal this example.

(B) is incorrect. The phrase "but there is no peace" is a fact, not a consequence.

(C) is incorrect. In order to be an exception, the word *but* would have to be preceded by a general point or observation. In this case, *but* is preceded by a demand for peace.

(D) is correct. The argument or claim that the country should be at peace precedes the word *but*. *But* counters the demand for peace with the argument that there is no peace; the war has begun.

(E) is incorrect. *But* does not introduce a reason in this text; it introduces a contradictory point.

2. What argument does the author use to support his main point?

(A) Life in slavery is not the goal of the country.

(B) To die bravely is worthwhile.

(C) Life without freedom is intolerable.

(D) The cost of going to war is too great.

(E) People cannot live in peace without going to war.

Answers:

(A) is incorrect. The main point is that the country has to go to war with England to be free. The author does not support his point with a discussion of the goals of the country.

(B) is incorrect. This does not relate to the main point of going to war.

(C) is correct. The author indicates that life is not so dear, nor peace so sweet, "as to be purchased at the price of chains and slavery."

(D) is incorrect. This is inaccurate. The author insists that the cost of not fighting for freedom is too great.

(E) is incorrect. Those who opposed going to war believed that Americans could find a way to live peacefully, without a war; the author's main point is the opposite.

Evaluating Supporting Details

Besides using supporting details to help understand a main idea, the reader must evaluate them for relevance and consistency. An author selects details to help organize a passage and support its main idea. Sometimes, the author's bias results in details left out that don't directly support the main idea or that support an opposite idea. The reader has to be able to notice not only what the author says but also what the author leaves out.

To understand how a supporting detail relates to the main idea, the purpose of the passage should be discerned: what the author is trying to communicate and what the author wants from the reader. Every passage has a specific goal, and each paragraph in a passage is meant to support that goal. For each supporting detail, the position in the text, the signal words, and the specific content work together to alert the reader to the relationship between the supporting ideas and the main idea.

Close reading involves noticing the striking features of a text. For example, does a point made in the text appeal to the reader's sense of justice? Does a description seem rather exaggerated or overstated? Do certain words—such as *agonizing*—seem emotive? Are rhetorical questions being used to lead the reader to a certain conclusion?

Though the author generally includes details that support the text's main idea, the reader must decide how those details relate to one another as well as find any gaps in the support of the author's argument. This is particularly important in a persuasive piece of writing, when an author may allow bias to show through. Discovering the author's bias and how the supporting details reveal that bias is also key to understanding a text.

Examples

In England in the 'fifties came the Crimean War, with the deep stirring of national feeling which accompanied it, and the passion of gratitude and admiration which was poured forth on Miss Florence Nightingale for her work on behalf of our wounded soldiers. It was universally felt that there was work for women, even in war—the work of cleansing, setting in order, breaking down red tape, and soothing the vast sum of human suffering which every war is bound to cause. Miss Nightingale's work in war was work that never had been done until women came forward to do it, and her message to her countrywomen was educate yourselves, prepare, make ready; never imagine that your task can be done by instinct, without training and preparation. Painstaking study, she insisted, was just as necessary as a preparation for women's work as for men's work; and she bestowed the whole of the monetary gift offered her by the gratitude of the nation to form training-schools for nurses at St. Thomas's and King's College Hospitals.

—from *Women's Suffrage: A Short History of a Great Movement*
by Millicent Garrett Fawcett

1. Which of the following best states the bias of the passage?

   (A) Society underestimates the capacity of women.

   (B) Generally, women are not prepared to make substantial contributions to society.

   (C) If women want power, they need to prove themselves.

   (D) One strong woman cannot represent all women.

   (E) The strength of women is their ability to take care of others.

   Answers:

   (A) is correct. The author is suggesting that the work Florence Nightingale did had not been done before women came forward. Up till that point, what a woman could do had not been recognized.

   (B) is incorrect. This fact may have been true at the time this text was written, but only because educational opportunities were not available to women, and women were not encouraged to develop their abilities. Including this fact reveals the bias that women should be granted opportunities to train and to contribute.

   (C) is incorrect. This option does not apply; Florence Nightingale did more than prove herself.

   (D) is incorrect. The fact that Florence Nightingale donated the money awarded her to the training of women indicates that other women were preparing themselves to contribute.

   (E) is incorrect. This may or may not be true. It does not matter what kind of strength women have; the bias is that the strength of women wasn't really known.

2. Which of the following best summarizes what the author left out of the passage?

   (A) Women can fight in wars.

   (B) Other women should be recognized.

   (C) Women need to stop wasting time giving speeches at conventions and start proving themselves.

   (D) Without the contributions of women, society suffers.

   (E) Women are the ones who get the important work done.

   Answers:

   (A) is incorrect. "It was universally felt that there was work for women, even in war" suggests that women had much to offer and didn't need to be sheltered; however, "there was work" does not mean the author thought women should engage in combat.

   (B) is incorrect. Since the passage is specifically about Florence Nightingale, nothing in it suggests the author included information about what other women did.

   (C) is incorrect. Information about women's suffrage conventions is unrelated to the topic of the paragraph.

(D) is correct. The author emphasizes that "Miss Nightingale's work in war was work that never had been done until women came forward to do it."

(E) is incorrect. The author shows the importance of Miss Nightingale's work, but that does not suggest it was the only important work being done.

Facts and Opinions

Authors use both facts and opinions as supporting details. While it is usually a simple task to identify the two, authors may mix facts with opinions or state an opinion as if it were a fact. The difference between the two is simple: A FACT is a piece of information that can be verified as true or false, and it retains the quality of truthfulness or falsity no matter who verifies it. An OPINION reflects a belief held by the author and may or may not be something each reader agrees with.

 To distinguish between fact and opinion, the reader should rely on what can be proven. Subjectivity is determined by asking if an observation varies according to the situation or the person observing.

Examples

I remember thinking how comfortable it was, this division of labor which made it unnecessary for me to study fogs, winds, tides, and navigation, in order to visit my friend who lived across an arm of the sea. It was good that men should be specialists, I mused. The peculiar knowledge of the pilot and captain sufficed for many thousands of people who knew no more of the sea and navigation than I knew. On the other hand, instead of having to devote my energy to the learning of a multitude of things, I concentrated it upon a few particular things, such as, for instance, the analysis of Poe's place in American literature—an essay of mine, by the way, in the current *Atlantic*. Coming aboard, as I passed through the cabin, I had noticed with greedy eyes a stout gentleman reading the *Atlantic*, which was open at my very essay. And there it was again, the division of labor, the special knowledge of the pilot and captain which permitted the stout gentleman to read my special knowledge on Poe while they carried him safely from Sausalito to San Francisco.

—from *The Sea-Wolf* by Jack London

1. Which of the following best summarizes an opinion stated by the narrator?

   (A) Poe has a place in American literature.

   (B) People have the time to read magazines like the *Atlantic* because there are other people to take care of other tasks.

   (C) The narrator has no knowledge of the sea and navigation.

   (D) Having specialized knowledge sets people apart and makes them superior.

   (E) Division of labor is a beneficial practice.

Answers:

(A) is incorrect. This is a fact. The *significance* of Poe's place in American literature is an opinion.

(B) is incorrect. This is a fact. The reader is expected to agree with the point that if someone else had not been managing the boat, the people who wanted to get across the water would have had to do the work of getting themselves across.

(C) is incorrect. This is a fact. The narrator admits to "this division of labor which made it unnecessary for me to study fogs, winds, tides, and navigation."

(D) is incorrect. Although the narrator acknowledges that specialized knowledge exists, he does not indicate that he believes it creates superiority.

(E) is correct. The narrator provides several facts proving that he and the other passengers benefit from the specialized knowledge and labor of others.

2. Which of the following is an opinion expressed by the narrator that is NOT supported by facts within the passage?

   (A) People should live life focusing on and learning about only a few things.

   (B) Having general knowledge is good.

   (C) He has time to focus on writing about literature.

   (D) People depend on other people.

   (E) People can experience more freedom by depending on others.

Answers:

(A) is correct. When the narrator says "instead of having to devote my energy to the learning of a multitude of things, I concentrated it upon a few particular things," he conveys his view that he does not have to learn much. There are no facts to support the view that he has to learn only a few particular things in life.

(B) is incorrect. The narrator does not express this opinion. He is speaking about specialized knowledge.

(C) is incorrect. This is a fact that the narrator shares about his life.

(D) is incorrect. The passage does offer facts to support this; both the narrator and the passenger reading depend on the pilot to navigate the boat safely.

(E) is incorrect. This opinion is supported by the fact that the passenger has the freedom to sit back and read, and the narrator has the freedom to watch him read, while they both depend on the pilot.

TEXT STRUCTURE

The structure of a text determines how the reader understands the argument and how the various details interact to form the argument. There are many ways to arrange text, and various types of arrangements have distinct characteristics.

The organizing structure of a passage is defined by the order in which the author presents information and the transitions used to connect those pieces. Problem-and-solution and cause-and-effect structures use transitions that show causal relationships: *because, as a result, consequently, therefore*. These two types of structures may also use transitions that show contradiction. A problem-and-solution structure may provide alternative solutions; a cause-and-effect structure may explain alternative causes: *however, alternatively, although*.

 Authors often use repetition to reinforce an idea, including repeated words, phrases, or images.

Specific text structures include not only problem and solution and cause and effect, but also compare and contrast, descriptive, order of importance, and chronological. When analyzing a text, the reader should consider how text structure influences the author's meaning. Most important, the reader needs to be aware of how an author emphasizes an idea by the way he or she presents information. For instance, including a contrasting idea makes a central idea stand out, and including a series of concrete examples creates a force of facts to support an argument.

Examples

It was the green heart of the canyon, where the walls swerved back from the rigid plan and relieved their harshness of line by making a little sheltered nook and filling it to the brim with sweetness and roundness and softness. Here all things rested. Even the narrow stream ceased its turbulent down-rush long enough to form a quiet pool.... On one side, beginning at the very lip of the pool, was a tiny meadow, a cool, resilient surface of green that extended to the base of the frowning wall. Beyond the pool a gentle slope of earth ran up and up to meet the opposing wall. Fine grass covered the slope—grass that was spangled with flowers, with here and there patches of color, orange and purple and golden. Below, the canyon was shut in. There was no view. The walls leaned together abruptly and the canyon ended in a chaos of rocks, moss-covered and hidden by a green screen of vines and creepers and boughs of trees. Up the canyon rose far hills and peaks, the big foothills, pine-covered and remote. And far beyond, like clouds upon the border of the slay, towered minarets of white, where the Sierra's eternal snows flashed austerely the blazes of the sun.

—from "All Gold Canyon" by Jack London

1. The organizational structure of the passage is

   (A) order of importance.

   (B) cause and effect.

   (C) problem and solution.

   (D) descriptive.

   (E) chronological.

Answers:

(A) is incorrect. A series of reasons is not presented from most to least or least to most important. The passage describes a restful nook in the canyon.

(B) is incorrect. The passage does not explain the origin of this nook or its effect on anything, although the reader understands from the details what makes the nook so restful.

(C) is incorrect. The description of the nook presents no problem, although time in the nook could be seen as a solution for many problems.

(D) is correct. The description of the nook begins with a general impression, moves from one side, to the area beyond the pool, to below the heart of the canyon, and finally to what is above the canyon.

(E) is incorrect. The description does not include a sequence of events in time.

2. How does the text structure emphasize the central idea of the passage?

   (A) The logical reasons for needing to rest while hiking make the author's argument compelling.

   (B) By explaining the activities within the canyon, the author convinces the reader that the canyon is safe.

   (C) By describing the areas to the side, below, and above the canyon, the author is able to emphasize the softness at the heart of the canyon.

   (D) The concrete examples included in the passage demonstrate the author's view that beauty is found in nature.

   (E) The sensory details of the description make it easy for the reader to visualize and enjoy.

Answers:

(A) is incorrect. The passage does not indicate anything about a hike, although the valley is described as a restful place.

(B) is incorrect. The heart of the canyon is still, without activity; even the water stops rushing and forms a pool.

(C) is correct. The little restful nook is surrounded by the wall of the mountain, a "chaos of rocks," "boughs of trees," "far hills and peaks."

(D) is incorrect. The central idea of the passage is not finding beauty in nature but simply the restfulness of this nook.

(E) is incorrect. The passage does include sensory detail that's easy to visualize; however, this option does not indicate how the detail relates to the central idea.

DRAWING CONCLUSIONS

Reading text begins with making sense of the explicit meanings of information or a narrative. Understanding occurs as the reader draws conclusions and makes logical inferences. To draw a conclusion, the reader considers the details or facts. He or she then comes to a conclusion—the next logical point in the thought sequence. For example, in a Hemingway story, an old man sits alone in a café. A young waiter says that the café is closing, but the old man continues to drink. The waiter starts closing up, and the old man signals for a refill. Based on these details, the reader might conclude that the old man has not understood the young waiter's desire for him to leave.

When considering a character's motivations, the reader should ask what the character wants to achieve, what the character will get by accomplishing this, and what the character seems to value the most.

An inference is distinguished from a conclusion drawn. An **INFERENCE** is an assumption the reader makes based on details in the text as well as his or her own knowledge. It is more of an educated guess that extends the literal meaning. Inferences begin with the given details; however, the reader uses the facts to determine additional facts. What the reader already knows informs what is being suggested by the details of decisions or situations in the text. Returning to the example of the Hemingway story, the reader might infer that the old man is lonely, enjoys being in the café, and is reluctant to leave.

When reading fictional text, inferring character motivations is essential. The actions of the characters move the plot forward; a series of events is understood by making sense of why the characters did what they did. Hemingway includes contrasting details as the young waiter and an older waiter discuss the old man. The older waiter sympathizes with the old man; both men have no one at home and experience a sense of emptiness in life, which motivates them to seek the café.

Conclusions are drawn by thinking about how the author wants the reader to feel. A group of carefully selected facts can cause the reader to feel a certain way.

Another aspect of understanding text is connecting it to other texts. Readers may connect the Hemingway story about the old man in the café to other Hemingway stories about individuals struggling to deal with loss and loneliness in a dignified way. They can extend their initial connections to people they know or their personal experiences. When readers read a persuasive text, they often connect the arguments made to counterarguments and opposing evidence of which they are aware. They use these connections to infer meaning.

Examples

I believe it is difficult for those who publish their own memoirs to escape the imputation of vanity; nor is this the only disadvantage under which they labor: it is also their misfortune, that what is uncommon is rarely, if ever, believed, and what is obvious we are apt to turn from with disgust, and to charge the writer with impertinence. People generally think those memoirs only worthy to be read or remembered which abound in great or striking events, those, in short, which in a high degree excite either admiration or pity: all others they consign to contempt and oblivion. It is therefore, I confess, not a little hazardous in a private and obscure individual, and a stranger too, thus to solicit the indulgent attention of the public; especially when I own I offer here the history of neither a saint, a hero, nor a tyrant. I believe there are few events in my life, which have not happened to many: it is true the incidents of it are numerous; and, did I consider myself an European, I might say my sufferings were great: but when I compare my lot with that of most of my countrymen, I regard myself as a *particular favorite of Heaven*, and acknowledge the mercies of Providence in every occurrence of my life. If then the following narrative does not appear sufficiently interesting to engage general attention, let my motive be some excuse for its publication. I am not so foolishly vain as to expect from it either immortality or literary reputation. If it affords any satisfaction to my numerous friends, at whose request it has been written, or in the smallest degree promotes the interests of humanity, the ends for which it was undertaken will be fully attained, and every wish of my heart gratified. Let it therefore be remembered, that, in wishing to avoid censure, I do not aspire to praise.

—from *The Interesting Narrative of the Life of Olaudah Equiano, or Gustavus Vassa, The African* by Olaudah Equiano

1. Which of the following best explains the primary motivation of the narrator?

    (A) He wants his audience to know that he is not telling his story out of vanity.

    (B) He is hoping people will praise his courage.

    (C) He wants to give credit to God for protecting him.

    (D) He is honoring the wishes of his friends.

    (E) He is not seeking personal notoriety; he is hoping people will be influenced by his story and the human condition will improve.

    Answers:

    (A) is incorrect. That motive is how the passage begins, but it is not his primary motive.

    (B) is incorrect. He says he does not aspire to praise, and he does not suggest that he was courageous.

    (C) is incorrect. He does state that the "mercies of Providence" were always with him; however, that acknowledgement is not his primary motive.

    (D) is incorrect. Although he says that he wrote it at the request of friends, the story is meant to improve humanity.

    (E) is correct. In the passage "If it…in the smallest degree promotes the interests of humanity, the ends for which it was undertaken will be fully attained, and every wish of my heart gratified," the narrator's use of the word *humanity* could mean he wants to improve the human condition or he wants to increase human benevolence, or brotherly love.

2. Given the details of what the narrator says he is *not*, as well as what he claims his story is *not*, it can be inferred that his experience was

(A) a story that could lead to his success.

(B) an amazing story of survival and struggle that will be unfamiliar to many readers.

(C) an adventure that will thrill the audience.

(D) a narrow escape from suffering.

(E) an interesting story that is worthy of publication.

Answers:

(A) is incorrect. The narrator says that what is obvious in his story is what people "are apt to turn from with disgust, and to charge the writer with impertinence." The narrator is telling a story that his audience couldn't disagree with and might consider rude.

(B) is correct. By saying "what is uncommon is rarely, if ever, believed, and what is obvious we are apt to turn from with disgust," the narrator suggests that his experience wasn't common or ordinary and could cause disgust.

(C) is incorrect. The reader can infer that the experience was horrific; it will inspire disgust, not excitement.

(D) is incorrect. The narrator admits he suffered; he indicates that he narrowly escaped death. This is not an inference.

(E) is incorrect. By saying "If then the following narrative does not appear sufficiently interesting to engage general attention, let my motive be some excuse for its publication," the narrator makes clear that he does not think his narrative is interesting, but he believes his motive to help humanity makes it worthy of publication.

UNDERSTANDING THE AUTHOR

Many questions on the Reading Comprehension test will ask for an interpretation of an author's intentions and ideas. This requires an examination of the author's perspective and purpose as well as the way the author uses language to communicate these things.

In every passage, an author chooses words, structures, and content with specific purpose and intent. With this in mind, the reader can begin to comprehend why an author opts for particular words and structures and how these ultimately relate to the content.

The Author's Purpose

The author of a passage sets out with a specific goal in mind: to communicate a particular idea to an audience. The **AUTHOR'S PURPOSE** is determined by asking why the author wants the reader to understand the passage's main idea. There are four basic purposes to which an author can write: narrative, expository, technical, and persuasive. Within each of these general purposes, the author may direct the audience to take a clear action or respond in a certain way.

The purpose for which an author writes a passage is also connected to the structure of that text. In a **NARRATIVE**, the author seeks to tell a story, often to illustrate a theme or idea the reader needs to consider. In a narrative, the author uses characteristics of storytelling, such as chronological order, characters, and a defined setting, and these characteristics communicate the author's theme or main idea.

In an **EXPOSITORY** passage, on the other hand, the author simply seeks to explain an idea or topic to the reader. The main idea will probably be a factual statement or a direct assertion of a broadly held opinion. Expository writing can come in many forms, but one essential feature is a fair and balanced representation of a topic. The author may explore one detailed aspect or a broad range of characteristics, but he or she mainly seeks to prompt a decision from the reader.

Similarly, in **TECHNICAL** writing, the author's purpose is to explain specific processes, techniques, or equipment in order for the reader to use that process or equipment to obtain a desired result. Writing like this employs chronological or spatial structures, specialized vocabulary, and imperative or directive language.

In **PERSUASIVE** writing, though the reader is free to make decisions about the message and content, the author actively seeks to convince him or her to accept an opinion or belief. Much like expository writing, persuasive writing is presented in many organizational forms, but the author will use specific techniques, or **RHETORICAL STRATEGIES**, to build an argument. Readers can identify these strategies in order to clearly understand what an author wants them to believe, how the author's perspective and purpose may lead to bias, and whether the passage includes any logical fallacies.

Reading persuasive text requires an awareness of what the author believes about the topic.

Common rhetorical strategies include the appeals to ethos, logos, and pathos. An author uses these to build trust with the reader, explain the logical points of his or her argument, and convince the reader that his or her opinion is the best option.

An **ETHOS—ETHICAL—APPEAL** uses balanced, fair language and seeks to build a trusting relationship between the author and the reader. An author might explain his or her credentials, include the reader in an argument, or offer concessions to an opposing argument.

A **LOGOS—LOGICAL—APPEAL** builds on that trust by providing facts and support for the author's opinion, explaining the argument with clear connections and reasoning. At this point, the reader should beware of logical fallacies that connect unconnected ideas and build arguments on incorrect premises. With a logical appeal, an author strives to convince the reader to accept an opinion or belief by demonstrating that not only is it the most logical option but it also satisfies his or her emotional reaction to a topic.

Readers should consider how different audiences will react to a text. For example, how a slave owner's reactions to the narrative of Olaudah Equiano (on page 55) will differ from a slave trader's.

A **PATHOS—EMOTIONAL—APPEAL** does not depend on reasonable connections between ideas; rather, it seeks to remind the reader, through imagery, strong language, and personal connections, that the author's argument aligns with his or her best interests.

Many persuasive passages seek to use all three rhetorical strategies to best appeal to the reader.

Clues will help the reader determine many things about a passage, from the author's purpose to the passage's main idea, but understanding an author's purpose is essential to fully understanding the text.

Examples

Evident truth. Made so plain by our good Father in Heaven, that all *feel* and *understand* it, even down to brutes and creeping insects. The ant, who has toiled and dragged a crumb to his nest, will furiously defend the fruit of his labor, against whatever robber assails him. So plain, that the most dumb and stupid slave that ever toiled for a master, does constantly *know* that he is wronged. So plain that no one, high or low, ever does mistake it, except in a plainly *selfish* way; for although volume upon volume is written to prove slavery a very good thing, we never hear of the man who wishes to take the good of it, *by being a slave himself*.

Most governments have been based, practically, on the denial of the equal rights of men, as I have, in part, stated them; *ours* began, by *affirming* those rights. *They* said, some men are too *ignorant*, and *vicious*, to share in government. Possibly so, said we; and, by your system, you would always keep them ignorant and vicious. We proposed to give *all* a chance; and we expected the weak to grow stronger, the ignorant, wiser; and all better, and happier together.

We made the experiment; and the fruit is before us. Look at it. Think of it. Look at it, in its aggregate grandeur, of extent of country, and numbers of population, of ship, and steamboat.

—from Abraham Lincoln's speech fragment on slavery

1. The author's purpose is to
   (A) explain ideas.
   (B) narrate a story.
   (C) describe a situation.
   (D) persuade to accept an idea.
   (E) define a problem.

   Answers:

   (A) is incorrect. The injustice of slavery in America is made clear, but only to convince the audience that slavery cannot exist in America.

   (B) is incorrect. The author briefly mentions the narrative of America in terms of affirming the equal rights of all people, but he does not tell a story or relate the events that led to slavery.

   (C) is incorrect. The author does not describe the conditions of slaves or the many ways their human rights are denied.

   (D) is correct. The author provides logical reasons and evidence that slavery is wrong, that it violates the American belief in equal rights.

   (E) is incorrect. Although the author begins with a short definition of evident truth, he is simply laying the foundation for his persuasive argument that slavery violates the evident truth Americans believe.

2. To achieve his purpose, the author primarily uses
   (A) concrete analogies.
   (B) logical reasoning.
   (C) emotional appeals.
   (D) images.
   (E) figurative language.

Answers:

(A) is incorrect. The author mentions the ant's willingness to defend what is his but does not make an explicit and corresponding conclusion about the slave; instead, he says, "So plain, that the most dumb and stupid slave that ever toiled for a master, does constantly *know* that he is wronged." The implied parallel is between the ant's conviction about being wronged and the slave knowing he is wronged.

(B) is correct. The author uses logic when he points out that people who claim slavery is good never wish "to take the good of it, *by being a slave*." The author also points out that the principle of our country is to give everyone, including the "ignorant," opportunity; then he challenges his listeners to look at the fruit of this principle, saying, "Look at it, in its aggregate grandeur, of extent of country, and numbers of population, of ship, and steamboat."

(C) is incorrect. The author relies on logic and evidence, and makes no emotional appeals about the suffering of slaves.

(D) is incorrect. The author does offer evidence of his point with an image of the grandeur of America, but his primary appeal is logic.

(E) is incorrect. Initially, the author uses hyperbole when he says, "Evident truth. Made so plain by our good Father in Heaven, that all *feel* and *understand it*, even down to brutes and creeping insects." However, the author's primary appeal is logos.

The Audience

The structure, purpose, main idea, and language of a text all converge on one target: the intended audience. An author makes decisions about every aspect of a piece of writing based on that audience, and readers can evaluate the writing through the lens of that audience. By considering the probable reactions of an intended audience, readers can determine many things: whether or not they are part of that intended audience; the author's purpose for using specific techniques or devices; the biases of the author and how they appear in the writing; and how the author uses rhetorical strategies. While readers evaluate each of these things separately, identifying and considering the intended audience adds depth to the understanding of a text and helps highlight details with more clarity.

When reading a persuasive text, students should maintain awareness of what the author believes about the topic.

Several aspects identify the text's intended audience. First, when the main idea of the passage is known, the reader considers who most likely cares about that idea, benefits from it, or needs to know about it. Many authors begin with the main idea and then determine the audience in part based on these concerns.

Then the reader considers language. The author tailors language to appeal to the intended audience, so the reader can narrow down a broad understanding of that audience. The figurative language John Steinbeck uses in his novel *The Grapes of Wrath* reveals the suffering of the migrant Americans who traveled to California to find work during the Great Depression of the 1930s. Steinbeck spoke concretely to the Americans who were discriminating against the migrants. Instead of finding work in the "land of milk and honey," migrants faced unbearable poverty and injustice. The metaphor that gives the novel its title is "and in the eyes of the people there is the failure; and in the eyes of the hungry there is a

A logical argument includes a claim, a reason that supports the claim, and an assumption that the reader makes based on accepted beliefs. All parts of the argument need to make sense to the reader, so authors often consider the beliefs of their audience as they construct their arguments.

growing wrath. In the souls of the people the grapes of wrath are filling and growing heavy, growing heavy for the vintage." Steinbeck, used the image of ripening grapes, familiar to those surrounded by vineyards, to condemn this harsh treatment, provide an education of the human heart, and inspire compassion in his audience. Readers who weren't directly involved in the exodus of people from Oklahoma to the West, could have little difficulty grasping the meaning of Steinbeck's language in the description: "66 is the path of a people in flight, refugees from dust and shrinking land, from the thunder of tractors and invasion, from the twisting winds that howl up out of Texas, from floods that bring no richness to the land and steal what little richness is there."

Examples

In the following text, consideration should be made for how an English political leader of 1729 might have reacted.

It is a melancholy object to those, who walk through this great town, or travel in the country, when they see the streets, the roads and cabin-doors crowded with beggars of the female sex, followed by three, four, or six children, all in rags, and importuning every passenger for an alms. These mothers instead of being able to work for their honest livelihood, are forced to employ all their time in strolling to beg sustenance for their helpless infants who, as they grow up, either turn thieves for want of work, or leave their dear native country, to fight for the Pretender in Spain, or sell themselves to the Barbados.

I shall now therefore humbly propose my own thoughts, which I hope will not be liable to the least objection.

I have been assured by a very knowing American of my acquaintance in London, that a young healthy child well nursed, is, at a year old, a most delicious nourishing and wholesome food, whether stewed, roasted, baked, or boiled; and I make no doubt that it will equally serve in a fricassee.

I do therefore humbly offer it to public consideration, that of the hundred and twenty thousand children, already computed, twenty thousand may be reserved for breed, whereof only one fourth part to be males; which is more than we allow to sheep, black cattle, or swine, and my reason is, that these children are seldom the fruits of marriage, a circumstance not much regarded by our savages, therefore, one male will be sufficient to serve four females. That the remaining hundred thousand may, at a year old, be offered in sale to the persons of quality and fortune, through the kingdom, always advising the mother to let them suck plentifully in the last month, so as to render them plump, and fat for a good table. A child will make two dishes at an entertainment for friends, and when the family dines alone, the fore or hind quarter will make a reasonable dish, and seasoned with a little pepper or salt, will be very good boiled on the fourth day, especially in winter.

—from *A Modest Proposal for Preventing the Children of Poor People in Ireland From Being a Burden on Their Parents or Country, and for Making Them Beneficial to the Public* By Jonathan Swift

1. Which of the following best states the central idea of the passage?

   (A) Irish mothers are not able to support their children.

   (B) The Irish people lived like savages.

   (C) The people of England are quality people of fortune.

   (D) The poverty of the Irish forces their children to become criminals.

   (E) The kingdom of England has exploited the weaker country of Ireland to the point that the Irish people cannot support their families.

Answers:

(A) is incorrect. This is a fact alluded to in the passage, not a central idea.

(B) is incorrect. Although the author does refer to the Irish as savages, the reader recognizes that the author is being outrageously satirical.

(C) is incorrect. The author does say "That the remaining hundred thousand may, at a year old, be offered in sale to the persons of quality and fortune, through the kingdom," referring to the English. However, this is not the central idea; the opposite is, given that this is satire.

(D) is incorrect. The author does mention children growing up to be thieves, but this is not the central idea.

(E) is correct. The author is hoping to use satire to shame England.

2. The author's use of phrases like "humbly propose," "liable to the least objection," "wholesome food" suggests which of the following purposes?

   (A) to inform people about the attitudes of the English

   (B) to use satire to reveal the inhumane treatment of the Irish by the English

   (C) to persuade people to survive by any means

   (D) to express his admiration of the Irish people

   (E) to narrate the struggles of the English people

Answers:

(A) is incorrect. The author's subject is the poverty of the Irish, and his audience is the English who are responsible for the suffering of the Irish.

(B) is correct. The intended meaning of a satire sharply contradicts the literal meaning. Swift's proposal is not humble; it is meant to humble the arrogant. He expects the audience to be horrified. The children would make the worst imaginable food.

(C) is incorrect. The author is not serious. His intent is to shock his English audience.

(D) is incorrect. The author is expressing sympathy for the Irish.

(E) is incorrect. It is the Irish people who are struggling.

Tone and Mood

Two important aspects of the communication between author and audience occur subtly. The TONE of a passage describes the author's attitude toward the topic, distinct from the MOOD, which is the pervasive feeling or atmosphere in a passage that provokes specific emotions in the reader. The distinction between these two aspects lies once again in the audience: the mood influences the reader's emotional state in response to the piece, while the tone establishes a relationship between the audience and the author. Does the author intend to instruct the audience? Is the author more experienced than the audience, or does he or she wish to convey a friendly or equal relationship? In each of these cases, the author uses a different tone to reflect the desired level of communication.

 To determine the author's tone, students should examine what overall feeling they are experiencing.

Primarily DICTION, or word choice, determines mood and tone in a passage. Many readers make the mistake of thinking about the ideas an author puts forth and using those alone to determine particularly tone; a much better practice is to separate specific words from the text and look for patterns in connotation and emotion. By considering categories of words used by the author, the reader can discover both the overall emotional atmosphere of a text and the attitude of the author toward the subject.

To decide the connotation of a word, the reader examines whether the word conveys a positive or negative association in the mind. Adjectives are often used to influence the feelings of the reader, such as in the phrase "an ambitious attempt to achieve."

Every word has not only a literal meaning but also a CONNOTATIVE MEANING, relying on the common emotions, associations, and experiences an audience might associate with that word. The following words are all synonyms: *dog, puppy, cur, mutt, canine, pet*. Two of these words—*dog* and *canine*—are neutral words, without strong associations or emotions. Two others—*pet* and *puppy*—have positive associations. The last two—*cur* and *mutt*—have negative associations. A passage that uses one pair of these words versus another pair activates the positive or negative reactions of the audience.

Examples

Day had broken cold and grey, exceedingly cold and grey, when the man turned aside from the main Yukon trail and climbed the high earth-bank, where a dim and little-travelled trail led eastward through the fat spruce timberland. It was a steep bank, and he paused for breath at the top, excusing the act to himself by looking at his watch. It was nine o'clock. There was no sun nor hint of sun, though there was not a cloud in the sky. It was a clear day, and yet there seemed an intangible *pall* over the face of things, a subtle gloom that made the day dark, and that was due to the absence of sun. This fact did not worry the man. He was used to the lack of sun. It had been days since he had seen the sun, and he knew that a few more days must pass before that cheerful orb, due south, would just peep above the sky-line and dip immediately from view.

—from "To Build a Fire" by Jack London

1. Which of the following best describes the mood of the passage?

   (A) exciting and adventurous

   (B) fierce and determined

   (C) bleak and forbidding

   (D) grim yet hopeful

   (E) intense yet filled with fear

Answers:

(A) is incorrect. The man is on some adventure as he turns off the main trail, but the context is one of gloom and darkness, not excitement.

(B) is incorrect. The cold, dark day is fierce, and the man may be determined; however, the overall mood of the entire passage is one of grim danger.

(C) is correct. The man is oblivious to the gloom and darkness of the day, which was "exceedingly cold and grey."

(D) is incorrect. The atmosphere is grim, and there is no indication the man is hopeful about anything. He is aware only of his breath and steps forward.

(E) is incorrect. The cold, grey scene of a lone man walking off the trail is intense, but "this fact did not worry the man."

2. The connotation of the words *intangible pall* is

(A) a death-like covering.

(B) a vague sense of familiarity.

(C) an intimation of communal strength.

(D) an understanding of the struggle ahead.

(E) a refreshing sense of possibility.

Answers:

(A) is correct. Within the context of the sentence "It was a clear day, and yet there seemed an intangible *pall* over the face of things, a subtle gloom that made the day dark," the words *gloom* and *dark* are suggestive of death; the words *over the face* suggest a covering.

(B) is incorrect. The word *intangible* can mean a vague sense, but there is nothing especially familiar about a clear day that is dark, with no sunlight.

(C) is incorrect. The word *intangible* suggests intimation; however, from the beginning, the author shows the man alone, and reports, "the man turned aside from the main Yukon trail."

(D) is incorrect. A struggle may be indicated by the darkness and gloom, but the man has no understanding of this possibility. The text refers to the darkness, saying, "This fact did not worry the man. He was used to the lack of sun."

(E) is incorrect. The man is hiking this trail for some possibility, but he is not refreshed; he is pausing to catch his "breath at the top, excusing the act to himself by looking at his watch."

VOCABULARY IN CONTEXT

Vocabulary in context questions ask about the meaning of specific words in the passage. The questions will ask which answer choice is most similar in meaning to the specified word, or which answer choice could be substituted for that word in the passage.

When confronted with unfamiliar words, the passage itself can help clarify their meaning. Often, identifying the tone or main idea of the passage can help eliminate answer choices. For example, if the tone of the passage is generally positive, try eliminating the answer choices with a negative connotation. Or, if the passage is about a particular occupation, rule out words unrelated to that topic.

Passages may also provide specific **CONTEXT CLUES** that can help determine the meaning of a word.

One type of context clue is a **DEFINITION**, or **DESCRIPTION**, **CLUE**. Sometimes, authors use a difficult word, then include *that is* or *which is* to signal that they are providing a definition. An author also may provide a synonym or restate the idea in more familiar words:

> *Teachers often prefer teaching students with intrinsic motivation; these students have an internal desire to learn.*

The meaning of *intrinsic* is restated as an *internal desire*.

Similarly, authors may include an **EXAMPLE CLUE**, providing an example phrase that clarifies the meaning of the word:

Teachers may view extrinsic rewards as efficacious; however, an individual student may not be interested in what the teacher offers. For example, a student who is diabetic may not feel any incentive to work when offered a sweet treat.

Efficacious is explained with an example that demonstrates how an extrinsic reward may not be effective.

Another commonly used context clue is the CONTRAST, or ANTONYM, CLUE. In this case, authors indicate that the unfamiliar word is the opposite of a familiar word:

In contrast to intrinsic motivation, extrinsic motivation is contingent on teachers offering rewards that are appealing.

The phrase "in contrast" tells the reader that *extrinsic* is the opposite of *intrinsic*.

Examples

1. One challenge of teaching is finding ways to incentivize, or to motivate, learning.

   Which of the following is the meaning of *incentivize* as used in the sentence?

   (A) encourage

   (B) determine

   (C) challenge

   (D) improve

   (E) dissuade

   Answers:

   (A) is correct. The word *incentivize* is defined immediately with the synonym *motivate*, or *encourage*.

   (B) is incorrect. *Determine* is not a synonym for *motivate*. In addition, the phrase "to determine learning" does not make sense in the sentence.

   (C) is incorrect. *Challenge* is not a synonym for motivate.

   (D) is incorrect. *Improve* is closely related to motivation, but it is not the best synonym provided.

   (E) is incorrect. *Dissuade* is an antonym for motivate.

2. If an extrinsic reward is extremely desirable, a student may become so apprehensive he or she cannot focus. The student may experience such intense pressure to perform that the reward undermines its intent.

   Which of the following is the meaning of *apprehensive* as used in the sentence?

   (A) uncertain

   (B) distracted

   (C) anxious

   (D) forgetful

   (E) resentful

   Answers:

   (A) is incorrect. Nothing in the sentence suggests the student is uncertain.

   (B) is incorrect. *Distracted* is related to the clue "focus" but does not address the clue "pressure to perform."

(C) is correct. The reader can infer that the pressure to perform is making the student anxious.

(D) is incorrect. Nothing in the sentence suggests the student is forgetful.

(E) is incorrect. The clue describes the student as feeling pressured but does not suggest the student is resentful.

3

MECHANICAL COMPREHENSION

The Mechanical Comprehension section of the OAR tests candidates' understanding of the basic principles of physics and how those principles are applied to real-world situations. Topics include Newton's laws of motion, work and energy, and simple machines. The OAR includes approximately thirty mechanical comprehension questions to be answered in fifteen minutes.

FORCES

Newton's Laws

A fundamental concept of mechanics is **INERTIA**, which states that an object has a tendency to maintain its state of motion. An object at rest will stay at rest, and an object moving at constant velocity will continue to move at that velocity, unless something pushes or pulls on it. This push or pull is called a **FORCE**. The newton (N) is the SI unit for force (1 newton is 1 kg m/s²).

MASS is a fundamental property of matter and is a measure of the inertia of an object. The kilogram (kg) is the SI unit for mass. An object with a larger mass will resist a change in motion more than an object with a smaller mass will. For example, it is harder to throw an elephant than it is to throw a baseball (the elephant has much more mass than a baseball).

In 1687, Isaac Newton published three laws of motion that describe the behavior of force and mass. Newton's first law is also called the law of inertia. It states that an object will maintain its current state of motion unless acted on by an outside force.

Newton's second law is an equation:

$$F = ma$$

where F is the sum of the forces on an object (also called the net force), m is the mass of the object, and a is the acceleration. The law states that the net force on an object will lead

A **SYSTEM** is a collection of particles or objects that is isolated from its surroundings. All forces within a system are called internal forces, and forces outside the system are called external forces.

to an acceleration. Also, if an object has an acceleration, there must be a force that is causing it. Extending the previous example, if the same amount of force is applied to an elephant and a baseball, the baseball will have a much larger acceleration than the elephant (and so it is easier to throw).

An object in EQUILIBRIUM is either at rest or is moving at constant velocity; in other words, the object has no acceleration, or $a = 0$. Using Newton's second law, an object is in equilibrium if the net force on the object is 0, or $F = 0$ (this is called the equilibrium condition).

Newton's third law states that for every action (force), there will be an equal and opposite reaction (force). For instance, if a person is standing on the floor, there is a force of gravity pulling him toward the earth. However, he is not accelerating toward the earth; he is simply standing at rest on the floor (in equilibrium). So, the floor must provide a force that is equal in magnitude and in the opposite direction to the force of gravity.

> Newton's second law, $F = ma$, can be used to remember all three laws.
>
> If there is no outside force ($F = 0$), the object will not accelerate and thus will stay at rest or at a constant velocity (Newton's first law).
>
> If an object is resting on the floor, it is not moving, and $a = 0$. To maintain this equilibrium, the weight of the object must be matched by the force pushing up from the floor (Newton's third law).

Another example is a person kicking a wall. While it may seem like kicking a wall would only damage the wall, the force applied to the wall from the person's foot is identical to the force applied to the person's foot from the wall.

Examples

1. When a car moving forward stops abruptly, which of the following describes what happens to the driver if she is wearing a seat belt?

   (A) The driver's body will continue to move forward due to inertia, and the seat belt will apply the required force to keep her in her seat.

   (B) The driver is inside the car, so she will stop with the car whether or not she is wearing a seat belt.

   (C) The driver will be pushed against the seat when the car stops; the seat belt has no effect.

   Answers:

   (A) is correct. The driver's body will continue moving forward due to inertia. A force is required to slow the driver down (Newton's first law).

   (B) is incorrect. Being inside the car does not matter; a force is required to slow the driver down.

   (C) is incorrect. The driver will be pushed against the seat only if the car is moving in reverse and comes to an abrupt stop.

2. Which example describes an object in equilibrium?

   (A) a parachutist after he jumps from an airplane

   (B) a person sitting still in a chair

   (C) a soccer ball when it is kicked

   Answers:

   (A) is incorrect. The parachutist will accelerate toward the earth.

   (B) is correct. The person is not accelerating.

   (C) is incorrect. During a kick, the soccer ball is accelerating.

Types of Forces

There are four FUNDAMENTAL FORCES that form the basis for all other forces. The GRAVITATIONAL force is the force that pulls mass together. It is an attractive force and is what holds stars and planets together as spheres and keeps them in orbit. It also keeps humans on the surface of the earth. The WEAK force is beyond the scope of this text, but it plays a role in nuclear reactions (like those in stars). The ELECTROMAGNETIC force is the force between electric charges. It is repulsive when the charges are the same sign (positive-positive or negative-negative) and is attractive when the charges are the opposite sign (positive-negative). This force holds the positive nuclei and negative electrons of atoms together. Finally, the NUCLEAR (or strong) force is so named because it holds together the nucleus in an atom. The nuclear force has a larger magnitude than the electromagnetic force that pushes protons (positive charges) away from each other in the nucleus.

Non-fundamental forces are defined as forces that can be derived from the four fundamental forces. These forces include tension, friction, the normal force, and the buoyant force. TENSION (F_T or T) is found in ropes pulling or holding up an object, and FRICTION (F_F) is created by two objects moving against each other. The NORMAL FORCE (F_N or N) occurs when an object is resting on another object. The normal force is always equal and opposite to the force pushing onto the surface. The BUOYANT FORCE (F_B) is the upward force experienced by floating objects. Finally, an APPLIED FORCE (F_A) is any force applied to an object by another object.

When working with forces, it is helpful to draw a FREE-BODY DIAGRAM, which shows all the forces acting on an object. Because forces are vectors, it is important to consider the direction of the force when drawing a diagram.

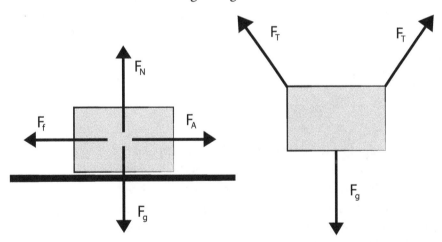

Figure 3.1. Free-Body Diagrams

Example

Which of the following forces causes oppositely charged ions to attract?

(A) nuclear

(B) electromagnetic

(C) tension

Answers:

(A) is incorrect. The nuclear force holds together the subatomic particles in an atom's nucleus.

(B) is correct. The electromagnetic force is the force between charged particles that causes them to attract or repel each other.

(C) is incorrect. Tension is a force that results from an object being pulled or hung from a rope or chain.

Weight

The gravitational force felt by an object on the surface of the earth is called the object's **WEIGHT**. The acceleration due to gravity on the surface of the earth is $g = 9.8$ m/s^2 and always points toward the center of the earth. Using Newton's second law, the weight W of an object of mass m is:

$$W = mg$$

Example

An object with a weight of 32 N on the moon is brought to Earth. If the acceleration due to gravity on the moon is 1.6 m/s^2, what is the weight of the object on Earth?

(A) 1.96 N

(B) 19.6 N

(C) 196 N

Answer:

(C) is correct.

$W = mg$ $32 = m(1.6)$ $m = 20$ kg	Use the formula for weight to find the object's mass using the acceleration due to gravity on the moon.
$W = mg$ $W = 20(9.8) =$ **196 N**	Use the object's mass to find its weight on Earth using $g = 9.8$ m/s^2.

Tension

A common type of applied force is **TENSION**, the force applied by a rope or chain as it pulls on an object. In a free-body diagram, the vector for tension always points along the rope away from the object. Tension plays an important role in pulley systems, as shown in the figure on the right. The tension in the pulley's rope acts against the mass's weight, and the magnitude of the two forces determines whether the mass moves up or down.

Example

In Figure 3.2, if mass M is much greater than mass m, what direction do both masses move?

(A) Mass M will move down, and mass m will move up.

(B) Mass M will move up, and mass m will move down.

(C) Neither mass will move; the system is in equilibrium.

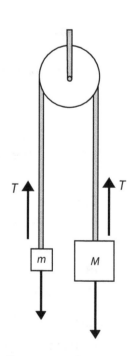

Figure 3.2. Pulley System

Answers:

(A) is correct. If mass *M* is larger, then the weight of mass *M* will produce a larger force than the weight of mass *m*. The larger force will move mass *M* down and mass *m* up.

(B) is incorrect. If mass *M* is larger, then the weight of mass *M* will produce a larger force than the weight of mass *m*. The larger force will move mass *M* down and mass *m* up.

(C) is incorrect. The forces are not balanced. Mass *M* will have a larger weight, so the system is not in equilibrium.

Friction

Microscopically, no surface is perfectly smooth. The irregular shape of the surfaces in contact will lead to interactions that resist movement. The resulting force is FRICTION. Friction opposes motion and describes the resistance of two surfaces in contact as they move across each other. On a free-body diagram, friction always points in the direction opposite the object's motion.

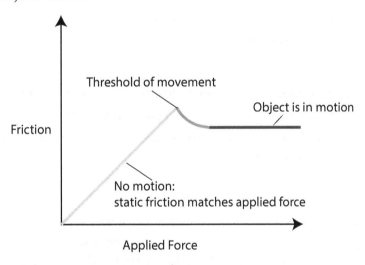

Figure 3.3. Static and Kinetic Friction

There are two types of friction: static and kinetic. STATIC FRICTION is applicable to an object that is not moving and is always equal to the force applied to the object. In other words, it is the amount of force that needs to be overcome for an object to move. For example, a small force applied to a large rock will not move the rock because static friction will match the applied force in the opposite direction. However, when enough force is applied, static friction can be overcome, and an object will begin moving. When this happens, the moving object experiences KINETIC friction.

The size of the friction force is dependent on an object's weight. Think of a couch being slid across a carpet. The couch becomes much harder to move if a person sits on the couch, and harder still if more people are added. This effect is written mathematically in terms of the normal force from the surface:

$$f_s \leq \mu_s N$$
$$f_k = \mu_k N$$

where f_s and f_k are the static and kinetic forces of friction, μ_s and μ_k are the static and kinetic coefficients of friction, and *N* is the normal force.

Examples

1. If a block is sliding down an inclined plane, in what direction will the friction vector point?

    (A) directly into (perpendicular to) the plane

    (B) down and parallel to the plane

    (C) up and parallel to the plane

    Answers:

    (A) is incorrect. This describes the direction of the component of the block's weight into the plane.

    (B) is incorrect. The force of friction will always oppose motion.

    (C) is correct. If the block is moving down the plane, the force of friction points up the plane.

2. In which of the following situations is an object experiencing static friction?

    (A) a rock sliding down a hill

    (B) a person in a moving car slamming on the brakes

    (C) a person leaning against a car

    Answers:

    (A) is incorrect. Kinetic friction will be in effect because the rock is moving.

    (B) is incorrect. Kinetic friction will be in effect because the car is moving.

    (C) is correct. The person is applying a force to the car, and static friction is keeping the car from moving.

Buoyant Force

When a boat or object is floating or under water or another liquid, the BUOYANT FORCE pushes vertically against the weight of the object. The magnitude of this force is calculated by considering the volume of the object that is submerged in the fluid. The object displaces a volume of liquid equal to its own volume, and the liquid pushes back by an amount that is exactly equal to the weight of the liquid that would exist in that volume. The buoyant force (always a vector pointing up), is given by:

Boats float by using the buoyant force. Ships that hold very large loads need a large buoyant force and so need to displace a large amount of water.

$$F_{buoyant} = m_{fluid} \, g = \rho V$$

where m_{fluid} is the mass of the fluid displaced, ρ is the density of the fluid, V is the volume of fluid that is displaced by the object, and g is the acceleration due to gravity.

Example

Which object will experience the largest buoyant force when fully submerged?

(A) a golf ball

(B) a baseball

(C) a basketball

Answer:

(C) ic correct. A basketball will have the largest volume and will displace the most water. This will lead to the largest buoyant force of the three.

Torque

TORQUE is the force required to rotate an object. The units for torque are N m (newton meters), and the equation is: $\tau = rF$, where r is the radius (the distance from the axis of rotation to the location of F), and F is the force. It is important to understand that r and F are vectors and that the equation is valid only in the case where r and F are perpendicular to each other.

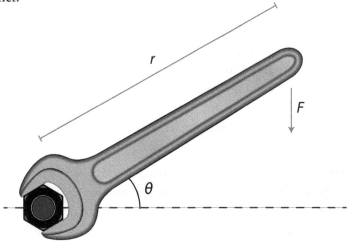

Figure 3.4. Torque

Remember that mass is a measure of inertia, where a larger mass is harder to accelerate with a force. MOMENT OF INERTIA is similarly used when discussing a rotating object to describe the object's inertia, or, its resistance to being rotated. A large amount of mass far away from the axis of rotation will have a larger moment of inertia than a smaller mass closer to the axis of rotation. For a single mass m at a distance r from a rotation axis, the moment of inertia is given by: $I = mr^2$.

For an object to be truly in equilibrium in terms of energy, it must not only be at rest or at constant velocity ($F = 0$); it must also not be rotating ($\tau = 0$). The object is then in ROTATIONAL EQUILIBRIUM.

Example

Which object has the highest moment of inertia? Assume all objects have the same mass.

(A) a solid disk with a radius of 5 cm

(B) a solid disk with a radius of 10 cm

(C) a hollow disk with a radius of 10 cm

Answers:

(A) is incorrect. An object's moment of inertia is largest when it has mass that is located far away from the axis of rotation. Compared to object C, the mass in this disk is closer to the axis of rotation.

(B) is incorrect. Compared to object C, most of the mass in this disk is closer to the axis of rotation.

(C) is correct. This object has identical mass to the other objects, but all the mass is located at a larger distance from the axis of rotation than the other objects.

WORK, ENERGY, AND POWER

Work

WORK is a scalar value that is defined as the application of a force over a distance. The SI unit for work is joule (J). The equation for work is:

$$W = Fd$$

where F is the force and d is the distance.

One example is a person lifting a book off the ground. As she lifts the book, the book has a weight, and her hand and arm are producing a force that is larger than that weight to make the book rise. In terms of work, the person's hand is doing work on the book to lift the book from the ground to its final position. If she drops the book, the force of gravity will push the book back to the ground. So, during a drop, gravity (the earth) is doing work on the book.

Another example is a person holding the book steady. Neither his hand nor gravity is doing work on the book because the book is not moving any distance. However, it is interesting to note that the person's hand and arm will get tired holding a book in the air. This is due to work that is done inside his body to keep his hand at its position while holding the book.

The sign of the work done is important. In the example of lifting a book, the person's hand is doing positive (+) work on the book. However, gravity is always pulling the book down, which means that during a lift, gravity is doing negative (−) work on the book. This can be expressed as such: If the force and the displacement are in the same direction, then the work is positive (+). If the force and the displacement are in opposite directions, then the work is negative (−). In the case of lifting a book, the net work done on the book is positive.

Example

Which situation requires the most work done on a car?

(A) pushing on the car, but it does not move

(B) towing the car up a steep hill for 100 meters

(C) pushing the car 5 meters across a parking lot

Answers:

(A) is incorrect. If the car does not move, then no work is done on the car.

(B) is correct. A steep hill requires a large force to counter the gravitational force. The large distance will also lead to a large amount of work done.

(C) is incorrect. Work will be done, but much less than in case B.

Energy

ENERGY is an abstract concept, but everything in nature has an energy associated with it. There are many types of energy, including mechanical, chemical, thermal, nuclear, electric, magnetic, and so on. The MECHANICAL ENERGY of an object is due to its motion (kinetic energy) and position (potential energy). Energy is a scalar and is given in the SI unit of joules (J).

There is an energy related to movement called the **KINETIC ENERGY**. Any object that has mass and is moving will have a kinetic energy. The equation for kinetic energy is:

$$KE = \tfrac{1}{2}mv^2$$

where m is the mass and v is the speed.

POTENTIAL ENERGY is understood as the potential for an object to gain kinetic energy. This can also be seen as energy stored in a system. There are several types of potential energy. **ELECTRIC POTENTIAL ENERGY** is derived from the interaction between positive and negative charges. Because opposite charges attract each other, and like charges repel, energy can be stored when opposite charges are moved apart or when like charges are pushed together. Similarly, compressing a spring stores **ELASTIC POTENTIAL ENERGY**. Energy is also stored in chemical bonds as **CHEMICAL POTENTIAL ENERGY**.

The energy stored in a book placed on a table is **GRAVITATIONAL POTENTIAL ENERGY**; it is derived from the pull of the earth's gravity on the book. The equation for gravitational potential energy is given by:

$$PE_g = mgh$$

where m is the mass, g is 9.8 m/s² (remember mg is an object's weight), and h is the height.

A simple way to understand gravitational potential energy is to consider an object's initial height. The speed of an object at a moment just before hitting the ground (and therefore the kinetic energy difference just before hitting the ground) after falling from a short stool to the ground may be compared to the speed of an object falling from the roof of a house to the ground. The jump from the roof will lead to a much higher kinetic energy, and so, the potential energy is higher on the roof.

Energy can be converted into other forms of energy, but it cannot be created or destroyed. This principle is called the **CONSERVATION OF ENERGY**. A swing provides a simple example of this principle. Throughout the swing's path, the total energy of the system remains the same. At the highest point of a swing's path, it has potential energy but no kinetic energy (because it has stopped moving momentarily as it changes direction). As the swing drops, that potential energy is converted to kinetic energy, and the swing's velocity increases. At the bottom of its path, all its potential energy has been converted into kinetic energy (meaning its potential energy is zero). This process repeats as the swing moves up and down. At any point in the swing's path, the kinetic and potential energies will sum to the same value.

Electrical power plants are energy converters. A hydroelectric plant converts gravitational energy (from water falling through the dam) into electrical energy. A nuclear power plant converts nuclear energy into electrical energy. Coal and gas power plants convert chemical energy into electrical energy. Solar panels convert light energy into electrical energy.

CONTINUE

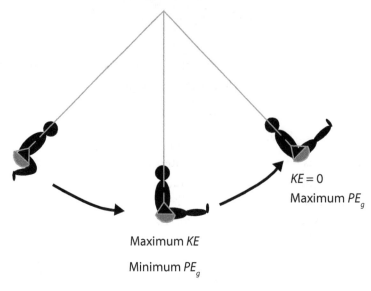

$KE = 0$

Maximum PE_g

Maximum KE

Minimum PE_g

Figure 3.5. Mechanical Energy in a Pendulum

In reality, there is air resistance against the swing, and there is friction between the swing's chain and the bar that holds the swing. Friction (and air resistance) convert mechanical energies into heat (thermal energy). This is why a swing will gradually slow down and reach lower heights with each back-and-forth motion. Energy loss through heat also occurs in electronics and motors.

Revisiting the concept of work, a change in position with the application of a force will necessarily lead to a velocity and therefore to kinetic energy. So, work is effectively an energy and can be related to kinetic energy with the following equation:

$$W = \Delta KE = \tfrac{1}{2}mv_2^2 - \tfrac{1}{2}mv_1^2$$

Examples

1. Imagine a roller coaster that does not have its own power and starts on a hill at a height of 100 meters. There is no air resistance or friction. It falls down to a height of 50 meters in the first dip and begins to move up the next hill that is 200 meters high. What will happen to the coaster on the next hill?

   (A) It will make it up to 150 m up the hill and move back down to the first dip.

   (B) It will make it up to 100 m up the hill and move back down to the first dip.

   (C) It will make it up to 75 m up the hill and move back down to the first dip.

   Answers:

   (A) is incorrect. It will not have enough energy to make it to 150 m.

   (B) is correct. Its maximum energy is from its starting point, the potential energy at 100 m, so it can never move higher than 100 m.

   (C) is incorrect. It has enough energy to make it past 75 m.

2. A pendulum with mass *m* is swinging back and forth. If it experiences both air resistance and friction, which of the following statements about the pendulum's speed is true?

   (A) The pendulum's maximum speed will always occur where the height of the mass off the ground is the lowest.

   (B) The pendulum's maximum speed will always occur where the height of the mass off the ground is the highest.

   (C) The mass will always travel at the same speed.

Power

As stated before, energy cannot be created or destroyed but can only change forms. A measure of this transfer of energy is called POWER, which is the rate of work done or energy conversion per time. The SI unit for power is a watt, W. Because work is defined as a force applied along a distance, power can also be written as a force multiplied by a speed. Power is a scalar with an equation that is given by:

$$P = \frac{W}{t} = Fv$$

where W is the work done (or energy converted) over an amount of time t, F is a force, and v is the speed.

Power is a commonly used measure of electrical devices. For example, light bulbs are labeled in terms of their wattage (40 W, 60 W, etc.). A 60 W light bulb will use 60 joules of electrical energy per second, and this energy will be converted into light energy (that is the light bulb's purpose), but also a great deal of that energy is converted into thermal energy (heat). The heat from light bulbs is wasted energy.

Electrical power from power companies is commonly charged in terms of kilowatt hours (kWh). From the equation for power above, the energy used during a time period can be calculated by multiplying the power by time. As an example, the energy used can be expressed as the amount kilowatts used multiplied by the number of hours. So, kilowatt hours is a unit of energy (1kWh = 3,600,000 J).

Examples

1. Which of the following is NOT a unit of energy?

    (A) joule

    (B) kilowatt hour

    (C) newton

    Answers:

    (A) is incorrect. A joule is the unit for energy.

    (B) is incorrect. Any form of watt multiplied by an amount of time is suitable for representing energy.

    (C) is correct. A newton is the unit for force.

2. A constant external force of 10 N is applied to an object to keep it moving at a constant speed of 10 m/s. Which of the following statements about the object is true?

    (A) No power is used to move the object.

    (B) The external force supplies power to keep the object moving at 10 m/s.

    (C) The object is not accelerating, so no power is used.

MOMENTUM AND COLLISIONS

The term *MOMENTUM* is a common one in the English language, but it has a specific meaning in mechanics: the mass of an object multiplied by its velocity. Any object that has mass and is also moving has momentum. Momentum is a vector and is given by the equation:

$$p = mv$$

where m is the mass and v is the velocity.

The concept of momentum can be used to describe a change in motion. For example, a baseball has a certain momentum when it is traveling through the air, but it has zero momentum once it has been caught. A change in velocity requires a force to cause an acceleration over a period of time, t. The change in momentum is called the **IMPULSE** and can be written as:

$$I = \Delta p = mv_2 - mv_1 = Ft$$

where p is the momentum; m and v are mass and speed, respectively; and F is the force over a time, t.

The relationship for impulse has interesting implications. If an object has a momentum change, then there was a force applied over a time t to cause that change. So, for an identical impulse value, a longer time requires less force to be used. Similarly, a shorter time requires more force. This is why a baseball catcher will wear a thick mitt and other padding to increase the interaction time that slows the ball. As a result, the catcher's hand feels a much smaller force than it would without the glove. Using the same reasoning, but in reverse, a baseball bat has no padding, which decreases the interaction time and relatively increases the force applied to the ball.

✔ You are an astronaut in space and are holding a baseball in your hand. If you make the motion to throw the ball but never actually throw it, will you still move away as if you did?

Like energy, **MOMENTUM IS CONSERVED**. However, momentum is conserved only when there are no outside forces on the system. Conservation of momentum states that if an object in a system is given momentum, then all the other objects in the system will have a net momentum that will be opposite to the object. The total momentum of the system remains unchanged. For example, the sidebar on this page addresses an astronaut is at rest in space. If she throws an object to her right, her body will also move to the left in response.

Examples

1. Modern cars are designed to crumple during a collision. Using the concept of impulse, how does this protect the passengers?

   (A) By decreasing the interaction time, the crumple maximizes the force felt by the passengers.

   (B) By decreasing the interaction time, the crumple minimizes the force felt by the passengers.

   (C) By increasing the interaction time, the crumple minimizes the force felt by the passengers.

   Answers:

   (A) is incorrect. The crumple will increase the interaction time. A decrease in interaction time will increase the amount of force felt by the passengers.

   (B) is incorrect. The crumple will increase the interaction time. A decrease in interaction time will increase the amount of force felt by the passengers.

   (C) is correct. The crumple increases the time of interaction and so decreases the force felt by the passengers.

2. A man is sitting in a boat next to a dock and decides to jump from the boat to the dock. The boat is much lighter than the man. Using conservation of momentum, what will be the most likely result?

   (A) The man will most likely fall into the water.

   (B) The man will reach the dock.

   (C) The boat will slam into the dock.

   Answers:

   (A) is correct. The boat will move behind the man at high speed, while the man will move forward at low speed. He will most likely end up falling in the water.

   (B) is incorrect. The boat will move behind the man at high speed, while the man will move forward at low speed. He will most likely end up falling in the water.

   (C) is incorrect. If the man jumps toward the dock, the boat will move away from the dock.

SIMPLE MACHINES

A simple machine changes the magnitude or direction of an applied force, with the result leading to a **MECHANICAL ADVANTAGE** for the user. This advantage is the ratio of force that is output from the machine relative to the force input. The equation for mechanical advantage is given by:

$$MA = \frac{F_{output}}{F_{input}}$$

A **LEVER** is a simple machine based on the concept of torque. The axis of rotation and also where the lever rests is called the **FULCRUM**. Using the figure as a guide, $r_{input} F_{input} = r_{output} F_{output}$. Using the previous definition for mechanical advantages gives:

$$MA = \frac{r_{input}}{r_{output}}$$

There are three types of levers. A **FIRST-CLASS LEVER** has the fulcrum between the input and output forces, and the input force is in the opposite direction of the output force. A

SECOND-CLASS LEVER has the input and output forces on one common side of the fulcrum, and both are in the same direction. The output force is closer to the fulcrum than the input force is. Like the second-class lever, a **THIRD-CLASS LEVER** has the input and output forces on one common side of the fulcrum, and both are in the same direction. The input force is closer to the fulcrum than the output force is.

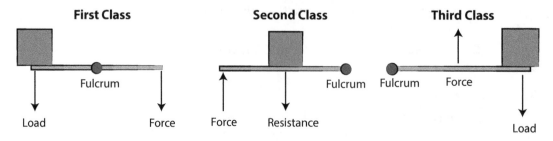

Figure 3.6. Types of Levers

An **INCLINED PLANE** is a simple machine (a ramp) that reduces the amount of force needed to raise a mass to a certain height. Earlier in this text it was shown that the weight of a mass on an inclined plane has a portion that pushes into the plane. Only a fraction of the weight is in the direction down the plane. This is the operating principle for this

The idea of simple machines was invented by Archimedes in the third century BCE.

simple machine. In terms of work, the input work to move an object up an inclined plane of length L is $W_{in} = F_{input} \times L$. The output work is what is required to lift the object up to a height h, $W_{output} = F_{output} \times h$, where F_{output} is the object's weight. Combining these gives the mechanical advantage:

$$MA = \frac{L}{h}$$

where L is the length of the inclined plane and h is the height.

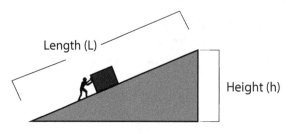

Figure 3.7. An Inclined Plane

A **PULLEY** is a simple machine that redirects force by supporting a rope that can move freely by rotating the pulley. A single pulley lifting a weight will have a mechanical advantage of 1. When a second pulley is added in a block-and-tackle configuration, the input force required to lift the weight is halved, and so the mechanical advantage is 2. Similarly, a three-pulley system will have a mechanical advantage of 3.

$$MA = \text{number of pulleys}$$

A **WEDGE** is a simple machine that converts an input force onto one surface into a force that is perpendicular to its other surfaces. A wedge is often used to separate material; common examples are an ax or knife. Using the same reasoning as used for an inclined plane

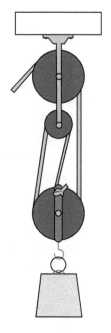

Figure 3.8. A Three-Pulley System

(a wedge is effectively two inclined planes on top of each other), the mechanical advantage is

$$MA = \frac{L}{W}$$

where L is the length of the inclined plane on the wedge, and W is the width (the length of the back edge).

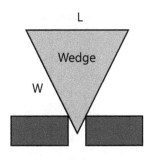

Figure 3.9. A Simple Wedge

A **WHEEL AND AXLE** is a simple machine that has a rotating structure with two different radii. The larger radius is the wheel, and the smaller radius is the axle. It is similar conceptually to a lever, where the different radii convert the torque on the wheel into a torque on the axle (or vice versa). The mechanical advantage is the same as for the lever:

$$MA = \frac{r_{input}}{r_{output}}$$

where r_{input} is the radius of the input, and r_{output} is the radius of the output.

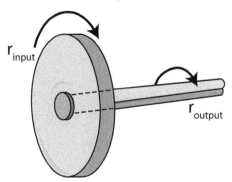

Figure 3.10. A Wheel and Axle

GEARS are simple machines that are circular and have notches or teeth along the outer edge. Several gears in contact form a gear train. Again, the force applied along a gear train is related to the torque, where a large-radius gear will apply a large torque to a smaller gear on the train. The number of teeth on a gear is directly related to the radius of the gear, allowing the mechanical advantage to be written as:

$$MA = \frac{\tau_{output}}{\tau_{input}} = \frac{N_{output}}{N_{input}}$$

where τ are the torques from each gear, and N is the number of teeth on each gear.

Another concept for a gear train is the **GEAR RATIO**, or speed ratio, which is a ratio of the angular velocity of the input gear to the angular velocity of the output gear. At the point of contact, the linear velocity must be the same, so $v = \omega_{input} \, r_{input} = \omega_{output} \, r_{output}$. So, the gear ratio is:

$$\frac{\omega_{input}}{\omega_{output}} = \frac{r_{output}}{r_{input}} = \frac{N_{output}}{N_{input}}$$

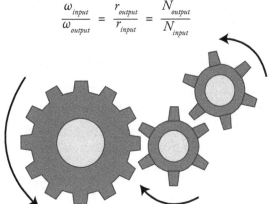

Figure 3.11. A Gear Train

A **SCREW** is a simple machine that converts rotational motion into linear motion. In general, a screw is a cylinder with an inclined plane wrapped around it. The wrapped inclined plane is called the thread, while the distance between the planes is called the pitch. The pitch is directed along the length of the screw. Again considering the work done, $W_{input} = F_{input} 2\pi r$, where r is the radius of the screw; and $W_{output} = F_{output} h$, where h is the pitch. The mechanical advantage then becomes:

$$MA = \frac{2\pi r}{h}$$

where r is the radius of the screw, and h is the pitch.

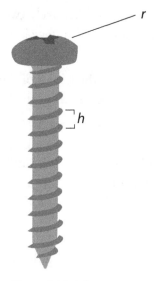

Figure 3.12. A Screw

Examples

1. Which is an example of a first-class lever?

   (A) wheelbarrow

   (B) scissors

   (C) tweezers

   Answers:

   (A) is incorrect. This is a second-class lever.

   (B) **is correct.** This is a first-class lever.

   (C) is incorrect. This is a third-class lever.

2. Which mechanical advantage is the best for the user?

   (A) 10

   (B) 5

   (C) 2

   Answer:

   (A) **is correct.** The highest mechanical advantage is the best for the user.

THE BASICS OF ELECTRICITY

Electric Charge

Electric **CHARGE** is a fundamental property of matter, like mass. When something is without charge, it is called **NEUTRAL**. Experimentally it was determined that there are two types of charges, named positive (+) and negative (–). As more was discovered about electric charge, it was shown that negative charge came from **ELECTRONS**, and positive charge came from **PROTONS**.

The unit of charge, e, is a fundamental constant (meaning it never changes) and has a value of $e = 1.602 \times 10^{-19}$ C, where C is coulombs. The charge of an electron is –e, and the charge of a proton is +e. Therefore, the total charge is always a multiple of e, and fractional values of e do not exist. For example, a charge of 14 e means there are 14 protons providing that charge.

As discussed in previous chapters, mass attracts other mass via the gravitational force. Similarly, an electric charge interacts with other electric charges through an electric force. Through experiments scientists determined that like charges repel (positive charges will repel positive charges and negative charges will repel negative charges), and unlike charges attract (positive charges will attract negative charges).

The magnitude of the electrical force, F, between charges is given in newtons, N, and is given by the equation:

$$F = \frac{k q_a q_b}{r^2}$$

where q_a and q_b are the charges, and r is the separation between them. k is a proportionality constant; $k = 9 \times 10^9$ Nm²/C². It is important to consider direction when applying the force equation. For example, two electrons will each experience a force due to the other that pushes them apart. An electron and a proton will each experience a force due to the other that pulls them together.

Charges interact through this force through an **ELECTRIC FIELD** that is created by each individual charge. The electric field has direction and always moves away from positive charges and toward negative charges. The magnitude of the electric field (units N/C) at distance r from a charge q is given by:

$$E = \frac{kq}{r^2}$$

⚠ The words *force* and *field* are commonly used in our language. Think of your understanding of the words compared to how they are described here. It will help you remember!

If another charge, q', is placed at r, the previous equation for the electric force is recovered:

$$F = q'E$$

Charges behave differently when placed in an electric field. A positive charge will be pushed along the direction of the electric field, while a negative charge will be pushed in the opposite direction of the electric field.

Examples

1. Consider two scenarios: A) a proton and electron separated by 1 meter and B) two protons separated by 1 meter. What can be said about the electric force for each case?

   (A) The electric force will be the same strength, but for A) it will pull them together and for B) it will push them apart.

   (B) The electric force will be the same strength, but for A) it will push them apart and for B) it will pull them together.

   (C) The electric force will be stronger for case B) than case A).

   Answers:

   (A) is correct. The electric force equation will give the same value for both cases. Opposite charges attract and like charges repel.

   (B) is incorrect. The electric force equation will give the same value for both cases. Opposite charges attract and like charges repel.

   (C) is incorrect. The electric force equation will give the same value for both cases.

2. What comment about the electric field is true?

  (A) The electric field can turn a proton turn into an electron.

  (B) The electric field gets stronger the farther it is from a charge.

  (C) The electric field always points from positive to negative charges.

  Answers:

  (A) is incorrect. An electric field cannot turn a proton into an electron.

  (B) is incorrect. The electric field gets weaker the farther it is from a charge.

  (C) is correct. The electric field does point from positive to negative charges.

Atomic Structure

Opposite charges attract, where the electric force will pull them together. However, this does not mean they will collide and stick together. Although the reasons are beyond the scope of this text, opposite charges will form systems called **ATOMS** when they are brought close together. In atoms, negatively charged electrons will orbit around a positively charged nucleus that contains protons and neutral particles called **NEUTRONS**.

> ⚠
> The neutron will radioactively decay into a positively charged proton and negatively charged electron (among other things).

Although it is possible for the number of protons in an atom to change (through nuclear reactions, like in the sun or a nuclear weapon), it is uncommon in daily experience. Outside of nuclear reactions, it is important to remember that electrons and protons are not created or destroyed.

The mass of a proton is 1.673×10^{-27} kg, and the mass of an electron is almost 2,000 times lighter, at 9.109×10^{-31} kg. Although their charges are equal and opposite, it is much harder to move the proton than the electron. Therefore, the much heavier nucleus may be considered rigid while the electrons move freely.

Electrons move around the nucleus in levels called shells. An atom's outermost shell is occupied by **VALENCE ELECTRONS**, which are farthest from the nucleus and therefore the most reactive of the atom's electrons. Atoms with a full valence shell are unreactive. Valence shells that are close to full will more easily accept electrons, and nearly empty valence shells will more easily lose electrons.

Valence shells determine a material's conductivity. The atoms in an **INSULATOR** have nearly full valence shells, meaning the electrons do not easily move. In a **CONDUCTOR**, the atoms have nearly empty valence shells, and electrons move freely. A **SEMICONDUCTOR'S** atoms are neither full nor empty, making them poor conductors and insulators. A semiconductor on its own will not conduct charge. However, other elements, or *dopants*, are added to change the material's electrical properties.

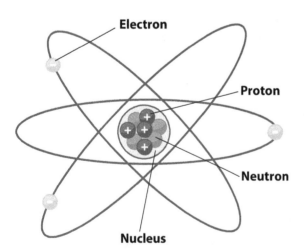

Figure 3.13. Atomic Structure

Examples

1. What configuration of particles can make an atom?

   (A) two neutrons

   (B) one proton and one electron

   (C) one neutron and one electron

   Answers:

   (A) is incorrect. Neutrons are neutral and will not attract and create an atom.

   (B) is correct. The proton and electron will attract and create an atomic system (in this case, a hydrogen atom).

   (C) is incorrect. The neutron has no charge, so it will not attract the electron to form an atom.

2. What best describes the properties of a semiconductor?

   (A) It is an insulator unless dopants are added.

   (B) It is a conductor unless dopants are added.

   (C) It has half the conducting properties of a conductor.

   Answers:

   (A) is correct. A semiconductor is an insulator whose conducting properties can be altered with dopants.

   (B) is incorrect. A semiconductor without dopants is an insulator.

   (C) is incorrect. Despite the name, a semiconductor does not have half the conducting properties of a conductor.

Current

CURRENT (I) is the amount of charge flow per time and is given by the equation:

$$I = \frac{\Delta q}{\Delta t}$$

where Δq is the amount of charge that moved past a location in Δt, the amount of time passed. Current is measured in amperes (amps), A.

Although current, by definition, does not need to be inside a material, for electronics, current flow is considered within a conductor (or semiconductor). As discussed previously, electrons are much lighter and therefore move much more easily than the heavy nuclei (nuclei are seen as basically rigid). Thus current flow is actually the flow of electrons. However, historically in electronics and circuits, current flow is positive in the direction of positive charge flow. This is called **CONVENTIONAL CURRENT**.

If a straight segment of conducting wire has an electric field applied along the wire, the electrons will move in the opposite direction of the field. If the nuclei are rigid and do not move, how is there positive charge flow? A simple analogy is bubbles in a liquid. The bubbles (air) are moving up through the liquid. The liquid moves down to fill the space left by the air. In electronics, the electrons act as the liquid, and the air (lack of electrons, also called **HOLES**) moves in the opposite direction. Therefore, conventional current flow is the direction of the flow of holes through a circuit.

Conceptually, a single electron or hole does not travel through the entire wire to create current. For example, a hole does not start at the battery and then move through the circuit back to the battery. Instead, the holes are colliding and moving at high speed in generally random directions in the wire. The electric field introduces a trend, or drift, in the hole movement that will make the holes move in the direction of the field, but rather slowly. Therefore, the electric field that is introducing the slow drift direction to the charge movement throughout the entire wire or circuit is what is measured as current flow.

There are two types of current sources, **DIRECT CURRENT (DC)** and **ALTERNATING CURRENT (AC)**. Direct current is a constant current value, like that from a battery. For example, a battery will supply a constant 10mA to a circuit as long as the battery is good. In alternating current sources, the current value changes sign at a certain frequency.

Voltage from a battery, power supply, or across a circuit element is usually notated with + and – signs. Current always flows from + to – in the circuit.

As shown later in this chapter, alternating current is created by alternators, like those in a car and in power plants. Power outlets in our homes and businesses are AC sources (with typical frequencies of f = 60 Hz, ω = 377 Hz). It is common to have electronic devices that convert AC sources to DC sources to power electronics, like laptops and smartphones.

Example

If charge is moving through a circuit at rate of 0.5 C every 2 seconds, what is the current in the circuit?

(A) 0.1 A

(B) 0.25 A

(C) 2.5 A

Answer:

(B) is correct. Use the formula for calculating current.

$$I = \frac{\Delta q}{\Delta t} = \frac{0.5}{2} = \mathbf{0.25\ A}$$

Resistance

RESISTIVITY is a measure of how easily an electron can move through a material. An insulator, where electrons are held close to the nuclei, will have a high resistivity. A conductor, where electrons can freely move throughout the entire material, has a low resistivity. The reciprocal of resistivity is called the conductivity; insulators have low conductivity and conductors have high conductivity. Resistivity is a material property and can vary by a huge amount.

Table 3.1. Resistivity of Common Materials

	MATERIAL	RESISTIVITY ($\Omega \times$ M)
Conductors	Copper	1.72×10^{-8}
	Gold	2.44×10^{-8}
Semiconductors	Silicon	2300
Insulators	Glass	$10^{10} - 10^{14}$
	Teflon	$>10^{13}$

RESISTANCE has units of ohms, Ω, and includes the material resistivity as well as the actual size of the device. For the case of a wire of length, L, cross-sectional area, A, and resistivity, ρ, the resistance is given by:

$$R = \frac{\rho L}{A}$$

Therefore, the resistance of a wire increases if the wire is made longer or if the wire is made thinner. Relatively, short and fat wires will have less resistance that long and thin wires.

Example

What is the best type of wire to use to get the highest resistance? Assume the material resistivity in the wire is identical.

(A) long, thin wire

(B) long, thick wire

(C) short, thin wire

Answers:

(A) is correct. From the equation $R = \frac{\rho L}{A}$, a larger length, L, means a higher resistance, R. A thinner wire (smaller A) will also have a higher resistance, R.

(B) is incorrect. The long wire will increase resistance, but a thick wire will have less resistance than a thin wire.

(C) is incorrect. The thin wire will increase resistance, but a short wire will decrease it.

Voltage

To understand voltage, it is helpful to revisit the concept of gravitational potential energy. Consider an individual standing on a box. She is not moving and therefore has zero kinetic energy. However, she has potential energy because if the box moves, she would fall to the floor. When the box moves, the person falls, and her potential energy becomes kinetic energy. As she falls, her kinetic energy increases and her potential energy decreases until she reaches the floor. There, her potential energy is zero because she cannot fall any further. (Her kinetic energy changes to other types of energy when she strikes the floor.)

Kinetic energy is the energy associated with moving objects. Potential energy is the energy stored in an object.

Potential energy is defined by the relative position of the object. The woman on the box would have more potential energy if the box was tall because she would be farther from the floor; she'd have less potential energy if she was standing on a shorter box. In this analogy, potential (not potential energy) is defined only by the height of the box, not by the size of the person standing on the box.

In electronics, the electrical potential energy is conceptually the same. If two charges are separated by a distance, there is the potential for their energy to be turned into kinetic energy. For example, two opposite charges at a distance r that start at rest will be pulled together and have kinetic energy. Also, two similar charges (both positive or both negative) that start at rest at a distance r will move away and gain kinetic energy.

The ELECTRICAL POTENTIAL is defined as the electrical potential energy per unit charge. A higher electrical potential at a location means that a charge placed at that location has a higher potential energy. The potential difference is defined as the difference between the potentials at two separate locations. In electronics, the **ELECTRIC POTENTIAL DIFFERENCE** is called **VOLTAGE** and is given in volts, V.

It is important to remember that voltage is a relative measurement. If a measurement of voltage is relative to zero potential, for example, the reading may be 1,000 V at point A. If the same measurement is made at point B, the reading may be 1,001 V. The potential difference, or voltage, between points A and B is only 1 V. Therefore, a charged particle moving from A to B would have much less kinetic energy than a charged particle moving from A to zero potential (a difference of 1,000 V).

An important concept to consider is called the **ELECTROMOTIVE FORCE**, or **EMF**. EMF is also measured in volts. If the terminals of a AAA battery (1.5 V) are connected with a conducting copper wire, the electrons in the wire will move from the negative terminal to the positive terminal through the wire. (The electric field goes from the positive to the negative terminal through the wire, and the negatively charged electrons move opposite to the electric field.)

But why do the electrons flow through the wire and not directly through the battery itself? The field inside the battery will oppose the flow of electrons in the wire, so how does this work? The battery has a chemical process that moves the electrons in the opposite direction of the field (they move from the positive to negative terminals, not vice versa). This chemical process provides the EMF that drives the electrons through the wire (a simple circuit). EMF can be provided by photovoltaic cells (solar power), batteries (chemical processes), and generators (mechanical processes). As shown later in this chapter, the EMF in generators is created by a changing magnetic field.

Example

What is the source of the electromotive force in a battery?

(A) changing magnetic field

(B) mechanical movement

(C) chemical processes

Answers:

(A) is incorrect. Generators (not batteries) supply an electromotive force through a changing magnetic field.

(B) is incorrect. Generators (not batteries) supply an electromotive force by converting mechanical movement into electricity.

(C) is correct. A battery contains chemicals that produce an electromotive force through chemical reactions.

CIRCUITS

Circuit Basics

An electronic **CIRCUIT** is made up of conducting wires that connect circuit elements, such as resistors, capacitors, and inductors. To operate, an electric circuit requires a source of power. Some common circuit symbols are shown in Figure 3.14.

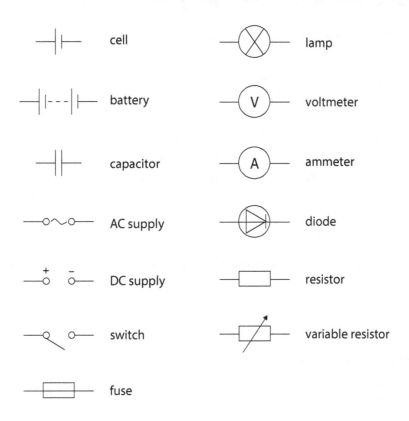

—┤├—	cell	—⊗—	lamp
—┤├---┤├—	battery	—Ⓥ—	voltmeter
—┤├—	capacitor	—Ⓐ—	ammeter
—o∿o—	AC supply	—◁—	diode
—o⁺ o⁻—	DC supply	—▭—	resistor
—switch—	switch	—variable resistor—	variable resistor
—fuse—	fuse		

Figure 3.14. Common Circuit Element Symbols

An important concept for circuits is **GROUND**. This is when the circuit is connected to the ground, or earth, which is ideally where charge of any amount can flow. Many buildings literally have a wire that goes into the earth outside as their ground. Ground is at zero potential.

There are many types of **VOLTAGE SOURCES**. The most common is the power outlet in our homes and businesses, and it provides $V_{rms} = 120$ V at 60Hz AC (the voltage goes from positive to negative to positive again at 60 times per second). Common DC sources include 9 V AA, AAA, C, and D batteries as well as batteries for our automobiles, smartphones, tablets, and laptops. These sources maintain a constant voltage. All voltage sources have an internal resistance, which is often assumed to be zero. However, this internal resistance can lead to actual voltage values that are less than expected. For example, a 1.5 V AAA battery may have a voltage measured at 1.3 V while connected to a device.

The electrical **LOAD** in a circuit consists of everything except for the power supply. The load is effectively the part of the circuit that uses power and performs a function. As shown later in this chapter, a complicated load circuit can often be reduced to a simpler, but equivalent, circuit. An example circuit with a power supply, an internal resistance, and a load resistance is shown in Figure 3.15.

A common circuit element is a **SWITCH**. It can either be an actual lever moved to connect or disconnect two wires, or it can be automated electronically. When the switch is open, the circuit is an open circuit, and current will not flow

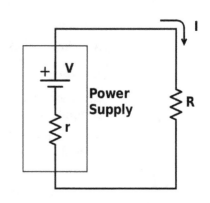

Figure 3.15. A Simple Circuit

through it. When the switch is closed, the circuit is a closed circuit, allowing current to flow.

A FUSE is a device that breaks the circuit (creates an open circuit) when too much current is flowing through it. At high currents, the heat caused by the power dissipated in the material will vaporize the material. Fuses can only be used once, and it is often easy to see when fuses have blown (the thin wire disappears). In homes, 10A and 20A to 40A fuses are common. A CIRCUIT BREAKER serves the same function as a fuse; however, it is a switch that is opened at high current and can be reused. It is common to have to manually reset the circuit breaker switch in homes.

Examples

1. Which circuit in the figure below shows a closed circuit with a power source and a load?

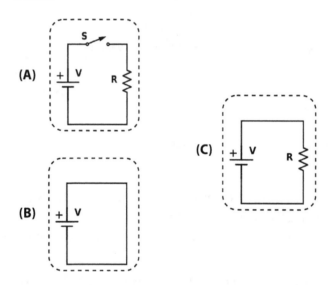

Answers:

(A) is incorrect. The circuit is not closed.

(B) is incorrect. There is no load on the power supply in this circuit.

(C) is correct. This circuit contains a power supply and a load.

2. Which electrical component would best turn a computer on and off?

   (A) switch

   (B) fuse

   (C) circuit breaker

Answers:

(A) is correct. A switch would allow power to flow through the circuit when the computer is on, and it would not allow power to flow when it is off.

(B) is incorrect. A fuse is used to protect a circuit, and it breaks when too much current is applied.

(C) is incorrect. A circuit breaker is used to protect a circuit, and it flips a switch when too much current is applied.

Ohm's Law

OHM'S LAW is perhaps the most commonly used equation in electronics. When a voltage is applied across a resistive circuit element, the electrons in that material begin to move in the opposite direction of the electric field created. This creates a flow of charge and therefore a current flow. Remember that current is positive in the opposite direction of the flow of electrons.

The voltage from the power supply provides the energy to move the charges to create current, but the material limits the amount of current that can flow. This limitation is represented as the material's resistance. Through experimentation, current flow was found to be directly proportional to the voltage applied. This is understandable, as a stronger field should lead to more charge movement. Current flow was also found to be inversely proportional to the resistance of the material. Again, this is understandable, as less resistance from the material should allow more charge flow. Writing this mathematically gives Ohm's law:

When two values are directly proportional, they increase or decrease at the same time. When two values are indirectly proportional, one goes up when the other goes down (and vice versa).

$$V = IR$$

Where V is the voltage across the resistive element, I is the current through the element, and R is the element's resistance.

Example

What is the current flowing through a 100 kΩ resistor when a voltage of 2 V is applied across it?

(A) 20 μA

(B) 200 mA

(C) 20 A

Answer:

(A) is correct.

$V = IR$	Identify the appropriate equation.
$I = \dfrac{V}{R}$ $I = \dfrac{2V}{100\ k\Omega} = 0.00002\ A = $ **20 μA**	Rewrite equation in terms of I, plug in values, and solve for the current.

Power

POWER is defined as the energy per unit of time (joules per second) and is measured in watts, W. Power is described by the equation:

$$P = \frac{energy}{time} = VI$$

where V is the voltage and I is the current through a circuit.

Power companies sell electric energy in units of kilowatt hours (kWh). 1 kWh = 3.6 × 10⁶ J.

Using Ohm's law to replace V and I in the above equation, the equation for power can be written as:

$$P = VI = I^2R = \frac{V^2}{R}$$

where R is the resistance.

As charges move through a material, they collide with other charges and nuclei, which leads to heat. Therefore, the majority of electrical power used is converted into heat (except for an electrical motor, where electrical power is turned into mechanical power). This is why electronics get hot during use.

Example

What is the power dissipated in a 1 kΩ resistor when a voltage of 350 V is applied across it?

(A) 350 μW

(B) 0.35 W

(C) 122.5 W

Answer:

(C) is correct.

$P = \frac{V^2}{R}$	Identify the appropriate equation.
$P = \frac{(350V)^2}{1k\Omega} = \mathbf{122.5\,W}$	Plug in values and solve for power.

Series Circuits

When elements are in a **SERIES CIRCUIT**, the current flows through the elements along a single path. The current through elements in series will always be constant, and the total voltage for the resistors can be found by adding the voltage at each individual resistor.

The **EQUIVALENT RESISTANCE** of the circuit, which models a complicated circuit with many resistors as a single resistor, is found by adding the resistance of each resistor. This equivalent resistance can then be used to find the power for the circuit.

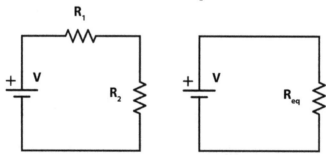

Figure 3.16. A Simple Series Circuit and Its Equivalent

Table 3.2. Series Circuits

Current	$I_1 = I_2 = I_3 = \ldots = I_n$
Voltage	$V_t = V_1 + V_2 + V_3 + \ldots + V_n$
Resistance	$R_{eq} = R_1 + R_2 + R_3 + \ldots + R_n$

Example

Find the equivalent resistance for the circuit in the figure below.

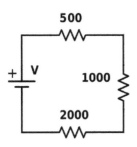

(A) 1.5 kΩ

(B) 2.5 kΩ

(C) 3.5 kΩ

Answer:

(C) is correct.

$R_{eq} = R_1 + R_2 + R_3$	Identify the appropriate equation.
$R_{eq} = 500\ \Omega + 1\ k\Omega + 2\ k\Omega = 3{,}500\ \Omega = \textbf{3.5 k}\Omega$	Plug in values and solve for equivalent resistance.

Parallel Circuits

When elements are in a **PARALLEL CIRCUIT**, current may flow through multiple paths. For this type of circuit, the voltage across each element is constant, and the current for the circuit is found by adding the current passing through each resistor. Because electricity can flow through multiple paths (meaning it passes through each resistor) the equivalent resistance of the circuit will decrease as resistors are added.

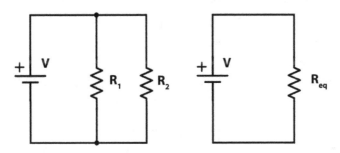

Figure 3.17. A Simple Parallel Circuit and Its Equivalent

Table 3.3. Parallel Circuits

Current	$I_t = I_1 + I_2 + I_3 + \ldots + I_n$
Voltage	$V_1 = V_2 = V_3 = \ldots = V_n$
Resistance	$\dfrac{1}{R_{eq}} = \dfrac{1}{R_1} + \dfrac{1}{R_2} + \ldots + \dfrac{1}{R_N}$

Example

Find the equivalent resistance for the circuit in the figure below.

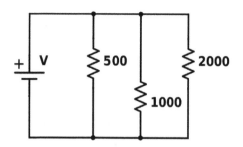

(A) 285.7 Ω

(B) 571.4 Ω

(C) 1.45 kΩ

Answer:

(A) is correct.

$\dfrac{1}{R_{eq}} = \dfrac{1}{R_1} + \dfrac{1}{R_2} + \dfrac{1}{R_3}$	Identify the appropriate equation.
$\dfrac{1}{R_{eq}} = \dfrac{1}{500\ \Omega} + \dfrac{1}{1\ \text{k}\Omega} + \dfrac{1}{2\ \text{k}\Omega} = 0.0035\ \dfrac{1}{\Omega}$ $R_{eq} = \textbf{285.7 Ω}$	Plug in values to solve for equivalent resistance.

Complex Circuits

Series and parallel circuits can be combined to make more complex circuits. To determine the properties of these circuits, they must be broken down into individual series and parallel circuits that can be used to find the properties of each resistor or the overall circuit.

In the figure below, resistors R_2 and R_3 are in parallel, and both are wired in series with resistor R_1. To find the equivalent resistance of the circuit, find $R_{2,3}$ for R_2 and R_3 using the rules for parallel circuits. $R_{2,3}$ and R_1 are now in series, so the equivalent resistance of the entire circuit can be found using the rules for series circuits, as shown below.

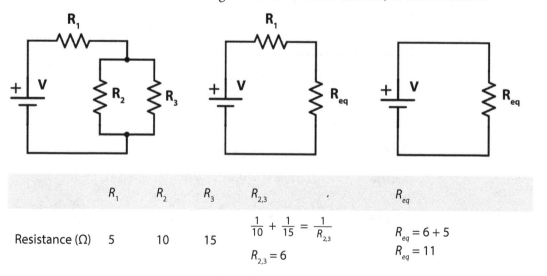

	R_1	R_2	R_3	$R_{2,3}$		R_{eq}
Resistance (Ω)	5	10	15	$\dfrac{1}{10} + \dfrac{1}{15} = \dfrac{1}{R_{2,3}}$ $R_{2,3} = 6$		$R_{eq} = 6 + 5$ $R_{eq} = 11$

Figure 3.18A. A Complex Circuit and Its Equivalent

In the next example below, resistor R_1 is in parallel with two resistors in series, R_2 and R_3. Again, the trick to finding the R_{eq} for this circuit is to work in steps. Using the equation for R_{eq} for series resistors, first reduce R_2 and R_3 to an equivalent resistance $R_{2,3}$. Now, R_1 and $R_{2,3}$ are in parallel, so use the rules for parallel circuits to find the equivalent resistance for the circuit.

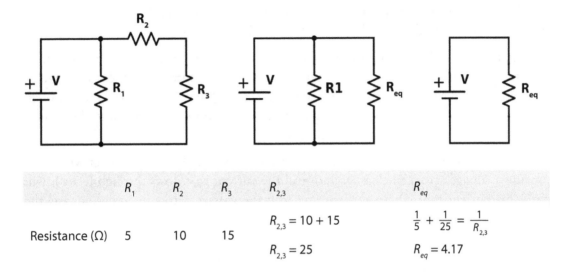

	R_1	R_2	R_3	$R_{2,3}$		R_{eq}
				$R_{2,3} = 10 + 15$		$\frac{1}{5} + \frac{1}{25} = \frac{1}{R_{2,3}}$
Resistance (Ω)	5	10	15			
				$R_{2,3} = 25$		$R_{eq} = 4.17$

Figure 3.18B. A Complex Circuit and Its Equivalent

Example

Find the equivalent resistance for the circuit in the figure below.

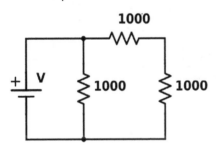

(A) 0.7 kΩ

(B) 1.5 kΩ

(C) 3.1 kΩ

Answer:

(B) is correct.

$\dfrac{1}{R_{eq}} = \dfrac{1}{R_1} + \dfrac{1}{R_2} + \dfrac{1}{R_3}$ $R_{eq} = R_1 + R_2$	Identify the appropriate equations.
$\dfrac{1}{R_{eq}} = \dfrac{1}{1\text{ k}\Omega} + \dfrac{1}{1\text{ k}\Omega} = 0.0021\dfrac{1}{\Omega}$ $R_{eq} = 500\ \Omega$	First, find the equivalent resistance of the parallel resistors.
$R'_{eq} = R + R_{eq} = 1\text{ k}\Omega + 500\ \Omega = \textbf{1.5 k}\boldsymbol{\Omega}$	Next, use that equivalent resistance in series with the last resistor to find the overall equivalent resistance.

Electrical Measurements

The previous sections discussed resistance, voltage, and current, all of which can be measured with a device called a **MULTIMETER**.

Electrical current is measured using a device called an **AMMETER**. An ammeter must be placed in series with the circuit element to accurately measure the current. An ammeter should have approximately zero internal resistance. Conceptually, the current going through the element also must be going through the ammeter.

Electric voltage is measured using a device called a **VOLTMETER**. A voltmeter must be placed in parallel to the circuit element to correctly measure the element's voltage. A voltmeter should have infinite resistance (an open circuit) so no current will flow through it. Because no current moves through the detector, a voltmeter can measure the voltage across the element without changing the circuit.

Resistance is measured using a device called an **OHMMETER**. An ohmmeter will either provide a voltage across an element and read the current that flows through it, or it will provide a current through an element and read the voltage across it. In either case, the resistance is calculated using Ohm's law.

Example

Which two diagrams in the figure below show the correct usage of an ammeter and a voltmeter to read the current through and voltage across the resistor shown?

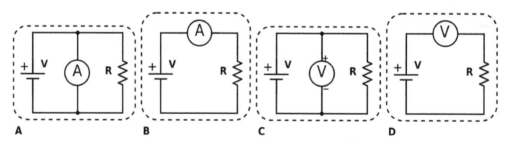

(A) A, C

(B) B, C

(C) A, D

Answers:

(A) is incorrect. An ammeter must be used in series, and a voltmeter must be used in parallel.

(B) is correct. An ammeter must be used in series, and a voltmeter must be used in parallel.

(C) is incorrect. An ammeter must be used in series, and a voltmeter must be used in parallel.

PRACTICE TEST

MATH SKILLS

40 minutes

This section measures your knowledge of mathematical terms and principles. Each question is followed by four possible answers. You are to decide which one of the four choices is correct.

1. Simplify: $-(3^2) + (5 - 7)^2 - 3(4 - 8)$
   - (A) −17
   - (B) −1
   - (C) 7
   - (D) 25

2. If a person reads 40 pages in 45 minutes, approximately how many minutes will it take her to read 265 pages?
   - (A) 202
   - (B) 236
   - (C) 265
   - (D) 298

3. W, X, Y, and Z lie on a circle with center A. If the diameter of the circle is 75, what is the sum of $\overline{AW}$, $\overline{AX}$, $\overline{AY}$, and $\overline{AZ}$?
   - (A) 75
   - (B) 300
   - (C) 150
   - (D) 106.5

4. A worker was paid $15,036 for 7 months of work. If he received the same amount each month, how much was he paid for the first 2 months?
   - (A) $2,148
   - (B) $4,296
   - (C) $6,444
   - (D) $8,592

5. 40% of what number is equal to 17?
   - (A) 2.35
   - (B) 6.8
   - (C) 42.5
   - (D) 680

6. The measures of two angles of a triangle are 25° and 110°. What is the measure of the third angle?
   - (A) 40°
   - (B) 45°
   - (C) 50°
   - (D) 55°

7. Michael is making cupcakes. He plans to give $\frac{1}{2}$ of the cupcakes to a friend and $\frac{1}{3}$ of the cupcakes to his coworkers. If he makes 48 cupcakes, how many will he have left over?

(A) 8

(B) 10

(C) 16

(D) 24

8. Which of the following is closest in value to $129,113 + 34,602$?

(A) 162,000

(B) 163,000

(C) 164,000

(D) 165,000

9. If $j = 4$, what is the value of $2(j-4)^4 - j + \frac{1}{2}j$?

(A) 0

(B) –2

(C) 2

(D) 4

10. Which of the following is equivalent to $(5^2 - 2)^2 + 3^3$?

(A) 25

(B) 30

(C) 556

(D) 538

11. In the fall, 425 students pass the math benchmark. In the spring, 680 students pass the same benchmark. What is the percentage increase in passing scores from fall to spring?

(A) 37.5%

(B) 55%

(C) 60%

(D) 62.5%

12. What is the area of the shape?

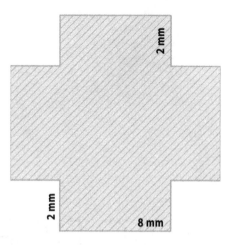

(A) 6 mm²

(B) 16 mm²

(C) 64 mm²

(D) 128 mm²

13. A fruit stand sells apples, bananas, and oranges at a ratio of 3:2:1. If the fruit stand sells 20 bananas, how many total pieces of fruit does the fruit stand sell?

(A) 10

(B) 30

(C) 40

(D) 60

14. Erica is at work for $8\frac{1}{2}$ hours a day. If she takes one 30-minute lunch break and two 15-minute breaks during the day, how many hours does she work?

(A) 6 hours, 30 minutes

(B) 6 hours, 45 minutes

(C) 7 hours, 15 minutes

(D) 7 hours, 30 minutes

15. If the value of y is between 0.0047 and 0.0162, which of the following could be the value of y?

(A) 0.0035

(B) 0.0055

(C) 0.0185

(D) 0.0238

16. A car traveled at 65 miles per hour for $1\frac{1}{2}$ hours and then traveled at 50 miles per hour for $2\frac{1}{2}$ hours. How many miles did the car travel?

(A) 190.5 miles

(B) 215.0 miles

(C) 222.5 miles

(D) 237.5 miles

17. A bike store is having a 30%-off sale, and one of the bikes is on sale for $385. What was the original price of this bike?

(A) $253.00

(B) $450.00

(C) $500.50

(D) $550.00

18. Adam is painting the outside walls of a 4-walled shed. The shed is 5 feet wide, 4 feet deep, and 7 feet high. How many square feet of paint will Adam need?

(A) 46 square feet

(B) 63 square feet

(C) 126 square feet

(D) 140 square feet

19. A grocery store sold 30% of its pears and had 455 pears remaining. How many pears did the grocery store start with?

(A) 602

(B) 650

(C) 692

(D) 700

20. A landscaping company charges 5 cents per square foot for fertilizer. How much would they charge to fertilize a 30-foot-by-50-foot lawn?

(A) $7.50

(B) $15.00

(C) $75.00

(D) $150.00

21. What is the value of the expression $0.5^x + 1$ when $x = -2$?

(A) 0.75

(B) 1.25

(C) 4

(D) 5

22. John and Ethan are working at a car wash. It takes John 1 hour to wash 3 cars. Ethan can wash 3 cars in 45 minutes. If they work together, how many cars can they wash in 1 hour?

(A) 6

(B) 7

(C) 9

(D) 12

23. Tiles are $12.51 per square yard. What will it cost to cover the floor of a room with tiles if the room is 10 feet wide and 12 feet long?

(A) $166.80

(B) $178.70

(C) $184.60

(D) $190.90

24. How many digits are in the sum $951.4 + 98.908 + 1.053$?

(A) 4

(B) 5

(C) 6

(D) 7

25. Melissa is ordering fencing to enclose a square area of 5,625 square feet. How many feet of fencing does she need?

(A) 75 feet

(B) 150 feet

(C) 300 feet

(D) 5,625 feet

READING COMPREHENSION

30 minutes

This section measures your ability to read and understand written material. Passages are followed by a series of multiple-choice questions. You are to choose the option that best answers the question based on the passage. No additional information or specific knowledge is needed.

The Battle of Little Bighorn, commonly called Custer's Last Stand, was a battle between the Lakota, the Northern Cheyenne, the Arapaho, and the Seventh Calvary Regiment of the US Army. Led by war leaders Crazy Horse and Chief Gall and the religious leader Sitting Bull, the allied tribes of the Plains Indians decisively defeated their US foes. Two hundred and sixty-eight US soldiers were killed, including General George Armstrong Custer, two of his brothers, his nephew, his brother-in-law, and six Indian scouts.

1. What is the main idea of this passage?
    (A) Most of General Custer's family died in the Battle of Little Bighorn.
    (B) The Seventh Calvary regiment was formed to fight Native American tribes.
    (C) Sitting Bull and George Custer were fierce enemies.
    (D) The Battle of Little Bighorn was a significant victory for the Plains Indians.

In 1953, doctors surgically removed the hippocampus of patient Henry Molaison in an attempt to stop his frequent seizures. Unexpectedly, he lost the ability to form new memories, leading to the biggest breakthrough in the science of memory. Molaison's long-term memory—of events more than a year before his surgery—was unchanged as was his ability to learn physical skills. From this, scientists learned that different types of memory are handled by different parts of the brain, with the hippocampus responsible for *episodic memory,* the short-term recall of events. They have since discovered that some memories are then channeled to the cortex, the outer layers of the brain that handle higher functions, where they are gradually integrated with related information to build lasting knowledge about our world.

2. The main idea of the passage is that
    (A) Molaison's surgery posed significant risk to the functioning of his brain.
    (B) short-term and long-term memory are stored in different parts of the brain.
    (C) long-term memory forms over a longer period than short-term memory.
    (D) memories of physical skills are processed differently than memories of events.

Archaeologists have discovered the oldest known specimens of bedbugs in a cave in Oregon where humans once lived. The three different species date back to between 5,000 and 11,000 years ago. The finding gives scientists a clue as to how bedbugs became human parasites. These bedbugs, like those that plague humans today, originated as bat parasites. Scientists hypothesize that it was the co-habitation of humans and bats in the caves that encouraged the bugs to begin feeding on the humans. The three species found in the Oregon caves are actually still around today, although they continue to prefer bats. Humans only lived seasonally in the Oregon cave system, however, which might explain why these insects did not fully transfer to human hosts like bedbugs elsewhere did.

3. With which of the following claims about bedbugs would the author most likely agree?

    (A) Modern bedbugs that prefer humans thrive better in areas with extensive light.

    (B) Bedbugs are a relatively fragile species that has struggled to survive over time.

    (C) The transition to humans significantly accelerated the growth of bedbug populations.

    (D) Bedbugs that prefer humans originated in caves that humans occupied year-round.

The Bastille, Paris's famous historical prison, was originally built in 1370 as a fortification, called a *bastide* in Old French, to protect the city from English invasion during the Hundred Years' War. It rose 100 feet into the air, had eight towers, and was surrounded by a moat more than eighty feet wide. In the seventeenth century, the government converted the fortress into an elite prison for upper-class felons, political disruptors, and spies. Residents of the Bastille arrived by direct order of the king and usually were left there to languish without a trial.

4. In the first sentence, the word *fortification* most nearly means

    (A) royal castle.

    (B) national symbol.

    (C) seat of government.

    (D) defensive structure.

Taking a person's temperature is one of the most basic and common health care tasks. Everyone from nurses to emergency medical technicians to concerned parents should be able to grab a thermometer to take a patient or loved one's temperature. But what's the best way to get an accurate reading? The answer depends on the situation.

The most common way people measure body temperature is orally. A simple digital or disposable thermometer is placed under the tongue for a few minutes, and the task is done. There are many situations, however, when measuring temperature orally isn't an option. For example, when a person can't breathe through his nose, he won't be able to keep his mouth closed long enough to get an accurate reading. In these situations, it's often preferable to place the thermometer in the rectum or armpit. Using the rectum also has the added benefit of providing a much more accurate reading than other locations can provide.

It's also often the case that certain people, like agitated patients or fussy babies, won't be able to sit still long enough for an accurate reading. In these situations, it's best to use a thermometer that works much more quickly, such as one that measures temperature in the ear or at the temporal artery. No matter which method is chosen, however, it's important to check the average temperature for each region, as it can vary by several degrees.

5. Which statement is NOT a detail from the passage?

    (A) Taking a temperature in the ear or at the temporal artery is more accurate than taking it orally.

    (B) If an individual cannot breathe through the nose, taking his or her temperature orally will likely give an inaccurate reading.

    (C) The standard human body temperature varies depending on whether it's measured in the mouth, rectum, armpit, ear, or temporal artery.

    (D) The most common way to measure temperature is by placing a thermometer in the mouth.

6.   What is the author's primary purpose in writing this essay?

   (A) to advocate for the use of thermometers that measure temperature in the ear or at the temporal artery

   (B) to explain the methods available to measure a person's temperature and the situation where each method is appropriate

   (C) to warn readers that the average temperature of the human body varies by region

   (D) to discuss how nurses use different types of thermometers depending on the type of patient they are examining

7.   What is the meaning of the word *agitated* in the last paragraph?

   (A) obviously upset

   (B) quickly moving

   (C) violently ill

   (D) slightly dirty

8.   According to the passage, why is it sometimes preferable to take a person's temperature rectally?

   (A) Rectal readings are more accurate than oral readings.

   (B) Many people cannot sit still long enough to have their temperatures taken orally.

   (C) Temperature readings can vary widely between regions of the body.

   (D) Many people do not have access to quick-acting thermometers.

One of the most dramatic acts of nonviolent resistance in India's movement for independence from Britain came in 1930, when independence leader Mahatma Gandhi organized a 240-mile march to the Arabian Sea. The goal of the march was to make salt from seawater, in defiance of British law. The British prohibited Indians from collecting or selling salt—a vital part of the Indian diet—requiring them instead to buy it from British merchants and pay a heavy salt tax. The crowd of marchers grew along the way to tens of thousands of people. In Dandi, Gandhi picked up a small chunk of salt and broke British law. Thousands in Dandi followed his lead as did millions of fellow protestors in coastal towns throughout India. In an attempt to quell the civil disobedience, authorities arrested more than 60,000 people across the country, including Gandhi himself.

9.   With which of the following claims about civil disobedience would the author most likely agree?

   (A) Civil disobedience is a disorganized form of protest easily quashed by government.

   (B) Civil disobedience requires extreme violations of existing law to be effective.

   (C) Civil disobedience is an effective strategy for effecting political change.

   (D) Civil disobedience is only effective in countries that already have democracy.

The odds of success for any new restaurant are slim. Competition in the city is fierce, and the low margin of return means that aspiring restaurateurs must be exact and ruthless with their budget and pricing. The fact that The City Café has lasted as long as it has is a testament to its owners' skills.

10. Which of the following conclusions is well supported by the passage?
   (A) The City Café offers the best casual dining in town.
   (B) The City Café has a well-managed budget and prices items on its menu appropriately.
   (C) The popularity of The City Café will likely fall as new restaurants open in the city.
   (D) The City Café has a larger margin of return than other restaurants in the city.

11. Which of the following is the meaning of *testament* as used in the last sentence?
   (A) story
   (B) surprise
   (C) artifact
   (D) evidence

We've been told for years that the recipe for weight loss is fewer calories in than calories out. In other words, eat less and exercise more, and your body will take care of the rest. As many of those who've tried to diet can attest, this edict doesn't always produce results. If you're one of those folks, you might have felt that you just weren't doing it right—that the failure was all your fault.

However, several new studies released this year have suggested that it might not be your fault at all. For example, a study of people who'd lost a high percentage of their body weight (>17%) in a short period of time found that they could not physically maintain their new weight. Scientists measured their resting metabolic rate and found that they'd need to consume only a few hundred calories a day to meet their metabolic needs. Basically, their bodies were in starvation mode and seemed to desperately hang on to each and every calorie. Eating even a single healthy, well-balanced meal a day would cause these subjects to start packing back on the pounds.

Other studies have shown that factors like intestinal bacteria, distribution of body fat, and hormone levels can affect the manner in which our bodies process calories. There's also the fact that it's actually quite difficult to measure the number of calories consumed during a particular meal and the number used while exercising.

12. Which of the following would be the best summary statement to conclude the passage?
   (A) It turns out that conventional dieting wisdom doesn't capture the whole picture of how our bodies function.
   (B) Still, counting calories and tracking exercise is a good idea if you want to lose weight.
   (C) In conclusion, it's important to lose weight responsibly: losing too much weight at once can negatively impact the body.
   (D) It's easy to see that diets don't work, so we should focus less on weight loss and more on overall health.

13. Which of the following would weaken the author's argument?

    (A) a new diet pill from a pharmaceutical company that promises to help patients lose weight by changing intestinal bacteria

    (B) the personal experience of a man who was able to lose a significant amount of weight by taking in fewer calories than he used

    (C) a study showing that people in different geographic locations lose different amounts of weight when on the same diet

    (D) a study showing that people often misreport their food intake when part of a scientific study on weight loss

When a fire destroyed San Francisco's American Indian Center in October of 1969, American Indian groups set their sights on the recently closed island prison of Alcatraz as a site of a new Indian cultural center and school. Ignored by the government, an activist group known as Indians of All Tribes sailed to Alcatraz in the early morning hours with eighty-nine men, women, and children. They landed on Alcatraz, claiming it for all the tribes of North America. Their demands were ignored, and so the group continued to occupy the island for the next nineteen months, its numbers swelling up to 600 as others joined. By January of 1970, many of the original protestors had left, and on June 11, 1971, federal marshals forcibly removed the last residents.

14. The main idea of this passage is that

    (A) the government refused to listen to the demands of American Indians.

    (B) American Indians occupied Alcatraz in protest of government policy.

    (C) few people joined the occupation of Alcatraz, weakening its effectiveness.

    (D) the government took violent action against protestors at Alcatraz.

In an effort to increase women's presence in government, several countries in Latin America, including Argentina, Brazil, and Mexico, have implemented legislated candidate quotas. These quotas require that at least 30 percent of a party's candidate list in any election cycle consists of women who have a legitimate chance at election. As a result, Latin America has the greatest number of female heads of government in the world, and the second highest percentage of female members of parliament after Nordic Europe. However, these trends do not carry over outside of politics. While 25 percent of legislators in Latin America are now women, less than 2 percent of CEOs in the region are female.

15. What is the main idea of the passage?

    (A) In Latin America, political parties must nominate women for office.

    (B) Latin America is the region with the greatest gender equality.

    (C) Women in Latin America have greater economic influence than political influence.

    (D) Women have a significant presence in Latin American politics.

Tourists flock to Yellowstone National Park each year to view the geysers that bubble and erupt throughout it. What most of these tourists do not know is that these geysers are formed by a caldera, a hot crater in the earth's crust, that was created by a series of three eruptions of an ancient supervolcano. These eruptions, which began 2.1 million years ago, spewed between 1,000 to 2,450 cubic kilometers of volcanic matter at such a rate that the volcano's magma chamber collapsed, creating the craters.

16.   The main idea of the passage is that
    (A) Yellowstone National Park is a popular tourist destination.
    (B) The geysers in Yellowstone National Park rest on a caldera in the earth's crust.
    (C) A supervolcano once sat in the area covered by Yellowstone National Park.
    (D) The earth's crust is weaker in Yellowstone National Park.

When the Spanish-American War broke out in 1898, the US Army was small and understaffed. President William McKinley called for 1,250 volunteers primarily from the Southwest to serve in the First US Volunteer Calvary. Eager to fight, the ranks were quickly filled by a diverse group of cowboys, gold prospectors, hunters, gamblers, Native Americans, veterans, police officers, and college students looking for an adventure. The officer corps was composed of veterans of the Civil War and the Indian Wars. With more volunteers than it could accept, the army set high standards: all the recruits had to be skilled on horseback and with guns. Consequently, they became known as the Rough Riders.

17.   According to the passage, all the recruits were required to
    (A) have previously fought in a war.
    (B) be American citizens.
    (C) live in the Southwest.
    (D) ride a horse well.

At first glance, the landscape of the northern end of the Rift Valley appears to be a stretch of barren land. Paleoanthropologists, however, have discovered an abundance of fossils just beneath the dusty surface. They believe this area once contained open grasslands near lakes and rivers, populated with grazing animals. Forty miles from this spot, in 1974, scientists uncovered a 3.2 million-year-old non-human hominid they nicknamed "Lucy." And, in 2013, researchers found the oldest fossil in the human ancestral line. Before this, the oldest fossil from the genus *Homo*—of which *Homo sapiens* are the only remaining species—dated only back to 2.3 million years ago, leaving a 700,000-year gap between Lucy's species and the advent of humans. The new fossil dated back to 2.75 and 2.8 million years ago, pushing the appearance of humans back 400,000 years.

18.   According to the passage, the discovery of Lucy
    (A) gave scientists new information about the development of humans.
    (B) provided evidence of a different ecosystem in the ancient Rift Valley.
    (C) supported the belief that other hominids existed significantly before humans.
    (D) closed the gap between the development of other hominids and humans.

CONTINUE

The social and political discourse of America continues to be permeated with idealism. An idealistic viewpoint asserts that the ideals of freedom, equality, justice, and human dignity are the truths that Americans must continue to aspire to. Idealists argue that truth is what should be, not necessarily what is. In general, they work to improve things and to make them as close to ideal as possible.

19. Which of the following best captures the author's purpose?

   (A) to advocate for freedom, equality, justice, and human rights
   (B) to explain what an idealist believes in
   (C) to explain what's wrong with social and political discourse in America
   (D) to persuade readers to believe in certain truths

Alexander Hamilton and James Madison called for the Constitutional Convention to write a constitution as the foundation of a stronger federal government. Madison and other Federalists like John Adams believed in separation of powers, republicanism, and a strong federal government. Despite the separation of powers that would be provided for in the US Constitution, anti-Federalists like Thomas Jefferson called for even more limitations on the power of the federal government.

20. In the context of the passage below, which of the following would most likely NOT support a strong federal government?

   (A) Alexander Hamilton
   (B) James Madison
   (C) John Adams
   (D) Thomas Jefferson

The cisco, a foot-long freshwater fish native to the Great Lakes, once thrived throughout the basin but had virtually disappeared by the 1950s. However, today fishermen are pulling them up by the net-load in Lake Michigan and Lake Ontario. It is highly unusual for a native species to revive, and the reason for the cisco's reemergence is even more unlikely. The cisco have an invasive species, quagga mussels, to thank for their return. Quagga mussels depleted nutrients in the lakes, harming other species highly dependent on these nutrients. Cisco, however, thrive in low-nutrient environments. As other species—many invasive—diminished, cisco flourished in their place.

21. It can be inferred from the passage that most invasive species

   (A) support the growth of native species.
   (B) do not impact the development of native species.
   (C) struggle to survive in their new environments.
   (D) cause the decline of native species.

After looking at five houses, Robert and I have decided to buy the one on Forest Road. The first two homes we visited didn't have the space we need—the first had only one bathroom, and the second did not have a guest bedroom. The third house, on Pine Street, had enough space inside but didn't have a big enough yard for our three dogs. The fourth house we looked at, on Rice Avenue, was stunning but well above our price range. The last home, on Forest Road, wasn't in the neighborhood we wanted to live in. However, it had the right amount of space for the right price.

22. What is the author's conclusion about the house on Pine Street?

(A) The house did not have enough bedrooms.

(B) The house did not have a big enough yard.

(C) The house was not in the right neighborhood.

(D) The house was too expensive.

It could be said that the great battle between the North and South we call the Civil War was a battle for individual identity. The states of the South had their own culture, one based on farming, independence, and the rights of both man and state to determine their own paths. Similarly, the North had forged its own identity as a center of centralized commerce and manufacturing. This clash of lifestyles was bound to create tension, and this tension was bound to lead to war. But people who try to sell you this narrative are wrong. The Civil War was not a battle of cultural identities—it was a battle about slavery. All other explanations for the war are either a direct consequence of the South's desire for wealth at the expense of her fellow man or a fanciful invention to cover up this sad portion of our nation's history. And it cannot be denied that this time in our past was very sad indeed.

23. What is the meaning of the word *fanciful* in the passage?

(A) complicated

(B) imaginative

(C) successful

(D) unfortunate

24. What is the author's primary purpose in writing this essay?

(A) to convince readers that slavery was the main cause of the Civil War

(B) to illustrate the cultural differences between the North and the South before the Civil War

(C) to persuade readers that the North deserved to win the Civil War

(D) to demonstrate that the history of the Civil War is too complicated to be understood clearly

The greatest changes in sensory, motor, and perceptual development happen in the first two years of life. When babies are first born, most of their senses operate in a similar way to those of adults. For example, babies are able to hear before they are born; studies show that babies turn toward the sound of their mothers' voices just minutes after being born, indicating they recognize the mother's voice from their time in the womb.

The exception to this rule is vision. A baby's vision changes significantly in its first year of life; initially it has a range of vision of only 8 – 12 inches and no depth perception. As a result, infants rely primarily on hearing; vision does not become the dominant sense until around the age of 12 months. Babies also prefer faces to other objects. This preference, along with their limited vision range, means that their sight is initially focused on their caregiver.

25. Which of the following senses do babies primarily rely on?

(A) vision

(B) hearing

(C) touch

(D) smell

MECHANICAL COMPREHENSION

15 minutes

This section measures your understanding of basic mechanical principles. Each question is followed by three possible answers. You are to decide which one of the three choices is correct.

1.

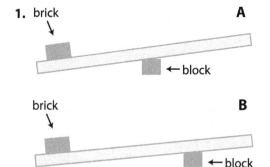

Compared to figure A above, the brick in figure B will

(A) be lifted the same height, and it will take the same amount of effort to do so.

(B) be lifted higher, and it will take more effort to do so.

(C) not be lifted as high, and it will take more effort to do so.

2. Because a crowbar has a fulcrum in the middle of the effort and the resistance, it is an example of a

(A) first-class lever.

(B) second-class lever.

(C) third-class lever.

3.

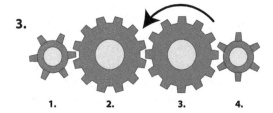

Which of the other gears is moving in the same direction as Gear 3?

(A) Gear 1 only

(B) Gear 2 only

(C) Gear 4 only

4.

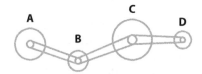

If Pulley B is the driver and turns clockwise, which pulley turns the slowest?

(A) Pulley A turns the slowest.

(B) Pulley C turns the slowest.

(C) Pulley D turns the slowest.

5.

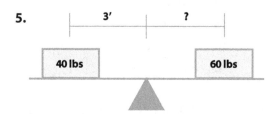

A 40-pound block and a 60-pound block are placed on a uniform board as shown above. How far to the right of the fulcrum must the 60-pound block be placed in order for the board to be balanced?

(A) 1 foot

(B) 2 feet

(C) 4 feet

6.

The simple machine shown above is an example of

(A) a lever.

(B) a pulley.

(C) an inclined plane.

7.

pulley

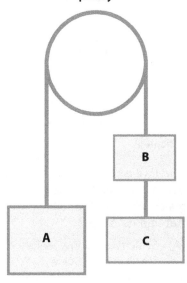

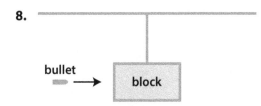

Blocks A, B, and C are hanging from a pulley as shown in the figure. If Block A weighs 70 pounds and Block B weighs 20 pounds, what must the weight of Block C be in order for the blocks to be at rest?

(A) 30 pounds

(B) 35 pounds

(C) 50 pounds

8.

bullet → block

A bullet is shot at a stationary block that is hanging from the ceiling as shown. What direction will the block swing after the bullet hits the block?

(A) down and to the right

(B) down and to the left

(C) up and to the right

9. Why is it so difficult to hold a beach ball under water?

(A) The ball is full of air, which is much less dense than water.

(B) The ball expands under water, so it rises faster.

(C) The cool water will cool the air in the ball, making it rise.

10.

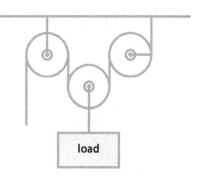

A block is hanging from a pulley system as shown in the figure. The theoretical mechanical advantage of the system is

(A) 1.

(B) 2.

(C) 3.

11. On Earth, Objects A and B have the same mass and weight. If Object B is moved to the moon, which of the following statements is true?

(A) Both objects have the same mass, but Object A now has the greater weight.

(B) Both objects have the same weight, but Object A now has the greater mass.

(C) Both objects still have the same mass and weight.

12.

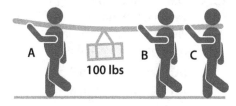

An object is being carried by three people as shown above. Which person bears the most weight?

(A) A

(B) B and C

(C) All three bear the same weight.

CONTINUE

13.

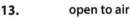

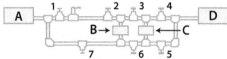

In the figure shown below, assume that all valves are closed. For the air to flow from A to D without flowing through B and C, it is necessary to open valves

(A) 1, 2, and 5.

(B) 1, 2, 3, and 4.

(C) 5, 6, and 7.

14. A steel ball with a temperature of 150°C is dropped into a liquid with a temperature of 120°C. Which of the following statements about the equilibrium temperature has to be true?

(A) The equilibrium temperature is exactly 135°C.

(B) The equilibrium temperature is between 120°C and 150°C.

(C) The equilibrium temperature is exactly 270°C.

15. Water is flowing through Pipe A, which has a diameter of 15 cm, into Pipe B, which has a diameter of 20 cm. The water will flow

(A) faster through Pipe A.

(B) faster through Pipe B.

(C) at the same speed through Pipe A and Pipe B.

16. Water flows out of a water tower at a rate of 3 gallons per minute and flows in at a rate of 140 gallons per hour. After one hour, the volume of water in the tank will be

(A) the same.

(B) 40 gallons less.

(C) 40 gallons more.

17.

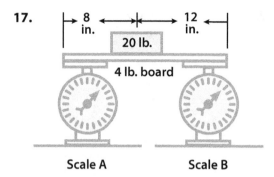

A weight is placed on a uniform board between two identical scales. Which of the following statements is true?

(A) Scale A will show a higher reading than Scale B because more weight is to the left of the fulcrum.

(B) Scale B will show a higher reading than Scale A because more weight is to the left of the fulcrum.

(C) The scales read the same weight.

18.

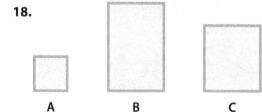

The three containers shown above are filled with the same gas. Which statement is true?

(A) Container A will experience the greatest pressure.

(B) Container B will experience the greatest pressure.

(C) Container C will experience the greatest pressure.

19. Two charges are held at a distance of 1 m from each other. Charge q_1 is −2e and charge q_2 is −2e. What will happen when the charges are released and free to move?

(A) q_1 and q_2 will remain at rest and not move.

(B) q_1 and q_2 will attract and move closer together.

(C) q_1 and q_2 will repel and move farther apart.

20.

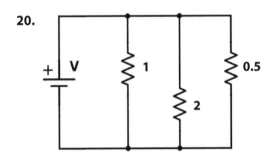

Find the equivalent resistance, R_{eq}, for the circuit in the figure above.

(A) 0.5 kΩ

(B) 1 kΩ

(C) 3.5 kΩ

21. What is the key electrical difference between a conducting material and an insulating material?

(A) A conducting material will conduct electricity, and an insulating material will not.

(B) A conducting material creates electrons, and an insulating material destroys them.

(C) An insulating material will create heat when electricity flows through it, and a conducting material will not.

22. An 80-pound object is placed on a scale inside an elevator that begins to travel upward. The scale will read that the weight of the object is

(A) 80 pounds.

(B) greater than 80 pounds.

(C) less than 80 pounds.

23. Two ropes are connected on either side of a mass of 100 kg resting on a flat surface. Each rope is pulling on the mass with 50 N of force, parallel to the ground. What can be said about the motion of the mass?

(A) The mass will accelerate to left.

(B) The mass is in equilibrium.

(C) The mass will accelerate to the right.

24.

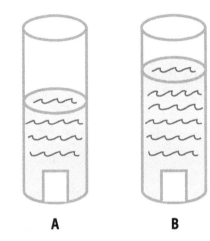

A   B

Objects A and B have the same mass and are placed in separate graduated cylinders that are each filled with 50 mL of water. If the water level rises higher in the cylinder containing Object B, which statement is true?

(A) Object A has a higher density than Object B.

(B) Object B has a higher density than Object A.

(C) Objects A and B have the same density.

25. A boat is crossing a river with a fast-moving current. If the captain aims the boat at a point of the opposite bank directly across from his starting point, where will the boat land?

(A) Downstream from his starting point

(B) Upstream from his starting point

(C) Directly across from his starting point

ANSWER KEY

MATH SKILLS

1. **(C)**

   Simplify using PEMDAS.
   $-(3^2) + (5 - 7)^2 - 3(4 - 8)$
   $= -(3^2) + (-2)^2 - 3(-4)$
   $= -9 + 4 - 3(-4)$
   $= -9 + 4 + 12 = \mathbf{7}$

2. **(D)**

   Write a proportion and then solve for x.
   $\frac{40}{45} = \frac{265}{x}$
   $40x = 11{,}925$
   $x = 298.125 \approx \mathbf{298}$

3. **(C)**

   All the points lie on the circle, so each line segment is a radius. The sum of the 4 lines will be 4 times the radius.
   $r = \frac{75}{2} = 37.5$
   $4r = \mathbf{150}$

4. **(B)**

   Write a proportion and then solve for x.
   $\frac{15{,}036}{7} = \frac{x}{2}$
   $7x = 30{,}072$
   $x = \mathbf{4{,}296}$

5. **(C)**

   Use the equation for percentages.
   $whole = \frac{part}{percentage} = \frac{17}{0.4} = \mathbf{42.5}$

6. **(B)**

   The sum of the measures of the three angles in a triangle is 180°. Subtract the two given angle measures from 180 to find the measure of the third angle.
   $180° - 25° - 110° = \mathbf{45°}$

7. **(A)**

   Add the number of cupcakes he will give to his friend and to his coworkers, then subtract that value from 48.
   # of cupcakes for his friend:
   $\frac{1}{2} \times 48 = 24$
   # of cupcakes for his coworkers:
   $\frac{1}{3} \times 48 = 16$
   $48 - (24 + 16) = \mathbf{8}$

8. **(C)**

   Round each value and add.
   $129{,}113 \approx 129{,}000$
   $34{,}602 \approx 35{,}000$
   $129{,}000 + 35{,}000 = \mathbf{164{,}000}$

9. (B)

Plug 4 in for j and simplify.

$2(j - 4)^4 - j + \frac{1}{2}j$

$2(4 - 4)^4 - 4 + \frac{1}{2}(4) = \mathbf{-2}$

10. (C)

Simplify using PEMDAS.

$(5^2 - 2)^2 + 3^3$

$(25 - 2)^2 + 3^3$

$(23)^2 + 3^3$

$529 + 27 = \mathbf{556}$

11. (C)

Use the formula for percent change.

$percent\ change = \frac{amount\ of\ change}{original\ amount}$

$= \frac{(680 - 425)}{425}$

$= \frac{255}{425} = 0.60 = \mathbf{60\%}$

12. (D)

Find the area of the square as if it did not have the corners cut out.

$12\ mm \times 12\ mm = 144\ mm^2$

Find the area of the four cut out corners.

$2\ mm \times 2\ mm = 4\ mm^2$

$4(4\ mm^2) = 16\ mm^2$

Subtract the area of the cut out corners from the large square to find the area of the shape.

$144\ mm^2 - 16\ mm^2 = \mathbf{128\ mm^2}$

13. (D)

Assign variables and write the ratios as fractions. Then, cross multiply to solve for the number of apples and oranges sold.

x = apples

$\frac{apples}{bananas} = \frac{3}{2} = \frac{x}{20}$

$60 = 2x$

$x = 30$ apples

y = oranges

$\frac{oranges}{bananas} = \frac{1}{2} = \frac{y}{20}$

$2y = 20$

$y = 10$ oranges

To find the total, add the number of apples, oranges, and bananas together. $30 + 20 + 10 = \mathbf{60\ pieces}$ **of fruit**

14. (D)

Find the time that Erica spends on break and subtract this from her total time at work.

$30 + 2(15) = 1$ hour

$8\frac{1}{2} - 1 = 7\frac{1}{2} = \mathbf{7\ hours,\ 30\ minutes}$

15. (B)

All of the decimal numbers are expressed in ten-thousandths. 55 is between 47 and 162, so **0.0055** is between 0.0047 and 0.0162.

16. (C)

Multiply the car's speed by the time traveled to find the distance.

$1.5(65) = 97.5$ miles

$2.5(50) = 125$ miles

$97.5 + 125 = \mathbf{222.5\ miles}$

17. (D)

Set up an equation. The original price (p) minus 30% of the original price is $385.

$p - 0.3p = 385$

$p = \frac{385}{0.7} = \mathbf{\$550}$

18. (C)

Two of the walls are 5 feet by 7 feet. The other two walls are 4 feet by 7 feet. Therefore, the total area of the four walls is:

$2(5)(7) + 2(4)(7) = 70 + 56 =$ **126 square feet**

19. (B)

Set up an equation. If p is the original number of pears, the store has sold $0.30p$ pears. The original number minus the number sold will equal 455.

$p - 0.30p = 455$

$p = \frac{455}{0.7} = \mathbf{650\ pears}$

20. (C)

Multiply the area by the charge per square foot.

Area $= 50 \times 30 = 1{,}500$ square feet
$1{,}500 \times 0.05 =$ **\$75.00**

21. **(D)**

    Substitute -2 for x and evaluate.
    $0.5^{-2} + 1 = 4 + 1 =$ **5**

22. **(B)**

    Use a proportion to find the number of cars that Ethan can wash in 1 hour (60 minutes). Then add to answer the question.
    $\frac{3}{45} = \frac{x}{60}$
    $3(60) = x(45)$
    $180 = 45x$
    $4 = x$
    $3 + 4 =$ **7**

23. **(A)**

    Find the area of the room in square feet and convert it to square yards (1 square yard = 9 square feet). Then multiply by the cost per square yard.

Area $= 10 \times 12 = 120$ square feet
$\frac{120}{9} = \frac{40}{3}$ square yards
$\frac{40}{3} \times \$12.51 = \frac{\$500.40}{3} =$ **\$166.80**

24. **(D)**

    Add zeros as needed so that each number is expressed in thousandths; then add the numbers.
    $951.400 + 98.908 + 1.053 =$
    $1{,}051.361 \rightarrow$ **7 digits**

25. **(C)**

    Use the area to find the length of a side of the square. Then find the perimeter of the square.
    $x^2 = 5{,}625$
    $x = \sqrt{5{,}625} = 75$
    Perimeter $= 4x = 4(75) =$ **300 feet**

1. (A) is incorrect. While the text does list several family members of Custer who died in the battle, this is not the main idea.

(B) is incorrect. The author does not explain why the cavalry was formed.

(C) is incorrect. The author does not describe the personal relationship between Sitting Bull and Custer.

(D) is correct. The author writes, "the allied tribes…decisively defeated their US foes."

2. (A) is incorrect. While the author does describe his memory loss, this is not the main idea of the passage.

(B) is correct. The author writes, "From this, scientists learned that different types of memory are handled by different parts of the brain."

(C) is incorrect. The author does explain the differences in long-term and short-term memory formation, but not until the end of the passage.

(D) is incorrect. While it is implied that memories of physical skills are processed differently than memories of events, this is not the main idea of the passage.

3. (A) is incorrect. The author does not address the impact of light on bedbugs.

(B) is incorrect. The author explains that the three discovered species still exist today.

(C) is incorrect. The author does not address the growth rate of bedbug populations.

(D) is correct. The author writes, "Humans only lived seasonally in the Oregon cave system, however, which might explain why these insects did not fully transfer to human hosts like bedbugs elsewhere did."

4. (A) is incorrect. There is no indication that the Bastille was occupied by royalty.

(B) is incorrect. There is no indication that the structure was intended to represent anything.

(C) is incorrect. There is no indication that the Bastille was used for governing.

(D) is correct. The author writes that the Bastille was originally built "to protect the city from English invasion during the Hundred Years' War."

5. **(A) is correct.** This detail is not stated in the passage.

(B) is incorrect. The second paragraph states that "when a person can't breathe through his nose, he won't be able to keep his mouth closed long enough to get an accurate reading."

(C) is incorrect. The final paragraph states that "[no] matter which method [of taking a temperature] is chosen, however, it's important to check the average temperature for each region, as it can vary by several degrees."

(D) is incorrect. The second paragraph states that "[t]he most common way people measure body temperature is orally."

6. (A) is incorrect. Thermometers that measure temperature in the ear and temporal artery are mentioned in the passage; however, they are a supporting detail for the author's primary purpose.

(B) is correct. In the first paragraph, the author writes, "But what's the best way to get an accurate reading? The answer depends on the situation." She then goes on to describe various options and their applications.

(C) is incorrect. Though this detail is mentioned, it is not the author's primary focus.

(D) is incorrect. The author writes about how many people—not only nurses—use different types of thermometers in different situations.

7. **(A) is correct.** The final paragraph states that "agitated patients...won't be able to sit still long enough for an accurate reading." The reader can infer that an agitated patient is a patient who is visibly upset, annoyed, or uncomfortable.

(B) is incorrect. While some agitated patients may move quickly, this is not necessarily the meaning of the word in context.

(C) is incorrect. The term *violently ill* does not necessarily explain why a patient would have a difficult time sitting still.

(D) is incorrect. The team *slightly dirty* does not explain why a patient would have a difficult time sitting still.

8. **(A) is correct.** The second paragraph of the passage states that "[u]sing the rectum also has the added benefit of providing a much more accurate reading than other locations can provide."

(B) is incorrect. In the final paragraph, the author suggests that "certain people, like agitated patients or fussy babies" might have a difficult time sitting still but does not suggest that this is a problem for "many" people.

(C) is incorrect. In the final paragraph, the author writes that "it's important to check the average temperature for each region, as it can vary by several degrees," but does not cite this as a reason to use a rectal thermometer.

(D) is incorrect. The author does not mention access to thermometers as a consideration.

9. (A) is incorrect. The author writes that the protest spread in spite of government attempts to end it.

(B) is incorrect. The author writes, "In Dandi, Gandhi picked up a small chunk of salt and broke British law." Picking up a piece of salt is not itself an extreme act; Gandhi was able to make a big statement with a small action.

(C) is correct. The author describes a situation in which civil disobedience had an enormous impact.

(D) is incorrect. The action the author describes occurred in India when it was controlled by Britain, a colonial and nondemocratic power.

10. (A) is incorrect. The author points to the skills of the owner as the reason for The City Café's long-term success, not the quality of the dining experience.

(B) is correct. The passage states that restaurateurs must be "exact and ruthless with their budget and pricing." The success of The City Café implies that its owners have done that.

(C) is incorrect. The passage suggests that most new restaurants struggle but does not discuss how new restaurants affect the popularity of existing restaurants.

(D) is incorrect. The passage implies that all restaurateurs must work with the low margin of return and simply suggests that the owners of The City Café have made the most of it, not that they have any advantage in this respect.

11. (A) is incorrect. This answer choice does not fit in the context of the sentence; the author has not told a story about The City Café's success.

(B) is incorrect. This answer choice does not fit in the context of the sentence; the author does not indicate surprise.

(C) is incorrect. This answer choice does not fit in the context of the sentence.

(D) is correct. *Evidence* best describes the idea that The City Café's longevity is proof of its owners' skills.

12. **(A) is correct.** The bulk of the passage is dedicated to showing that conventional wisdom about "fewer calories in than calories out" isn't true for many people and is

more complicated than previously believed.

(B) is incorrect. The author indicates that calorie counting is not an effective way to lose weight.

(C) is incorrect. Though the author indicates that this may be the case, the negative impacts of losing weight quickly are not the main point of the passage; a more inclusive sentence is needed to conclude the passage successfully.

(D) is incorrect. The author does not indicate that diets don't work at all, simply that the scientific understanding of dieting is still limited.

13. (A) is incorrect. A new diet pill would have no effect on the existing studies and would not prove anything about conventional dieting wisdom.

(B) is incorrect. A single anecdotal example would not be enough to contradict the results of well-designed studies; if anything, the account would provide another example of how complex the topics of dieting and weight loss are.

(C) is incorrect. This answer choice would strengthen the author's argument by highlighting the complexity of the topic of dieting.

(D) is correct. People misreporting the amount of food they ate would introduce error into studies on weight loss and might make the studies the author cites unreliable.

14. (A) is incorrect. While the author states this, it is not the main idea.

(B) is correct. The author states, "Ignored by the government, an activist group known as Indians of All Tribes sailed to Alcatraz in the early morning hours with eighty-nine men, women, and children." The author goes on to describe the nineteen-month occupation of the island.

(C) is incorrect. The author states that up to 600 people joined the occupation.

(D) is incorrect. The author does not describe any violent action towards protestors.

15. (A) is incorrect. While this fact is stated in the passage, it is not the main idea.

(B) is incorrect. The author writes, "However, these trends do not carry over outside of politics."

(C) is incorrect. The author explains that women have a large amount of political influence but less economic influence.

(D) is correct. The passage discusses the large number of women in political positions in Latin America.

16. (A) is incorrect. While this is stated in the first sentence, it is not the main idea.

(B) is correct. The passage describes the origin of Yellowstone's geysers.

(C) is incorrect. While the author states this in the passage, it is not the main idea.

(D) is incorrect. This is not stated in the passage.

17. (A) is incorrect. The author writes that the officers, not the volunteers, were veterans.

(B) is incorrect. The passage does not mention a citizenship requirement.

(C) is incorrect. While most of the volunteers were indeed from the Southwest, the passage does not say this was a requirement.

(D) is correct. The author writes, "the army set high standards: all of the recruits had to be skilled on horseback...."

18. (A) is incorrect. The author writes, "scientists uncovered a 3.2 million-year-old non-human hominid they nicknamed 'Lucy.'"

(B) is incorrect. The author does not connect Lucy's discovery with the knowledge about the area's past ecosystem.

(C) is correct. The author writes that before Lucy's discovery, the oldest known fossil from the genus Homo "dated only back to 2.3 million years ago, leaving a 700,000-year gap between Lucy's species and the advent of humans."

(D) is incorrect. The author explains it was the 2013 discovery that narrowed the gap.

19. (A) is incorrect. The author identifies the ideals associated with idealism but does not offer an opinion on or advocate for them.

(B) is correct. The purpose of the passage is to explain what an idealist believes in. The author does not offer any opinions or try to persuade readers about the importance of certain values.

(C) is incorrect. The author states that social and political discourse are "permeated with idealism" but does not suggest that this is destructive or wrong.

(D) is incorrect. The author provides the reader with information but does not seek to change the reader's opinions or behaviors.

20. (A) is incorrect. The author states that "Alexander Hamilton…called for the Constitutional Convention to write a constitution as the foundation of a stronger federal government."

(B) is incorrect. The author states that "James Madison called for the Constitutional Convention to write a constitution as the foundation of a stronger federal government."

(C) is incorrect. The author states that "Federalists like John Adams believed in… a strong federal government."

(D) is correct. In the passage, Thomas Jefferson is defined as an anti-Federalist, in contrast with Federalists who believed in a strong federal government.

21. (A) is incorrect. The author provides no evidence that invasive species typically help native species.

(B) is incorrect. The author writes that the quagga mussels, an invasive species, harmed native species.

(C) is incorrect. The author implies that quagga mussels are thriving.

(D) is correct. The author writes that "the reason for the cisco's reemergence is even more unlikely. The cisco have an invasive species, quagga mussels, to thank for their return."

22. (A) is incorrect. The author indicates that the house on Pine Street "had enough space inside[.]"

(B) is correct. The author says that the house on Pine Street "had enough space inside but didn't have a big enough yard for [their] three dogs."

(C) is incorrect. The author does not mention the neighborhood of the Pine Street house.

(D) is incorrect. The author does not mention the price of the Pine Street house.

23. (A) is incorrect. The author does not suggest that the narrative of the Civil War as "a battle for individual identity" is a complicated one, only that it is untrue.

(B) is correct. The author writes, "All other explanations for the war are either a direct consequence of the South's desire for wealth at the expense of her fellow man or a fanciful invention to cover up this sad portion of our nation's history."

(C) is incorrect. The author does not discuss the extent to which the attempt to "cover up this sad portion of our nation's history" was successful or unsuccessful.

(D) is incorrect. Though the author may agree that the invention of the identity narrative is unfortunate, this is not the best answer choice to highlight her main assertion that it is untrue.

24. **(A) is correct.** The author writes, "But people who try to sell you this narrative are wrong. The Civil War was not a battle of cultural identities—it was a battle about slavery."

(B) is incorrect. Though the author describes the cultural differences between the North and South in the first half of the passage, her primary purpose is revealed when she states, "But people who try to sell you this narrative are wrong."

(C) is incorrect. The author makes no comment on the outcome of the Civil War.

(D) is incorrect. The author asserts that, despite the popular identity narrative, the cause of the Civil War was actually very clear: "The Civil War was not a battle of cultural identities—it was a battle about slavery."

25. (A) is incorrect. The passage states that "vision does not become the dominant sense until around the age of 12 months."

(B) is correct. The passage states that "infants rely primarily on hearing."

(C) is incorrect. The sense of touch in not mentioned in the passage.

(D) is incorrect. The sense of smell is not mentioned in the passage.

Mechanical Comprehension

1. **(B) is correct.** Moving the block farther from the brick changes the location of the fulcrum. The weight of the brick will have more torque since it is farther from the fulcrum; therefore it is going to take more force to lift. The increase in distance also will lift the board higher than before.

2. **(A) is correct.** Levers with a fulcrum that is between the effort and the resistance are always first-class levers.

3. **(A) is correct.** Adjacent gears rotate in the opposite directions. Gears 2 and 4 will move in the same direction, and Gears 1 and 3 will both move in the direction that is opposite to Gears 2 and 4.

4. **(B) is correct.** The larger the radius of a pulley, the slower it will turn. Because Pulley C has the largest radius, it will turn the slowest.

5. **(B) is correct.** The board is balanced when the net torque is zero, meaning the torque from each block is equal.
$$T_1 = T_2$$
$$F_1 l_1 = F_2 l_2$$
$$40(3) = 60 l_2$$
$$l_2 = \frac{120}{60} = \textbf{2 ft.}$$

6. **(C) is correct.** The figure shows a ramp acting as an inclined plane.

7. **(C) is correct.** The blocks will be at rest when the net force on the system is zero, meaning the total weight on the left side of the pulley must be equal to the weight on the right side. Block C needs to be 50 pounds so that there are 70 pounds on both sides of the pulley.

8. **(C) is correct.** When the bullet moves right and collides with the block, it will move the block the same direction. Since the block is attached to the string, it will also swing up.

9. **(A) is correct.** The weight of the air in the ball is much less than the same volume of water that was displaced. Therefore, the buoyant upward force is very large.

10. **(B) is correct.** The theoretical mechanical advantage is the total number of ropes that are in contact with the load, so the advantage is 2.

11. **(A) is correct.** The mass of an object is constant. The weight of an object depends on the force of gravity that the object experiences. The gravity of the moon is less than Earth's, so Object B will have the same mass but a smaller weight.

12. **(A) is correct.** The weight is evenly distributed on both sides of the object. Because B and C are helping each other carry the weight on the right side, A is bearing the most weight.

13. **(C) is correct.** To make air flow in the desired direction, open a valve on the opposite path. This causes a difference in pressure that will keep the air flowing on the desired path. To make the air flow through the top path, open all the valves on the bottom: 5, 6, and 7.

14. **(B) is correct.** Heat will transfer from the steel ball to the liquid. The equilibrium temperature depends on the masses of the objects and the specific heat of each object. Without knowing these values, the only guarantee is that the temperatures of the objects will be somewhere between 120°C and 150°C.

15. **(A) is correct.** The velocity of a fluid through a pipe is inversely related to the size of the pipe, so the water's velocity will go down when the diameter of the pipe goes up.

16. **(B) is correct.** Water flows into the tower at a rate of 140 gallons per hour and out at a rate of 3 gallons per minute, or 180 gallons per hour. The tower is losing 180 − 140 = 40 gallons of water per hour.

17. **(A) is correct.** The weight is closer to Scale A than it is to Scale B, so Scale A will have a higher reading. The fulcrum in this case is the center of the rod, so there is more weight on the left side of the fulcrum.

18. **(A) is correct.** The gas that is compressed into the smallest space will have the greatest pressure. Container A has the smallest volume, so it has the greatest pressure.

19. **(C) is correct.** The two charges are the same type, negative, and will therefore repel and move farther apart.

20. **(C) is correct.** Plug in the values for the resistors to get the equivalent resistance.

$$R_{eq} = R_1 + R_2 + \ldots + R_n$$
$$R_{eq} = 1\ k\Omega + 2\ k\Omega + 0.5\ k\Omega = 3.5\ k\Omega$$

21. **(A) is correct.** A conductor has free electrons that easily move current, while an insulator has restricted electrons that do not allow current to flow.

(B) is incorrect. Electrons are not created or destroyed by electronics materials. (They can be created or destroyed in nuclear reactions, like in the sun.)

(C) is incorrect. All materials will have heat created when electricity flows through them.

22. **(B) is correct.** A scale gives the weight of an object, not its mass. The scale reading is the same as the normal force that the object experiences. The object is moving upward, so the normal force has to be greater than the downward force of the weight. Thus, the scale will read a weight that is greater than 80 pounds.

23. **(B) is correct.** The net force on the object will be zero, so the mass is in equilibrium and will not accelerate.

24. **(A) is correct.** The height of the water moves up relative to the volume the object displaces, so the object with the higher volume will raise the water level higher. Density is the ratio of mass to volume, so if Objects A and B have the same mass, Object B must have a larger volume and thus a lower density.

25. **(A) is correct.** The current in the river will carry the boat downstream.

Go to **www.triviumtestprep.com/oar-online-resources** to access your second SIFT practice test and other online study resources.

CPSIA information can be obtained
at www.ICGtesting.com
Printed in the USA